MEMOIR OF A BLACK CANADIAN ACTIVIST

by

Lyle Talbot with Carol Talbot

Cover Art by Tiffany Tremaine

Copyright © 2012 Carol Talbot

All rights reserved.

ISBN: 978-1-304-38604-5

Dedicated to George H. Crowell

Who encouraged me in my activism

And

Graduate studies as my professor in Christian Social Ethics

Preface

Why This Book

People have often expressed the opinion to me that there should be a book written by a black person about blacks in Canada that would tell what it has been like to be black in this country. It is my impression that people who are interested in race relations, human rights or the perception of discrimination by blacks more often than not have had limited interaction across racial lines. Furthermore, the books that they have read about blacks do not really provide answers to the kinds of questions that both blacks and whites are thinking but not always asking.

The experiences of blacks in Canada, especially as they relate to the broad concept of human rights, are an integral part of Canada's history. I propose to identify the roles played by blacks in Canadian society in the twentieth century as I have known them. Many of these events will provide some fresh insights into the Canadian black experience. In this account there will not be many outstanding heroes according to the usual standards since only a few individuals have been directly involved in the struggle to bring blacks from the state of almost total alienation from the mainstream of society to where they are today. The heroes whose stories I will tell are like the flowers in Thomas Gray's "Elegy Written in a Country Churchyard": "Full many a flower is born to blush unseen, /And waste its sweetness on the desert air."

Thousands of blacks will be able to identify with and relive the experiences typified by the examples used to illustrate my observations. Perhaps others, black or otherwise, will empathize with me as I review the first half of the twentieth century. I hope that the reader will vicariously experience what it has been like to be black in an almost all white society like Canada.

Many young black Canadians, and practically all West Indian and African immigrants since 1965, are almost totally unaware of actions taken by Canadians of other generations to try to break down the barriers of race that were once as pervasive as the Jim Crow laws in the southern United States. I have lived through several phases in race relations in this country and I have felt a constraint to write a book that will give a comprehensive picture of the struggle of blacks to gain full rights and privileges as citizens of Canada.

The concept of merit as the principal criterion for success in Canada is widely accepted: that is, that the most deserving person gets the job, the promotion, the apartment, and the honours in Canadian society. When someone alleges that he or she has not received due recognition of merit in any area of social economic life, that person is suspected of being paranoid. It is taken for granted that Canadians are fair, honest and equitable in decision-making situations. Therefore, when a black person accuses any employer, property owner, proprietor of a business or other decision maker of racial discrimination, the initial response from the average white Canadian is one of disbelief. It follows that the higher the status, prestige and economic position of the accused, the more likely it is that white Canadians will see the complainant as somewhat deluded in his or her perception of the situation.

Unfortunately, blacks and members of other visible minority groups do not all share the view that they have equal opportunity in this country. The records of human rights agencies indicate that race, color and ethnic origin are still the most prevalent grounds for allegations of discrimination in employment, accommodations, housing and service – ahead of gender – despite the publicity that the feminist movement has ascribed to the disparities based on gender. These realities of racism and discrimination are a part of being black, and most blacks have an unspoken knowledge and understanding of these issues.

Some of those who say that racism and discrimination are not and never have been a serious problem in Canada also claim that anyone who really tries can do anything he or she wants to do, and those who claim otherwise are simply too lazy or too lacking in initiative and resourcefulness to achieve their goals. Others like to think that blacks have come a long way since the days of slavery, and if we just keep on trying and improve our knowledge and skills, we will someday overcome all obstacles.

Other people postulate that the problems of blacks are no different from the problems of other people who are at similar socio-economic levels and who lived in similar areas and communities. They say, for example, that Nova Scotia is a generally depressed economic area and so one would expect poor people, black and white, to have the same problems in that province. This is not the case on examination of the situation in Halifax. There was no group of whites as badly off as the blacks in Africville.

People with a similar attitude point to Toronto and Montreal and say, "Look how many blacks have good jobs, how many are professionals, how many own nice homes, how many are in business." People who draw attention to the celebrities in attempting to justify the situation in Canada are much like the writers of textbooks who talk about only the outstanding feats of the majority group in society and neglect to tell all the relevant facts. In my view biased history textbooks are a disservice in the education of all children, and certainly omission and/or distortion of facts relevant to visible minorities causes serious damage to their sense of identity and even shame.

It is my purpose to fill in some of the gaps in the story of black Canadians by interweaving my own experiences with knowledge gained through personal relationships and analytical and theoretical assertions. I will begin by looking at some of the things I learned about being black in early childhood and will go on to develop an account of what it has been like being black and Canadian over my life. My observations will cover more of my experiences in Windsor and southwestern

Ontario where I spent the first half-century of my life. However, since my involvement in race relations, human rights, community activities and unions has helped me to keep somewhat well-informed about blacks wherever they live in Canada, my analyses will include a national perspective. A wide range of concepts will be examined such as the controversies regarding identification terminology and why it is that after generations of objecting to racial jokes, blacks are now telling racial jokes themselves.

My experience and background overlap racial lines, class distinctions, economic status and religious denomination. Perhaps that will provide some insight into those phenomena that give race relations in Canada its unique character. During my lifetime I have been a common labourer and a skilled professional, an employee and a supervisor, a businessperson and a customer, a very poor man and a relatively well-to-do man, a union activists and a management consultant. My religious experience and formal training extends from the literalist conservative-evangelical to the ultra -modern liberal-radical theologies of the death and rebirth of God. In the area of race relations I have been both a radical human rights activist and a controlled government administrator bound by regulations and protocol. I know what is meant when an aspiring young politician is advised to become proficient at walking with one's feet planted firmly on the ground, one's ear attuned to the winds of change, one's eyes fixed on the horizon and holding steadfast with both hands to past traditions while reaching out to new challenges.

This book is written to fill a literary and historical vacuum in this country. It is my attempt to provide some continuity to the story of blacks in Canada. I hope that this effort will become part of the structure of Canadian history as well as inspiring professionally skilled historians and writers to further research the events and situations related herein.

Table of Contents

Chapter 1   MY EARLY YEARS 1

Chapter 2   THE DIXIELAND OF CANADA 21

Chapter 3   PRINCE EDWARD PUBLIC SCHOOL YEARS 33

Chapter 4   AS FOR THE CHURCH 45

Chapter 5   HIGH SCHOOL YEARS 49

Chapter 6   VOICES IN THE WILDERNESS 65

Chapter 7   THE REAL WORLD 69

Chapter 8   "CLIMBING THE MOLASSES MOUNTAIN" 83

Chapter 9   LOVE AND MARRIAGE 93

Chapter 10 BLESS THIS HOUSE 111

Chapter 11 RESTRICTIVE COVENANTS 119

Chapter 12 BEYOND BELLHOP 129

Chapter 13 THE BIRTH OF A MOVEMENT 143

Chapter 14 GROWING PAINS 157

Chapter 15 BY THEIR FRUITS 167

Chapter 16 THE DRESDEN AFFAIR 171

Chapter 17 THE CREDIT UNION AFFAIR 177

Chapter 18	THE OTHER UNION – THE UAW	185
Chapter 19	A MODEL FOR TRANSPORTATION	191
Chapter 20	BLACK IS BEAUTIFUL	197
Chapter 21	A NEW HOME	201
Chapter 22	HOUSING AND INTERRELATED ISSUES	213
Chapter 23	NOTHING VENTURED NOTHING GAINED	217
Chapter 24	FAMILY AND FAITH	223
Chapter 25	CHAPTER 25	241
Chapter 26	VOICES IN THE WILDERNESS NO MORE	241
Chapter 27	UNFAIR EMPLOYMENT PRACTICES	247
Chapter 28	TOWARD A BETTER UNDERSTANDING	253
BIBLIOGRAPHY		256

MY EARLY YEARS

On August 4, 1914, Great Britain declared war on Germany. After the German army had invaded Austria, Canadian men across the nation began to volunteer for service in the armed forces to fight in the war that people generally believed to be the war to end all wars.

In the enthusiasm of the moment a group of men of colour from the area around Dresden, Ontario, drove by horse and wagon to the recruiting office in Chatham, about eighteen miles away, to enlist in the army. Henry Lorenzo Talbot, a thirty year old farmer, was a member of that group. When the recruiting officer interviewed him, the officer told Henry that if he were to be accepted into the army he would be assigned to a labour battalion.

Henry asked, "What does a labour battalion do?"

The officer replied, "They dig trenches, drive mules and do other types of physical work. That's what coloured soldiers do."

Henry responded, "Sir, I'm volunteering for service in the army to fight a war, not to dig ditches and drive mules. I can do that at home on the farm."

The officer then informed him that there was a law written in the Emancipation Act that prohibited a black man from taking up arms against a white man even in defense of his country. I don't know whether that law was still on the statute books, but I do know that when the first black police constable was being considered for Windsor in the 1940s the question as to whether he could legally use a gun in making an arrest was discussed. At any rate, Henry left the recruiting office and returned home. Exactly nine months later, on June 27, 1915, I was born in the old brown house on the 11th Concession in Chatham Township, just outside the town of Dresden, Ontario. I was the fourth child and second son of Henry and Adele Talbot.

Thus, racial discrimination, as noted above, played a significant role in my being born, and it was to play a significant role in almost every situation and event during my lifetime. I was nurtured in the midst of racial prejudice and educated in a racist system. I struggled to survive as a fully human black person in a white racist society. Every step of the way, as my life unfolded, I abhorred the inequity and injustice of it all. I have lived first hand through the experience of practically every phase and facet of interracial interaction, reaction, pro-action and inaction that one can encounter in this country. I know the sharply focused anger and frustration of a black child fighting to grow and live. I know the generalized, deep-rooted anger of a mature person who recognizes that the racist, especially in Canada, is a sick person who thinks that he/she is perfectly healthy and normal. However, I know that in fact he/she, like some victims of cancer, is dying of a malignant psychological and social disease, while at the same time being blissfully unaware of his/her condition.

When Dr. Martin Luther King was in Windsor, Ontario, a few months before his assassination, he suggested the formation of an International Association for the Advancement of Creative Maladjustment for people who refuse to adjust to such unjust conditions in society as racism, poverty, war and other manifestations of man's inhumanity to his fellow man. The organization never materialized during his lifetime, but, if it had, I would have been one of the first to join.

I was a member of the committee that invited Dr. King to speak, but I had to work that evening so I had my nephew Henry White record his speech on my little Sony tape recorder. I think I owned the only tape recording of the one speech he made in Canada.

***

My paternal grandfather was born near Paris, Ontario, in 1855. I thought that he had three brothers and four sisters but I had never been able to find out who his father was or where he was from until 2006. I learned from my nephew, Kenn

Stanton who has been researching the Talbot family tree, that my paternal great grandfather's name was Lorenzo after whom my father was named. That Lorenzo was born before his father Zebediah married. He was the eldest of Zebediah's eleven children. All of the other siblings had biblical names. Kenn researched the DNA of my brother Andrew's son, Ted, and found that there is no African DNA in the paternal line of Lorenzo's descendants. This fact lends credence to my opinion that my great great-grandfather Talbot was probably old Colonel Thomas Talbot himself, the white bachelor settler whose well known name graces a street, a town and several establishments in southwestern Ontario.

Figure 1
Simon Andrew Talbot and Sarah Ann Talbot, Lyle's paternal grandparents.

I was seventeen when my paternal grandfather died. I remember him well as a very blunt old man known for speaking his mind. Having a very fair complexion, he was about as prejudiced against dark skinned people as some white people were. He had to modify this attitude when three of his four children married brown-skinned persons. His name was Simon Andrew Talbot, and until 1973 that was all I knew of him.

While researching material at the University of Windsor that year, I came across an item in a book about the Elgin settlement that Colonel Thomas Talbot had established in the Brantford/Paris area. That item may be the missing link in my paternal ancestral chain. The Colonel was a bachelor, but he owned a number of slaves prior to the Emancipation Act of 1833 that freed all the slaves in the British Empire. Gossip around the settlement was that the Colonel had had affairs with several women including some of his slaves. It may have been merely gossip, but if there is any truth in it, it may provide an answer to the question regarding who my great great-grandfather Talbot was and why my grandfather never talked about him to anyone as far as I could ascertain. It makes this more intriguing when you know that my grandfather was light-skinned enough to have been half-white and that slaves usually assumed the surname of their last owner when they became free.

In 1971, while interviewing a woman in Toronto, I learned that she was from Jamaica, her maiden name was Talbot and her grandfather looked like a white man, but he was known as a black person. She added that he too would never tell where he was born or who his father was. He claimed that he was originally from Ontario and that he had relatives in Canada. He had moved to Jamaica and married a Jamaican woman. Jenna (nee Talbot) said that her grandmother had just recently confided in her that her husband had refused to talk about his ancestors because he had been born out of wedlock and could not legally claim his paternal ancestry.

There were also Talbot families in Nova Scotia and around Harrow Ontario, whose patriarchs all resembled one another enough to have had the same paternal origin but who did not recognize any blood relationships to one another. Could it be that our family, Jenna's family, the Nova Scotia Talbots and the Harrow Talbots are all descendants of the same old bachelor?

Simon Talbot married Sarah Ann, daughter of the Rev. Samuel Henry Davis who was born in New York State in 1810. He was the grandson of a slave owner. I never learned where Samuel's father was born, but I did learn from Samuel's partial autobiography that he changed his name a few times, apparently to avoid bounty hunters who were searching for former slaves. This information came from the research of my cousin, Bill Richardson. Like many slave owners' illegitimate sons, he attended a school in Maine that had been established especially for such boys. Also recently, I learned that Samuel Henry Davis was a strong anti-slavery abolitionist advocate who travelled around the northern United States before coming to Canada.

In 1841, after learning about the Underground Railroad, Samuel Davis migrated to the Windsor/Detroit area to minister to the escaped slaves as a missionary/teacher/preacher. He joined the newly formed Amherstburg Baptist Association and travelled regularly between Amherstburg and Toronto stopping at each black settlement along the way. He covered a three hundred mile distance at least once every year. My grandmother said that he often referred to his mission as, "one of preaching to black men, white men, Indians and dogs". He lived to be ninety-seven years old and it was said that he had never been sick a day in his life. My grandmother told me that he came into the farmhouse where they were living, one day after his daily walk, asked for his corncob pipe, took one puff and slumped over in his chair, dead.

Adele Brown, my mother, was the illegitimate child of Annie Brown of Dresden who married Samuel Freeman. Her father's identity was never revealed to me, but her mother was a mixture of aboriginal, Welsh and black. My mother and those of her blood relatives whom I came to know all looked more aboriginal than anything else though they were all part of the black community. I never actually questioned why it was; it could be that both racial mixing and illegitimacy were unacceptable in both the white and aboriginal communities so these people had no place to be accepted except by what was considered the bottom of the heap in Canadian society, the black community.

***

I experienced life before there were computers, satellites, TV or even household radios. One of my earliest memories of the world outside the old brown house in which I was born is sitting either on my mother's lap or on the floor of our family buggy. We were behind one of my dad's horses — either Dick or Jess, but probably Jess the mare, since she would more likely be the one hitched to the buggy. Dick was more of a workhorse. If you have never been that close to a horse's rear end, you have missed a very aromatic experience. Horses presented a unique exposure from where I sat.

Another aromatic experience of my early childhood was with Open Plumbing Openly Arrived At, more commonly known as outhouses or backhouses. They invariably had a crescent shaped opening near the top. Could that opening have been for light and ventilation? Well, it did not do much of either. I don't remember how we managed in the winter months, but I have a faint recollection of myself trying to follow Dad's footprints in the snow. Where else would I have been going?

Other familiar items in my early childhood were the old kerosene lamps, the wood burning cook stove in the kitchen and the big Quebec heater in the parlour. There was always a big sheet metal boiler on the kitchen stove for cooking, washing and the compulsory Saturday night bath that everyone had to take behind a curtain in a corner of the kitchen. In a metal tub on a bench in the kitchen there was a washboard on which the women used to scrub their washing. They had to wring the clothes out by hand, or by a hand driven wringer, and hang them outside to dry in both summer and winter. I can still see in my mind those frozen stiff things being brought in to finish drying on a line strung across the kitchen. Finally, there was a lovely washbasin, a water pitcher and a commode or chamber pot that adorned Mom and Dad's bedroom. When the lamps were turned off for the night, you had better remember where each of these useful, as well as ornamental, items was situated.

Before we leave that old brown house in Chatham Township, let me tell you about some of the events from that time that are still vivid in my memory. One day, when I was about two years old, Mom and Dad were out of the house. They were probably working in the fields, and my three sisters, Luella, Gladys and Dorothy, and my brother George had decided to cook some apples on top of the old wood burning cook stove in the kitchen. I must have climbed up on a chair to attempt to retrieve my apple because I remember touching the hot stovetop with my right hand. I still bear the scar (about the size of a twenty-five cent piece) from the burn where my wrist touched the stovetop.

About a year later we had what I remember calling a democrat, a wagon that would probably have been a pickup truck if it had been a motor-driven vehicle. Some of us children were playing around the democrat and somehow I fell off the cart and dislocated my shoulder. I can remember my mother binding my shoulder while I sat on the back stoop watching the other children playing in the yard.

Another significant event involved my Uncle Ernie Lucas and the killing of a pig. I was able to watch as Uncle Ernie slit the throat of the pig, and in my mind I can still hear the squeals as the pig writhed in its death throes. I was then sent to my room to take my afternoon nap, but before I went to bed I looked out the window, and there was the pig, hanging head down from a plank fixed between the windowsill and a tree. Later, when I asked Uncle Ernie what they were going to do with the pig, he replied, "We're gonna eat everything but the squeal."

Finally, about three weeks before my third birthday, I was taken with my mother to stay at Grandma Freeman's house. I remember loud screaming wakening me from sleep in a dark room. Then the screaming would stop for a few minutes, start again — louder and higher pitched, stop and start in an even rhythm. Suddenly all became quiet and I went back to sleep. When I awoke in the morning I was introduced to my new baby brother, Earl Andrew.

Our family left the farm and moved to Windsor, Ontario, when I was four years old. My dad, Henry L. Talbot, had felt the call to become a preacher of the gospel, but already with six children he had to have other work to support his family. The Ford Motor Company offered him that opportunity. Dad got a job at the plant that Henry Ford had opened in what became known as Ford City, on the eastern outskirts of Windsor, and was able to make the down payment on a house.

The house was located on Lillian Street about half of a long block from what is now Giles Blvd. but what was at that time a gully. Just like that, we had running water, electricity, natural gas for cooking and heating and a paved road in front of our house. Howard Avenue was the street behind our house and there was a bridge over the gully there. Windsor Grove Cemetery was on one side of Howard Avenue and Heavenly Rest Catholic Cemetery was on the other side at the south end of the bridge. My friends and I used to coast in our wagons from the centre of the bridge northward but never southward toward the cemeteries!

But the country life was not totally behind me. On a visit to my Uncle Ernie and Aunt Bertha's when I was around nine years old, I learned running water on their farm there meant that someone had to run down to the well and bring water up. It was during that visit that I witnessed my first and only grain-threshing bee. They let me ride on the big wagon bringing the sheaves of grain to the huge threshing machine. It was not the powerful combine that you see these days but one driven by a belt attached to the rear wheel of a Ford tractor. It was only many years later, after I had become involved in interracial activity, that I realized something very significant about that grain threshing bee. All morning the men, black and white, worked congenially side by side in the field, and the women, black and white, prepared dinner together, but when it came time to eat, the white men sat at one table and the black men at another.

It was also during that visit that I went with my cousin Chester to bring the horses in from the pasture. After we got all the horses in the lane along the log fence, Ches asked me if I wanted to ride one of them to the stable. I think it was Maud that he said was the easiest to manage. From the fence I was able to grasp Maud's mane and throw my leg across her big back which was at least two feet across. Ches took off at a slow trot on his horse; both of us were riding bareback of course. By holding on to her mane for dear life I managed to bounce around on Maud's back to the barnyard. All at once I realized that Maud was heading for the barn door. She was oblivious of the rider on her back. She must have been the last horse in the group because I was able to roll off onto the ground just outside the barn door without being trampled. This whole episode delighted cousin Ches who thought that he had played a good trick on his city cousin.

Another special memory from that visit in the country is the enjoyment of eating my Grandmother Freeman's raspberry pies. She and her husband Sam lived in the town of Dresden, and I stayed at their house for a few days. One morning Grandma asked me if I would like some raspberry pie for dinner. Of course I would, so she gave me a pail and told me to go pick some berries out in the garden. Maybe it was because those berries were freshly picked, but whatever it was, I've never tasted raspberry pie like my Grandmother Freeman's. Also during that visit I was introduced to the churn for making butter and the separator for making cottage cheese and skim milk.

One other memory of that visit that is not so pleasant. Grandma Freeman had made dandelion wine that had reached drinkable age. It was her custom each year to bring out a jug of her wine and allow her three adult sons and their two buddies from across the road to drink a glass or two each. Then she made them leave while she hid the jug. My distant cousin Roy, her nephew, was about eleven and was also visiting. He got the bright idea of hiding under the table to see where Grandma hid the jug.

When everyone had left the house Roy and I brought out the jug and decided to sample the wine. It must have tasted good because some time later while picking some cherries, I suffered from overindulgence and got quite nauseous. Grandma knew, of course, that we had found her jug of wine.

However, even those pies and all the other nice things Grandma did were not enough to keep me from getting homesick on my first visit away from my immediate family. If you have ever been homesick, you can empathize with how I felt. They had to send me home early on the train. That return trip between Dresden and Windsor was my first ride on a huge passenger train.

Life in Windsor brought with it many new experiences. Mom was soon able to buy an electric washing machine, but she still had to wring out the clothes with a hand wringer and then rinse them in two tubs of water. In addition, they still had to be hung outside to dry, but the electric iron replaced the old cast iron pressing iron that she formerly had to heat on the stovetop. Items to be pressed had to be sprinkled with water just enough to dampen them; collars and cuffs had to be starched. Wash and wear and no-iron clothing had not been dreamed of yet. One of my early chores, as with some of my siblings, was to turn the wringer for Mom as she did the washing. Every spring one of the first tasks was to hang the floor rugs out on the clothesline and beat the dirt out of them with a tool designed for that purpose. We had linoleum floor coverings in the kitchen and bathroom making these floors much easier to clean than wood or carpeted floors. Of course, only the well-to-do in town could procure hardwood floors.

Our 1920s house was in many ways more luxurious than the homes most of the people we knew. Along one side there was a parlour, then a middle room, which served as a dining room or a library/office for Dad as needed, then a rather large kitchen/eating area with a sink and a stove. Along the other side of the house was Mom and Dad's bedroom at the front, the middle bedroom where the three older girls slept and the smaller back bedroom where we three boys slept. We still had to heat water on the stove and take our weekly baths in a washtub in a corner of the kitchen. Can you imagine ten people, six females and four males, getting ready for work or school during the week and for church on Sundays with no bathroom, no hot running water, and very little time? Frankly, I have no recollection of how we did it in the 1920s and 1930s. Everyone dressed in their finest for church: the girls and Mom in nice dresses and the latest style hats, we boys in suits and ties and Dad, in the summer as well as the winter, in his Prince Albert frock coat, vest and striped trousers. When Dad became pastor of First Baptist Church in about 1923, we moved into the parsonage or manse. That residence had three bedrooms upstairs and one downstairs, a toilet, tub and vanity in the upstairs bathroom and a toilet and vanity downstairs.

When my dad arrived home from work the day that I turned five years old, , he took me up in his arms and put five brand new shiny pennies, the size of our present day quarters, in my hand. Then he gave me five whacks on my bottom, one for each year. I don't remember any other birthdays from my childhood, but I do remember that one over ninety years later. I always felt a special bond with my dad, cemented by things like the five pennies and the five whacks.

In those pre-school years I had no awareness of being different, but that changed when we moved into the parsonage in the heart of the black residential district in Windsor. I started at Tuscarora Street School even though we lived just one short block from Mercer Street School because the grade one class at Mercer Street was overcrowded. Tuscarora was an almost all-white school about three blocks from home. It was there that I suddenly became aware of children calling us black children niggers. Thus, from the time I was six years old, I never ceased to be aware of my blackness.

A large vacant lot separated Tuscarora Street School from St. Francis Roman Catholic School, and there were frequent fights and skirmishes between the Protestant and Catholic children. The name calling included words like "cat licker" and I don't remember the name used for the Protestants, but the Jewish kids got it from both groups, usually being called "kikes" or "Christ killers". Apart from one boy who became my friend, I was never included in any playground activities unless a teacher was present.

The next year I transferred to Mercer Street School which was approximately 95 percent black but with all white teachers. By 1925 most of Windsor's black elementary school children attended this school, one of the oldest buildings in the city. While there were two other schools like Mercer in the city, Mercer stayed open as a school long after the others were closed down. One of these was Park Street School; it was used as a storehouse for school supplies until after World War II.

When I attended Mercer Street School the black boys ruled the school grounds. Whenever a white boy transferred to our school (usually because his family had come upon hard times and had to move into a poorer neighbourhood like Mercer Street's) that white boy would become our property. One of us who was his size would pick a fight with him on some pretext. If the white boy won that fight, the next day a bigger or better fighter would engage him in combat. After beating the white boy, the bigger black child would welcome the newcomer into our gang and there would be no further racial confrontation with that particular white boy.

One such episode involving an Italian boy named Sammy is particularly memorable. Sammy was apparently small for his age, but when a boy his size picked a fight with him, Sammy beat him handily, and so a bigger boy tried with the same result. When Sammy did the same with a third, still bigger boy (Sammy must have had boxing lessons), Alf, the leader of our Mercer Street gang, shook Sammy's hand and welcomed him to the school and to the gang. Since he had moved into a house just a half block from our house, you can appreciate why I soon made Sammy one of my best friends and helped him build an underground bunk in his back yard.

I am reminded at this point of a story I once heard. A little black boy was playing on the street with a little Catholic boy one day when the parish priest happened to come by. The Catholic boy greeted the priest with, "Good morning, Father."

The priest replied, "Good morning, son."

The black boy also greeted the priest as his friend had done, "Good morning, Father."

The priest replied, "Good morning, son; I didn't know you were a Catholic."

The black boy responded, "Oh no! I'm not. It's bad enough being coloured!"

One of my most memorable teachers at Mercer Street School was a Miss Campbell, an auburn haired white woman, who in the eyes of this nine year old black boy, was about the most beautiful woman he had ever seen. In the classroom Miss Campbell was able to hold everyone's attention, including the boys who had given other teachers a hard time or whose conduct on the playground was less than perfect. But it was her treatment of us outside the classroom that was most remarkable, especially since she was a young white woman in a school with a virtually all black student body.

On several Friday afternoons Miss Campbell invited the class to come to her house on Saturday afternoons. I don't recall the stated purpose of the invitation, but usually about six to ten children, mostly boys (myself included), would make their way across town to the big house on Janette Avenue. Miss Campbell would spend time with us, both as a group and individually, and she always provided cookies or candy and milk for us to enjoy. Looking back over 90 years, it must have taken a great deal of courage to risk the criticism, perhaps even hostility, of neighbours by bringing a group of black boys not only into that all white middle class neighbourhood but also into her parlour!

Mr. E.M. Gibson became the principal of Mercer Street School during my Grade 3 year. He was a handsome man with a ruddy boyish face that seemed incongruous with his booming bass voice that we could hear clearly over the entire nine room school whenever he wanted someone's attention. Mr. Gibson loved music, so one of the first things he did during his time at Mercer Street was to organize a school choir. I joined the choir and continued to sing in school choirs throughout elementary school largely because Mr. Gibson transferred to Prince Edward School at the same time that we moved from the parsonage back to our house on Lillian Street and into that school's district.

As a youngster many stories in the Bible fascinated me, both those taught in Sunday school and the ones that I read on my own. In those early years I learned about the Bible heroes and many of the psalms that are familiar to all Christians. I also spent many hours listening to my dad and the other pulpit pounding preachers expounding on the Gospel and enjoyed the choirs and the congregation singing the hymns of the church. To me, as a lad of five to ten years of age, my dad was by far the best preacher, our choir was the best choir and our church was the best church around.

Seeing my dad come home wringing wet with perspiration from the exertion he put into his preaching left me with the impression that unless a preacher exercised some physical activity he wasn't really preaching. It took many years and many sermons before that impression receded from the forefront of my mind. Although I can listen with interest and attention to a pastor who speaks with little or no expression, I still prefer the preacher who proclaims the Word of God with some enthusiasm. I heard somewhere that the word enthusiasm comes from the root words '*en*' and '*Theo*' meaning God-filled; perhaps that is why the enthusiastic preachers are more impressive for me.

Sometimes my friends and I would find something in the Bible, such as in the *Song of Solomon*, and we would giggle and laugh among ourselves at some of the language. I remember my mother becoming concerned by our behaviour on such occasions, but when I would tell her that we were reading the Bible, her concerns seemed to abate. She never asked us what was so funny in the Bible that caused us to giggle. I think she knew somehow but chose to avoid any discussion of subjects that were taboo in those days such as sex, body parts and procreation.

In those days of awakening to adult realities, it so happened that one Saturday morning Mom sent me next door to run an errand for Aunt Media Milburn. (Children were required to call adult friends of the family with the descriptors aunt or uncle as terms of respect.) Aunt Media gave me a list of things to buy for her at the farmers' market, and off I went with my wagon. An hour or so later I arrived back home and saw Dr. Taylor coming out of our house. Aunt Media took her time emptying my wagon, and when she finally allowed me to go into our house, I found my mother in bed with my new baby sister, Mary Elizabeth. My questions about how the baby got there were never answered satisfactorily, but since I had abandoned my belief in the stork by that time, I somehow connected the doctor's visit with the new arrival. Bette, as she became known, was the first and until now, the only baby born in the First Baptist Church parsonage. Since babies are almost exclusively born in hospitals now, her distinction will probably last for all time.

Those taboo sections heightened my fascination with The Book, and my fascination led me to explore and study the Bible throughout my life. As the most fascinating book in the world for me, my reading of the Bible evolved from a searching arising out of curiosity to a passion for truth.

During its early years First Baptist Church grew both numerically and spiritually. At its peak membership of three hundred it was the largest black church in Canada. I can remember several baptismal services when as many as ten to twenty people of all ages followed their Lord in baptism by immersion. I remember sitting in our family pew, the fourth from the front on the right-hand side of the centre aisle, every Sunday morning. The singing of the white-robed choir filling the choir loft above the baptistry and the preaching of my dad and the other enthusiastic and exciting preachers who visited our church from time to time never ceased to thrill me.

Around the age of seven or eight, inspired by my church experiences, I would gather the children of the neighbourhood and preach to them from the old pulpit Bible that had been brought from the original building on McDougall Street. This was the same building that the escaped slaves had built in 1858. The old pulpit from that building was my pulpit from 1922 to 1923.

My father, Rev. Henry Lorenzo Talbot, preached the gospel for about forty years. He never travelled more than a couple of hundred miles from his birthplace and he never pastored a church other than the First Baptist Churches in Windsor, Amherstburg, Chatham, Dresden, North Buxton, and the little village of Shrewsbury at Rondeau Park. His formal education included only grade eight in the one room country school about a mile from his father's farm plus several correspondence courses that he took after he began preaching. He was well aware of his limitations though. One indication of this was his request that his children point out any errors in grammar, pronunciation or syntax that we detected in the delivery of his sermons.

Dad had the ability to block out any distractions when he was studying. This was a real blessing because throughout most of his ministry he had no private study. He prepared his sermon notes in the living room of our house on Lillian Street, mostly on Saturdays, with from five to eight children milling about the house. He was so adept at this that he could listen to the Detroit Tiger's baseball games without losing his train of thought or the important plays of the game.

Dad had to work at the Ford Motor Company during all the years that we children lived at home, leaving only evenings and Saturdays to concentrate on his preaching ministry. He must have made quite an impact on his fellow workers; when he retired in 1947 to devote himself to full-time ministry, his fellow workers gave him a beautiful Bible as a retirement gift. The picture in the Windsor Star marking this event showed his plant superintendent, Norm Douglass, and the union committeeman, Abe Modlinsky, an avowed communist, both holding the Bible as they presented it to him.

Figure 2
Rev. Henry Lorenzo Talbot

He Was My Dad

As I think back this Father's Day
To days gone by when I was young,
I think of Dad, home and love
And songs of praise that we had sung.
I watched him stand before the flock
And preach the Word of Life with vim;
He always seemed to work so hard,
For preaching took so much of him.

I think of the day that I turned five
When Dad at last from work came back;
I ran to greet him and received
A hug, five copper pennies and five whacks.

I'd gather neighbourhood children 'round
And down the stairs we'd go where
From my pulpit I would expound.

I think of how he'd leave for work
With little time to drink his tea,
And when the streetcar did not come
He'd run the miles, 'twas two or three.
I think of joyous teenage years,
And Sundays, they were special days
For with my Dad I travelled far
As he his churches served with praise.

I think of lean depression years;
The folk were poor, work hard to find,
But on our table they ensured
A bounteous fare, for they were kind.
Years passed; our family grew up
As one by one we loved and wed.
My dad and mom grew older too;
All eight of us to Christ they'd led.

One day the church in Dresden town
Began to build a lovely manse

To house their pastor and his wife
And their own fellowship enhance.
Dad would find a task to do
On weekdays when his calls he'd made;
And thus it was, that fateful day,
The day he fell and struck his head.
Months passed, and though he seemed to mend,
He never really did get well.
His health, his mind, his spirit waned;
He lost his skill the Word to tell.
In hospital we watched him fade,
His strength, tho' great, could not prevail.
And tho' God raised him several times,
It seemed that soon his life would fail

One day beside his bed I sat;
The Lord's my Shepherd, I began."
Dad could not finish . . . then I knew
The end was near for God's great man.
It was a cold and windy day
That God called Dad from labour here
To that blest home where all is peace
And joy and praise and love and cheer.

The church was filled with saddened flock,
Precious jewels to adorn his crown;
For half a century they had heard
And claimed the Gospel as their own.
For Dad 'twas not the end. Oh! No!
The clouds just rolled back like a scroll
To welcome him as he came home.
'Twas well. It is well with his soul!
Father's Day 1981

THE DIXIELAND OF CANADA

It was only natural that slaves fleeing to Canada would take the most direct route to freedom. That would lead them to enter Canada at Amherstburg. However, the Underground Railroad brought many slaves through the friendly state of Pennsylvania as well. The station at Williamsport, for example, was closer to the Niagara River crossing than that of the Detroit River. By taking the former route the escaping slaves could avoid having to cross the state of Ohio where slave-catching bounty hunters were a constant threat. That is probably why Harriet Tubman, nicknamed Black Moses, had her Canadian headquarters at or near St. Catherines in the Niagara Peninsula. She is believed to have led more than three thousand escaping slaves to Canada. Nonetheless, Amherstburg was one of the most popular points of entry into Canada.

In Windsor the members of First Baptist Church were largely comprised of the descendants of the escaped slaves who had come to Canada by way of the Underground Railroad. During the years between 1833, when the slaves were emancipated in the British Empire, and 1865 when they were freed in the United States, approximately sixty thousand African American people came to southwestern Ontario.

Those who came through Kentucky, Ohio and Michigan settled primarily in the areas around Windsor, Amherstburg, Colchester, Elmstead, North Buxton, Chatham, Dresden, London and Brantford. Those who came by way of Pennsylvania and New England crossed into Canada at the Niagara River and settled in Niagara Falls, Hamilton, St. Catherines and Toronto. Wherever the escaped slaves settled they established churches of Baptist and Methodist persuasions. It is of historical significance that the first Baptist church in each of these communities was a black church. White Baptists who came to these areas would join the black church until they were enough of them to start an all-white church.

Figure 3
Locations of early black settlements in southwestern Ontario

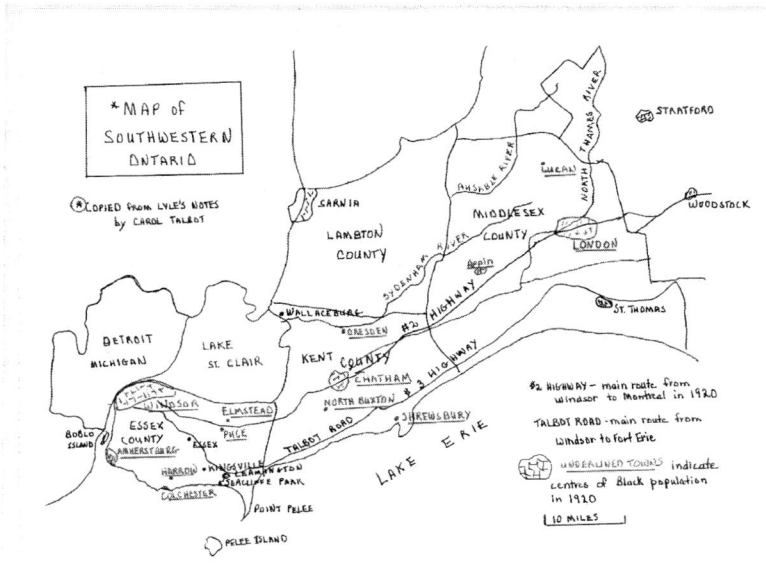

Ironically, after a few years those white churches would deny full membership to black people. This situation did not change for many years. For example, sometime around 1950, a white female member of the large and white Temple Baptist Church in Windsor had a daughter by a black porter who worked at the train station. As a teenager the girl became a Christian and was baptized, but when she applied for membership at Temple Baptist Church, she was told to go to First Baptist Church.

In the 1920's there were approximately three hundred blacks in the Amherstburg area and that population figure remained fairly constant for over five decades. Although there were black families living on almost every street east of what is now Highway 18, there were also two areas of denser concentration, one known locally as Back O' Town where some of the poorer families lived and the other was on King and George streets.

There was another community of about two hundred blacks around Colchester and Harrow, about ten miles east of Amherstburg. My earliest recollection of an experience in Harrow goes back to about 1933 when, with a carload of young people, we stopped at a soda fountain on the main street to get a bottle of pop. When the shopkeeper told us that we would have to drink the pop outside, we decided that we were not that thirsty and left.

Many hundreds of the escaped slaves returned to the United States between 1865 and 1900, but the greatest exodus from Ontario occurred during and after World War I, when employment opportunities became more numerous for black people south of the border. Many of them possessed skills in carpentry, masonry and other trades and were able to find more lucrative work there than in Canada.

Racism played a part even in this exodus of black people back to the United States. As late as the early 1900s there was no registration of the birth of babies designated as Negro in some states. Many Canadian born blacks, including some of my relatives, took advantage of this by claiming that they were born in one of those states in the year in which they were actually born. My Uncle Sam Freeman, who had operated a three or four chair barbershop in Hamtramck, a black suburb of Detroit Michigan, told me that he had paid an elderly client of his to sign an affidavit that he had been born in a county in Georgia.

The problem in Ontario was that, apart from farmers who set up homesteads, black people were hired only for the most menial types of labour. When we moved into the First Baptist Church's parsonage, there were no professional people in our church other than two public school teachers, both of whom were white in appearance. There was one insurance agent and the proprietor of a paint store, also both white in appearance, and one self-employed electrician. Two or three men had been able to find jobs in Detroit as waiters and bellhops and a few worked in the Ford Motor Company factories in either Detroit or Windsor.

In those days 95 percent of the black residents of the city of Windsor lived in an area three blocks wide and eight blocks long: two blocks east of Ouellette Avenue, the main street, stretching from one block south of the Detroit River to what is now Giles Boulevard. All but about half a dozen families, in a black population of over two thousand, lived within these boundaries. I use the term boundaries advisedly since tradition, restrictive covenants and outright racial segregation confined blacks within these limits.

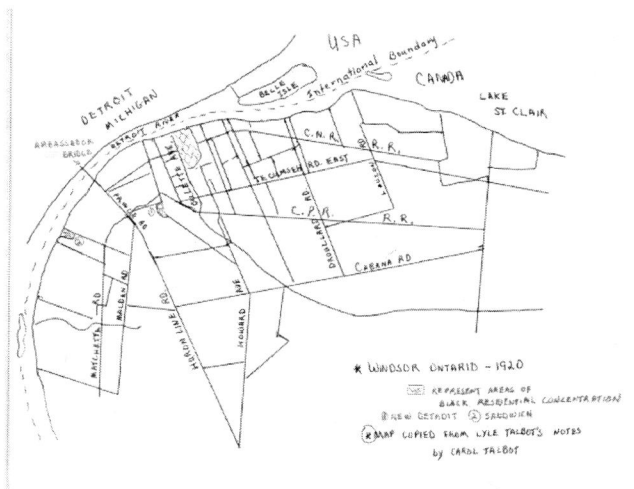

Figure 4
Concentration of black homes in 1920s Windsor

Except for about three years from 1922–1925, during which my father was a full-time pastor of First Baptist Church and we lived in the parsonage next to the church on Tuscarora Street, our family was one of the few black families who did not live within those boundaries. When my dad purchased the house on Lillian Street in 1919, I am inclined to believe that the seller was not aware that he was black. He may have taken him to be a dark complexioned Frenchman with a name like Talbot.

Elsewhere in Essex County, except for a small group of farmers at Elmstead and a few isolated families living near the towns we have named, there were no blacks. They were not allowed to own property in the towns of Essex, Kingsville, Leamington or Tilbury, and it was said that they were not allowed to stay after sundown in some of these towns. Except for a few families in Shrewsbury near Blenheim, blacks owned no property anywhere along the lakeshores in southwestern Ontario. The only places they were allowed to swim were at the foot of Bridge Avenue in Windsor, a place called Smitty's west of the town of Sandwich, Waterworks Park in Amherstburg and the provincial park beach at Colchester. These restrictions were in place even though there were good sandy beaches along the entire waterfront (i.e. along the seventy-five mile shoreline from Mitchell's Bay the northeast end of Lake St. Clair, along the Detroit River and along the north shore of Lake Erie)

I attended the first picnic ever held by a black group at Seacliff Park near Leamington in the early 1930s. The black churches of Kent County were given special permission to hold their annual picnic there. They made such a favorable impression by their conduct and the way they cleaned up at the end of the day that the park authorities invited them to come again, only as a church group of course. What stands out in my memory, though, is that as teenagers we were constantly reminded to keep quiet and keep the park clean, so much so that it almost spoiled the picnic for us. Just one summer before that picnic a group of black youths from Windsor had been denied the use of the washrooms and change house at that same park. No private picnic grounds, bathing beaches, golf courses, bowling alleys or other amusement centers were accessible to blacks. It was common to see "Whites Only" or "Restricted Clientele" signs all over the county.

An example of how open and deep-rooted racism and bigotry were in that part of Canada occurred in the old town of Walkerville, made famous as the home of Hiram Walker's Canadian club whiskey. In 1933 Walkerville was amalgamated with the city of Windsor when David Croll, Windsor's first Jewish mayor, was in office. The townspeople were so bitter that they erected a signboard at the former town limits where the highway entered the town. The sign read in huge letters for all to see, "Welcome to Walkerville, Inc. 1890, crucified 1933".

Kent County was as bad as Essex County. In fact the whole of southwestern Ontario earned the nickname Dixieland of Canada from the blacks who lived there. Chatham had about eight hundred blacks concentrated in the east end of town beyond the railway station. They endured severe restrictions in every aspect of life. It was practically impossible to get a restaurant meal or even a cup of coffee in the city of Chatham and no hotel in either Chatham or Windsor would rent a room to a black traveller. Also in Kent County there were black residents — almost all of them farmers — in and around Dresden, in a small hamlet near Blenheim at the western end of Rondeau Bay called Shrewsbury and at North Buxton, about ten miles southwest of Chatham.

Dresden became well known across Canada for two paradoxical reasons. First, it was the home of Josiah Henson who claimed to be the original Uncle Tom, and second, for the fact that it was one of the last frontiers of open and flagrant racism in Ontario. Some of Canada's most prosperous black farmers lived in and around the town, but let me make it quite clear: it was not the blacks of Dresden who made a celebrity of Henson.

Anyone who has seen the Detroit River when the ice flows are coming downstream past Boblo Island at six to eight miles per hour would be skeptical about the story of Eliza crossing to freedom in Canada by jumping from ice flow to ice flow with the slave catchers hot on her heels. Maybe that's not the way Harriett Beecher Stowe actually portrayed this scene in *Uncle Tom's Cabin*, but it is the way it was impressed upon the mind of a lad eight years old, born in Dresden, Ontario in 1915.

In spite of my early training in a rather strict Baptist pastor's home where tolerance, forbearance and forgiveness were taught as vital principles, somehow I just could not admire the hero of *Uncle Tom's Cabin*. Why did he submit to the lash of Simon Legree so patiently and docilely? He was stronger than his master, so why didn't he grasp the whip out of his hand, lay it on the evil old man but good, and then, before anyone found out, run away to freedom in Canada? I don't remember all the details of the story, but I do remember that Uncle Tom was portrayed in a sickeningly submissive role. No matter how much good Josiah Henson did for the Dawn Settlement, if he really was, as he claimed to be, the model for the novel, then I could never look up to him as a hero. That, no doubt, is why I preferred to believe my Grandmother Talbot's stories and those that were printed in the nineteenth century newspaper, "Voice of the Fugitive" (1851–1852). My grandmother knew Rev. Josiah Henson personally in her youth and some of the stories she told me about him did not enhance his image for me. These stories were about a trip that Henson took to England to raise money for the Dawn Institute. Apparently, so the story went, he also received a grant from Queen Victoria, but the money he raised was significantly more than the Institute received. According to Grandma Talbot, Henson purchased farmland for himself soon after the trip. Therefore, the term "Uncle Tom" became the pseudonym for a black person who exploits his relationships with the white power structure for his own personal advantage. His relationship is always one of subservience to "the man" (i.e. any white man or group of white men) and seeking patronage. In a later chapter about the sit-ins in Windsor in 1949, you will see the typical response of an Uncle Tom in a critical interracial situation.

Besides, white historians gave Uncle Tom to blacks as a hero. I think that he has perhaps been venerated as much for his early submissiveness to the yoke of slavery as for what he is reported to have done for the Dawn Institute. There must be some significant reason why more than a century after Henson claimed to be the original Uncle Tom, the term "Uncle Tom" is generally considered to be one of contempt and derision among blacks all over North America. Certainly my grandmother's stories fit the Uncle Tom stereotype more closely than the great benefactor stories.

Shrewsbury and North Buxton are the only all-black communities in Ontario that have survived since the earliest days of black migration to Canada. Since World War II, the village of Shrewsbury, about twenty miles east of Chatham, has been a community of black American cottagers who have taken advantage of a rare opportunity to purchase lakefront property by buying up all the land in the area as it became available. The reason they were able to do this was that the area had been settled by blacks who had come there as escaped slaves over a hundred years previously and the descendants of those settlers had managed to hold on to their properties. In an almost ideal setting they created a black vacationland where the fishing, swimming, boating and duck hunting are among the best in the great lakes region. Shrewsbury must have been completely forgotten by the white world; otherwise this development would not have occurred.

North Buxton, located about ten miles southeast of Chatham, is unique in other ways as well. Even though it had only a few dozen families, it had three churches, a community hall and two stores. Much of the success of North Buxtonites has been due to the competent fatherly training and sound counsel of a man named Arthur Alexander. Mr. Alexander was born and grew up in Amherstburg. He became a schoolteacher and later a principal of the North Buxton one-room school. He married a Buxton girl, Ethel Shreve, and for more than forty years he taught and encouraged the youth of the community before his retirement sometime in the 1960s. During the Depression, he worked for whatever the township could pay him, and for long periods at a time this was much less than enough for his family to live on. Poor as he was, not only did he and Ethel feed the minds of the young blacks of Buxton, but also the stomachs of many a hungry traveller who would stop by unannounced but who were never unwelcomed on a Sunday afternoon. The Alexander home was situated on Center Road going west out of North Buxton and my impression was that hardly a visitor to the village ever left without stopping at the Alexanders for a cup of tea.

In recent years the community has established one of the best museums of black history and artifacts in Canada. The population has remained fairly constant throughout the twentieth century in spite of the emigration of many of its people to large cities and the United States. An unusual number of talented and famous blacks had their origins in Buxton, but they had to leave home to gain recognition.

Families in Owen Sound and nearby Collingwood concentrated around the black British Methodist Church under highly restricted socio-economic conditions. Similarly, in London, Brantford, Hamilton, Niagara Falls and St. Catherines, descendants of escaped slaves who had crossed into Canada at the Niagara River had settled and remained in small clusters in and around the cities. They were relegated to living on the fringes of the mainstream of society just as they were in other parts of the province.

In Toronto there were about five thousand blacks, about half of whom had come from the West Indies. The black population of Toronto was concentrated mostly in the area just west of University Avenue and south of College Street. A few families lived outside this area, but there was by no means any type of open housing. Except for a few professionals, the elite of the black community were the men who had acquired the best runs on the railroads as sleeping car porters. These men provided a personal service to the middle and upper class travelling public. This gave them contacts with many influential people. They exploited these contacts to their advantage whenever the opportunity arose to do so. Stories told by the porters about their experiences were much like those of the black bellhops who worked in the larger hotels in southern Ontario during the same era.

Montreal was the only city in the province of Quebec that had a significant number of black residents. There may have been as many as in Toronto at that time. Blacks from elsewhere who visited Montreal received the impression that there was more freedom of movement there for them, especially in the field of entertainment. By comparison with other Canadian cities and certainly with American cities, Montreal was no doubt freer. However, according to residents whom I interviewed in the 1970s, housing and employment were just as restricted there as they were everywhere else in Canada. The difference was that a person had to live in Montreal in order to be aware of these restrictions.

In the Maritimes, since the earliest days of black migration to Canada, Nova Scotia has had the largest per capita black population. In the 1920s Halifax County was the area of greatest concentration with over seven thousand blacks. Antigonish, Amherst, Guysborough, New Glasgow, East Preston in Nova Scotia and Sydney on

Cape Breton Island had blacks living on the outskirts of town or in rural communities nearby.

The plight of Nova Scotia and New Brunswick blacks has always been worse than in any other province. In New Brunswick there were only a few hundred blacks concentrated mostly in the St. John and Sackville areas. There were no known blacks on Prince Edward Island in the 1920s, and even today there are probably less than one hundred. If there were any blacks in Newfoundland or the Territories, they have had no contact with blacks in other parts of the country.

So it was that Canada's black population in the 1920's consisted primarily of the descendants of escaped slaves or free men who had run away from slavery and oppression — to what? It is undeniable that they did not find equality, fraternity and full acceptance anywhere on Canadian soil. Whites considered blacks to be hewers of wood and drawers of water. A study done by the Dalhousie Institute of Public Affairs in 1962 stated, "The general community holds stereotyped ideas that as descendants of slaves, they were naturally inferior (intellectually and otherwise), dirty, lazy, only suitable for domestic service and other unskilled jobs but not adaptable to or acceptable in positions of higher prestige or responsibility." Clairmont and Magill observed that the basis for this attitude was the early existence of a slave society in combination with white supremacists' attitudes.

Since the liberalization of Canada's immigration policies toward non-white peoples in the 1960's, the black population has almost quadrupled. Almost all of these immigrants have settled in urban centers with the largest numbers going to the big metropolitan areas. The increase in the black population between the pre-World War II period and the 1970s suggests that it seemed rather abruptly that blacks were being seen in the downtown streets, shopping centers and wherever people go everywhere in Eastern Canada. Many thousands travelled to western Canada as well but not nearly in such large numbers as they did to Toronto, Montreal, Ottawa,

Hamilton and the other large eastern cities. More went to Toronto than to all the rest of Canada combined. Montreal was the second most popular destination and Ottawa the third.

More than 75 percent of Canada's black population has a very brief Canadian history. It has been my observation that many students of black culture in Canada generally do one of two things in the search for identifying their roots. They indulge in limited genealogical excursions by skipping over the last hundred years and adopting American black history as theirs, or they attempt to find historic identity in Africa and, in that process, assume that all blacks in North America must have originated in the prime slave yielding countries of West Central Africa. The myth that prompts this assumption is that if the history of a people is to be a cohesive force it must have continuity. While I do not deny the importance of continuity in a people's history, it is my opinion that an artificially conjured continuity will not bring about cohesion or a sense of homogeneity.

PRINCE EDWARD PUBLIC SCHOOL YEARS

Before we ever had a family car automobiles were something like spaceships are today. I knew they existed, but I had little or no personal knowledge about them. In about 1923 or 1924, when I was eight or nine, only two people in our whole community owned automobiles, and we saw only an occasional one on the streets of Windsor. Mr. I.C. Parker, who lived in a big house at the corner of Mercer and Ann (now Elliott), had a Dodge sedan that had one door in the middle on each side. I don't remember ever seeing anyone drive that car, but Walter Perry, who lived next to Mercer Street School, bought a Studebaker touring car, which today might be called a four door convertible. Walter lived just a half block from us, and we had the unique privilege of riding around the block with him a few times. These were my first times in a motor vehicle.

I knew airplanes existed and had been flown in World War I, but I never saw one until I was about ten years old. The memory of that event is vividly etched in my mind. I was playing in our backyard when an airplane flew overhead so low that I thought I might see the pilot. When the sound of the single engine seemed to stop suddenly, I thought for sure that the plane must have landed in a field nearby. It appeared to be going down as it passed overhead. Excitedly I ran to see what had happened, but there was no airplane there. I learned later that the plane had landed in Walker Airfield about five miles from where we lived. It wasn't long before airplanes were a common sight as we lived on the flight path for planes taking off and landing at the airport.

The first radio I remember was the one that my brother George made around 1925. Somehow George learned about how silicon crystal could be used to receive sound waves by radio. Our first radio was a little piece of silicon crystal with a needle attached to earphones. Our family would take turns listening to whatever

George found by moving the needle around on the crystal. Not long after that George learned how to build a battery operated radio, connected an amplifier to it and installed an antenna on the roof of the house. I still recall our excitement when the voice on the radio announced, "This is station KDKH in Shreveport, Louisiana."

The move back into our house on Lillian Street, when I was ten years old and going into Grade 5, ushered in a completely new phase of my life experience. The relative luxuries of the parsonage at First Baptist Church must have spoiled us because two of the first projects I helped Dad with (figuratively speaking)after we moved back were to install a tongue and groove wooden partition using four feet of the back bedroom. Then we added a tub and wash basin to the toilet that was in one corner of the room. By that time there were three teenage girls and two teenage boys, so the congestion continued. We three boys vied for sleeping space in the one double bed in that room which shrank to about six feet by ten feet after the bathroom wall was built. Added to this, Andy, the youngest, was a bed wetter until he was almost a teenager. As a result, I spent half of many nights on the floor.

Figure 3
12 year old Lyle

We still attended First Baptist Church and Sunday school even though it was a twenty minute walk from our house. I had to make new friends and adjust to a new school and a neighborhood where we were the only non-white family on the block except for the Jacobs family across the street. They had one son, Kenneth, the same age as my sister Bette. The Jacobs were very dark skinned and for the most part stayed aloof from the other families on the block until Ken started school around 1930. Mr. Jacobs attended First Baptist Church regularly and was a letter carrier somewhere in the city while Mrs. Jacobs attended the British Methodist Episcopal Church where her family members, the Walkers, were pillars of the church.

The change from Mercer Street School to Prince Edward School was a dramatic one. Mercer was one of the oldest buildings in the city. It had no gymnasium, no auditorium, and no extracurricular facilities. In extremely bad weather the children were allowed to assemble in the dingy basement to line up to march to their classrooms. It had nine rooms on two floors, a smaller library on the attic floor and a basement divided in two so that on cold or rainy days the boys could gather on one side and the girls on the other. The basement ceiling was too low for any games like basketball or volleyball, and so there were no regular physical education activities unless the weather outside was suitable. The only play area outside was a cinder covered schoolyard, approximately thirty-five yards square, on each side of the building. The boys and girls were required to stay on their own side of the building with severe penalties for violating this rule. There was hardly enough room for a softball game on the boys' side and the bigger boys often hit the ball to the other side of the street occasionally striking a window in the corner store, the house, the apartment building or the Burroughs Adding Machines building.

Attending Prince Edward was like experiencing a different world. The school had been built around 1920 and had been officially opened by Edward, Prince of Wales (later King Edward VIII) on his visit to Canada after World War I. It was one of the first schools to institute the rotary system in which the classes moved to special rooms for all subjects except mathematics, spelling and grammar. The specified rooms had specialist teachers and equipment. There was a large gymnasium for boys' activities and inter-school events, a smaller gymnasium for girls' activities and inter-class events, shower rooms, a basement play area for both boys and girls to use in bad weather and a huge playground laid out with three full sized softball diamonds. The school also had a large auditorium for assemblies, concerts and the study of the dramatic arts. The extracurricular activities at Mercer Street consisted of a school choir directed by Mr. Gibson himself and athletic teams with no adequate facilities for practice. At Prince Edward we had ample facilities in addition to instructors and coaches for music, drama, gymnastics, dancing and a wide range of sports. The students at Mercer Street had to walk several blocks to other schools, Dougall Avenue or Begley, for home economics and manual training while Prince Edward provided these classes. Can one say by any stretch of the imagination that the kids at Mercer Street enjoyed educational opportunities equal to those available at Prince Edward?

Nonetheless, the boys and girls from Mercer Street always came home with several winning ribbons and trophies at the annual public school track and field meets. Many of them continued to excel in high school and beyond. For example, James Watson, who later became Windsor's first and only black city solicitor, set Western Ontario Secondary School Association records in the one hundred and two hundred yard dashes. Those records stood unbroken for several years. Fred Thomas set a record for the most points in a basketball game while attending Assumption College (now the University of Windsor). Fred also excelled in track, football, and baseball at university, climaxing his athletic career by playing center field for the Cincinnati Reds after blacks were admitted to the major leagues in the 1950s. Gordon Lawson was a star quarterback for Patterson Collegiate Institute Panthers for three years and Ferguson Jenkins, the father of the Hall of Famer Fergie Jenkins, was the third baseman for the team from Chatham Ontario that won the Canadian championship in the mid-1930s.

At least at a school like Mercer the teachers had to recognize the abilities of the black pupils because they were in the majority. In Amherstburg, where my wife Marietta grew up, black children attended the one public school in the town where they were a small minority. There it was common for a white teacher to totally ignore a black child for weeks. The traumatic change between Mercer and Prince Edward involved more than facilities and a large white student body. I had to learn to adapt from being one of the majority racial group on the school grounds to being one of the only four black boys, including my brother Andrew, three years my junior, in a school of eight hundred to one thousand pupils. The other two black boys were also two or three years behind me and they moved to the new John Campbell school a year or two later. I had to learn how to deal with racial name calling, physical abuse from the bigger boys and even the mental abuse from white teachers who derived their concept of blacks from the prevalent stereotypes of the day.

At Mercer I had managed to stay at or near the top of the honour roll every year. When I went to Prince Edward I had to live down such commonly held stereotypes as blacks being lazy and not very bright even though I had no idea what a stereotype was. Imagine sitting through lesson after lesson in every subject and having the teacher virtually ignore you whenever you held up your hand to answer a question. This was my experience all through Prince Edward and on through high school, except for a very few teachers who made a sincere attempt to be fair.

Under the conditions cited above how did I gain respect and friendship? I wasn't a star athlete, so by excelling in as many subjects as I could and sharing my knowledge with whomever asked for help, I made friends and at the same time I was enhancing my status with the teachers. I was somewhat of a novelty, since black kids weren't supposed to be as bright as I was, and this seemed to inspire the teachers to challenge me with the most difficult questions; when I responded with the correct answer I had to be recognized. There were those teachers who tried to ignore the black students so I developed my own techniques for getting their attention. I would stare out the window, or off into space, or close my eyes feigning sleep, or rustle papers or hassle the students around me. The teacher, thinking that I wasn't paying attention, would suddenly call my name. Few were the times that I didn't respond with the answer to the question, or whatever was needed to show that I had really been paying attention. I got caught in as much mischief as any normal boy. But that's just it! I was a normal boy just trying to prove it to teachers and pupils alike who were conditioned to think that because I was not white I had to be different.

I had to learn to gain the respect of the white children instead of having them fear me. I had to learn to get along with those who didn't like me whether it was because I was black or for some other reason. I had to learn how to make friends, for, believe me, when you were the only black kid on the school grounds at recess or at noon hour, you needed friends, as many as you could get. Many times I was made to feel sorry for the part I had in mistreating the white kids at Mercer Street Public School.

During those years I did continue to excel in subjects for which answers could be objectively evaluated such as mathematics, science, spelling, grammar and geography. However, I was never able to achieve much more than a passing grade in those subjects that depended on the subjective evaluation of the teacher such as creative writing, art, history and literature. Nevertheless, I managed to graduate from grade eight with the general proficiency silver medal for the highest average among the boys. The girl who received the girls' medal, Dorothy May, had a less than a two percent higher average than I did.

But childhood is not just about school. Going to the movies was a regular form of entertainment for Windsor children in my era, but the racism of that time also tainted this experience. There were four movie theaters in Windsor, and for ten cents you could watch a double feature on Saturday afternoons. Those were the days of Charlie Chaplin, Tom Mix, Mary Pickford, and the legendary Rudolph Valentino, reputed to have been the most handsome actor of all time. They were all black and white movies, and both the sound and the action were jerky.

As a child I always resented and inwardly rebelled that, as a condition of seeing a movie, we black kids had to sit in the two front rows on the right side in the Capitol Theatre craning our necks to see the picture. At both the Palace and Windsor theatres we had to sit in a very small section at the very back of the balcony, derogatorily called the Crows' Nest. At the old Walkerville Theatre we weren't even allowed in. We weren't allowed to go to the Empire Theatre because it was within the area where the more seedy people hung out.

The one good thing about the Capitol Theatre was that, before technicolor movies came in, they had vaudeville shows as well as movies and we had the best seats in the house for that. They always showed a newsreel between the movies as well as a short comedy. Later, in about 1932, the Loop Theatre in downtown Detroit used to change double features on Wednesday nights. For one dime we could go at eight in the evening and watch four movies. We would arrive home about six on Thursday mornings after stopping at the White Tower for a fifteen cent breakfast of bacon, eggs, toast and coffee.

My first recollection of any attempt to break down the racial barriers and restrictions in Canada involved my parents, the Rev. Charles L. Wells and his wife. The movie was *The Birth of a Nation* in which the rise of the Ku Klux Klan was described during the reconstruction period following the emancipation of the slaves in the United States in 1865. Rev. Wells had purchased tickets for four reserved seats on the main floor centre of the Palace Theatre. When the two couples arrived at the theatre, the manager refused to let them occupy their reserved seats. The two clergymen, with Rev. Wells taking the leading role, insisted that they had a right to their seats. The manager insisted that there must have been some mistake in selling them the tickets, but he was willing to exchange their tickets for seats in the balcony. A heated argument ensued, the police were called and the two couples were forcibly removed from the premises. It was only because the two men were clergymen that they were not charged with causing a public disturbance.

But the matter was by no means closed. I don't recall the sequence of events that followed the showing of *The Birth of a Nation*, or the tactics that were used by the two clergymen or others whom they may have recruited. I do know that by 1925 the Crows' Nest at that Palace and then the Monkeys' Cage at the Capitol had been abolished. The Walkerville was tougher to break. It took several more years before that theatre accorded blacks a civil reception.

You might wonder what else we did for fun with no computer, television, recreation hall or community center and not even a mall at which to pass the time. So what did we do? We invented games and improvised entertainment. What we did have more of than today's kids was time and what we lacked almost completely was money. We played such games as Stuck in the Mud, Duck on the Rock, Run, My Sheepy, Run and Red Light.

I'll describe just one game played by boys, Duck on the Rock. Each boy in the group found a nice stone about the size of a softball. That was his duck. Then we employed the usual way of picking the one who was "it" (Eeny Meeny, Hand Over Hand, Odd Man Out etc.). The one who was "it" placed his duck on a big rock and stepped far enough away to avoid being hit by flying ducks. The other boys had to stand behind a toe line about twenty feet away and throw their ducks at the duck on the rock. When a duck was knocked off the rock, the "it" man had to retrieve his duck and tag the duck thrower before the thrower could place his own duck on the rock. If he got tagged, he became "it". Dangerous? Maybe it was dangerous, but the only time anyone was injured was once when my friend Tom got his thumb smashed between someone else's duck and his duck, or the rock. Tom's mother was angry with us kids for playing so rough, but her anger turned to gratification when Tom could no longer suck that thumb which he had been sucking since infancy.

The more usual sports were also a part of our outdoor play. Like my Dad I've always been a sports person even though I was never very good at any of them. I played baseball and hockey from the time I was eight or nine. We played hockey wearing our skates clamped to our walking shoes and with no ankle supports, no hockey gloves, no shin guards, no shoulder pads and, of course, no face masks for the goalies. The games are basically the same as they were then, but imagine being the catcher on the neighbourhood baseball team with no mask, no chest protector or protective cup. Well, that's exactly how I started. We kids gathered scrap metal, paper and rags to raise money for these things, first the mitt and then the mask, but we never got to the chest protector, shin guards or cup that every little league team starts out with today. Every kid had to get his own baseball glove somehow, but together we procured the ball and bat. This prevented any disgruntled kid from taking his bat or ball and going home. The only argument was over whose turn it was to take these two valuable items home.

We also played games as a family or with friends who came by for an evening. The game Pit was comprised of one hundred cards in ten suits for up to ten players. Pit was an imitation stock market in which the players traded cards in groups of two or more around the table trying to obtain a corner on a particular commodity, i.e. all ten cards in a suit. Then there was the bull which doubled your corner and the bear which doubled your losses. It was a noisy game but a lot of fun.

The most important event of my life took place in the year in which I graduated from Prince Edward Public School. For two or three years my dad had been travelling to North Buxton, a village about fifty miles east of Windsor, to minister in the Baptist church there. Whenever I was allowed I would accompany him in our old Model T Ford. January 13, 1928, was one of those occasions. Mom and my sister Dorothy were also with us on that day. Dad had chosen for his sermon text that morning, "Choose you this day whom you will serve . . . but as for me and my house, we will serve the Lord."(Joshua 24:15, *King James Bible*)

Dad expounded in his usual vehement style on the need to make a decision to serve the Lord or to serve self. Then he came to the climax of his message, saying something like, *"*Our text this morning tells us to choose today, not tomorrow, not next week, not next year, but this day. 'Choose you this day whom you will serve'. Whom will you choose to serve today?"

Dad seemed to be looking right into my eyes as he said, "I can say, 'As for me . . . I will serve the Lord', because I have determined many years ago that I would serve my Lord Jesus Christ all the days of my life. But can I say with Joshua, 'As for me and my house, we will serve the Lord?' Young man, young woman, boys and girls, can your parents say, 'As for me and my house, we will serve the Lord?' I challenge all of us here this morning to heed the call of the Lord through his servant Joshua to 'Choose this day whom you will serve. . . but as for me and my house . . . .'"

And he stopped there. After a long pause, which seemed like minutes to me, he extended the invitation, repeating simply, "Choose you this day whom you will serve. If you have chosen to serve the Lord this morning, stand up and make your way to the altar and let us pray for you."

I don't remember getting up out of my seat. I do remember standing at the front of the sanctuary and being greeted by one of the deacons. When I became aware of my surroundings I remember seeing my sister Dorothy, my future brother-in-law, Phillip Alexander, his sister Gloria, the Harding twins, Irene and Florine, whose birthdays incidentally were the same day as mine and Harriett (Hattie) Shreve lined up across the front. Loving deacons, parents and Sunday school teachers surrounded us, all rejoicing over the newborn babes in Christ.

Six months later on July 7, 1928, we were baptized in Lake Erie, three miles south of the church. My baptism too was a unique experience. One of the deacons and my dad stood in waist deep water about fifty feet from the shore. Another deacon waded out to the baptismal spot with each candidate and then assisted the candidate back to shore after he or she had been immersed. I wasn't the first candidate to be led out into the lake, nor was I the last. When my turn came I was led ahead with the attending deacon out to where dad and the other deacon were waiting. Dad told me to clasp my hands in front of my chest, and he grasped my hands with one of his hands and placed the other hand on my shoulder. Then he asked me, "Lyle Emerson Talbot, have you received the Lord Jesus Christ as your own personal Savior and Lord?"

"I have," I replied.

Dad continued, "On your profession of faith in the Lord Jesus Christ and in obedience to his command, I now baptize you in the name of the Father, and of the Son and of the Holy Ghost." At that precise moment a huge wave swept over me, Dad and the assisting the deacon. The wave was so strong that we were barely able to maintain our footing. As suddenly as the wave had come, it subsided and the lake was once more as calm as before. Everyone on the shore was so startled by the wave that no one was able to observe the cause of it. We speculated later that either this swell came from a freight ship passing by or from the speedboat of a curious boater that, in swinging in too close to shore, had sent a wash rolling up the beach. Whatever caused that large wave to wash over us, I have never ceased to believe that somehow God was involved. No human being could have timed it so that at the exact moment I was to be immersed in the water that wave happened. All Dad had to do was to say, "Amen!" to complete my baptism.

With my conversion experience sealed by my public profession of faith and baptism, I began my Christian life determined that, come what may, I would never deny that Jesus Christ was my Savior and Lord. I knew that I would be tempted to sin and that I would be subjected to criticism and ridicule from my neighborhood chums as well as from the young people that I had known from the old neighborhood around First Baptist Church. Being a preacher's kid I also expected that even the adults in the church would be keeping a watchful eye on me waiting for me to slip and fall. I must confess that, as a young Christian, I often gave all of those people grounds for their suspicions. But I kept my vow. Even when my behavior was other than Christian, I insisted that I was still a Christian because Christ had died for my sins and I had received his offer of salvation.

AS FOR THE CHURCH

In the sphere of religion many of the black churches were formed in Canada between 1840 and 1860 because of the racism expressed in the white churches. Many of these churches are still functioning after a century and a half. The number of black churches is very high relative to the black population even in those areas of black concentration. For example in the 1970s, Windsor, with an estimated black population of about 3000 had six black churches affiliated with three different denominations (two of each), i.e. more than Toronto which had at least 100,000 blacks and Montreal with over 30,000 blacks. Structural racism is more relevant than black population figures to the number of black churches in Canada.

The following passage taken from a letter to the white Long Point (now Western) Baptist Association from the black Amherstburg Baptist Association gives some idea of the effects of racism in the area of religion in the mid-19th century. The letter was written after the Long Point Association had refused to receive black applicants for membership in their churches.

> Extracts from "Pathfinders of Liberty and Truth: A History of the Amherstburg Regular Missionary Baptist Association, 1940":
>
> It is evident from the meagre minutes of 1845 that some differences of importance had arisen between Amherstburg Baptist Association and Long Point Baptist Association. . . .
>
> Elder H. H. Hawkins, the moderator in 1846, prepared the annual circular letter of that year. That circular letter is a curiosity . . . as a literary production coming from one of the supposedly ignorant people to its constituent members. The chief object of the writer seemed to be to abuse the Long Point Association

and its members. Few writers could have done the work better than the writer of that letter could.

It backs up a former statement that our forefathers who entered Canada during that period were not all unlearned men, as is commonly supposed; secondly, because it shows the firm stand taken by our pioneer leaders against what they considered a wrong . . . .

The letter:

The time has come when it becomes us as an Association, composed as we are denominated 'the people of colour', to stand like men of war in defense of truth, and our peculiar privileges, and to expose the base and ignominious misrepresentations of the Long Point Association in Canada West. Since we have come out from them and have formed ourselves into an independent Association and cast off the yoke of anti-Christian bondage; no longer to be set at naught in their Ecclesiastical Councils, to be looked up on with contempt, to be insulted whenever and wherever we meet with them, as we suppose to worship the true and living God.

They have raised the cry that we are not recognized as being in fellowship with them. We desire no fellowship with anti-Christians; if we had, we would have stayed with them and covered up their iniquities. But the true light has come, and we are no longer to be duped by those agents of the Archnacromancer of the infernal regions of malignity and impetuosity.

There have been persons of colour who gave evidence of being born again. They have made application for membership with that church, and were told that it was against the rules of that church to admit to its fellowship any person, or persons of colour, but they would baptize them and take them under their watchcare but not fellowship with them as Christians. What, in the name of truth, do they baptize them for if they are not Christians — to make a mockery of a divine institution? . . .

We shall consider that their religion has been carried off by the scape-goat of darkness, or buried near St. Thomas, or some other proper place, probably near the big marsh.

We would like to know if there are any more of the arch-heretics who sit as judges . . . If there are any more they had better arrayed themselves in their pontifical habiliments and stand as sentinels at Windsor, for our brethren from Detroit are determined to come over and help us in spite of Satan and his artillery.

From the foregoing it can be surmised that discrimination in religious circles in Canada was as deep rooted as it was in any other sphere of community life. Black clergymen in Canada as a rule supported the racial status quo probably, among other things, because small black congregations and their pastors depended on economic support from the white community to keep their doors open and provide a meagre livelihood for the minister. The generally lower academic status of black clergymen in Canada was also a result of the historically low socio-economic status of black parishioners.

Accordingly, there was no indication of any movement toward congregational integration between blacks and whites even within the same denominations. This phenomenon was later greatly due to the value of group-owned assets that blacks in Canada possessed. Market value of black-owned church properties was well in excess of two million dollars in 1970. This may account for the fact there are not more churches among West Indian immigrants; church buildings cost too much.

The likelihood of any more than a mere token number of blacks being found in any church located in a middle or upper class urban or suburban area is very slight, not because of conscious prejudice or ill will such as was prevalent a hundred years ago, but because of the lasting effects of past housing patterns and socio-economic conditions. Notwithstanding the fact that white churchmen have spoken in support of human rights in Canada, church members as distinctive groups, more by benign neglect than by deliberate intention have failed to counteract the racism of the society around them. Pious platitudes from the nation's pulpits will not bring about social change as far as blacks are concerned.

HIGH SCHOOL YEARS

Charles Dickens began The Tale of Two Cities with this sentence, "It was the best of times; it was the worst of times." My early teens as a new Christian and a high school student was also the best of times and the worst of times. While I enjoyed travelling with my dad whenever I was able to as he ministered to three congregations, North Buxton, Dresden and Shrewsbury, the rest of the time our family continued to attend First Baptist Church in Windsor.

The years from 1927 to 1937 were hectic ones for First Baptist Church in Windsor. After Dad resigned as pastor in 1925, the church had difficulty finding a replacement. In those days, and even up to the present, black churches felt that they had to have black pastors, but there were just too few Canadian black men who aspired to the ministry. To resolve this situation they looked to the United States to fill the void.

First there was Rev. H.L. McNeil, a young preacher from Detroit whose worldly ways bothered the more conservative members. His worldly ways consisted of playing checkers with some of the men and generally socializing with young couples both inside and outside the church. He stayed about two years.

Next was Rev. A.R. James, a young bachelor of Jamaican origin, recently graduated from McMaster University Divinity School, the recognized Baptist seminary in eastern Canada. Rev. James had a refined manner that the young fellows defined as sissy while some older people ridiculed it as intellectual snobbishness. After about two years a large percentage of the members wanted him to resign, but Rev. James refused. A bitter struggle ensued, lasting about a year, culminating in court action to force his resignation. Rev. James called a membership meeting to discuss the revision of the membership rolls. When the opposing group boycotted the meeting, Rev. James and his supporters passed a motion requiring all members to re-register in order to be recognized as members in good standing. The opposing group refused to comply and it seemed that Rev. James had won the battle. The church, however, was the loser, split almost in half between those who supported Rev. James and those who opposed him. Those who were neutral remained silent for the most part. Rev. James resigned a few months after the struggle quieted down, but the broken relationships within the body remained for a whole generation. At that time, Dad said that a whole generation would have to die before the church would be healed. He wasn't far off in his prediction.

After Rev. James there were two or three interim pastors from Detroit. Then in 1936 or 1937, Dad returned to attempt to reconcile the differences that had kept the members divided for almost a decade. Since both sides in the dispute had some confidence in Dad's pastoral abilities, as well as his preaching, there was a noticeable change for the better for the next two or three years. Then in 1938, Rev. C. L. Wells, the pastor whom Dad had succeeded in 1921 when Rev. Wells took education leave, returned to the church as pastor.

Back in 1915 Rev. Wells had led the church in the construction of the impressive brick edifice at the corner of Mercer and Tuscarora Streets. It stood as a symbol of God's love and grace after all the turmoil of the late 1920s and early 1930s. It was one of the largest Protestant church buildings in Windsor in 1915, seating about 360 people, and was still the largest black church in Canada in 1970. That church property, which included three houses as well as the church building, occupied a quarter of a block in the heart of the city and was the most valuable piece of real estate owned by any group of blacks anywhere in Canada in the 1940s. This was all due to the leadership, organizing and negotiating skills of one young thirty to forty year old preacher, Charles Levi Wells who had only high school education and was in his first term as pastor of a city church.

An example of his negotiating skill was that he was able to get the Armour Packing Company in Toronto, one of the largest meat packing companies in Canada, to donate the beautiful stained glass window on the front wall of the building, depicting an angel in front of the empty tomb and "HE IS RISEN" across the bottom. Rev. Wells told me that the window cost fifteen thousand dollars in 1915. He never did receive the esteem or recognition that he deserved.

Meanwhile, the Great Depression, that began in 1929 and lasted for us until the start of World War II, hit our family. Those were the worst of times for us financially. The farmers in dad's churches in North Buxton and Chatham Township were hard-pressed for money in those days, but they were generous with their meat, fowl, potatoes and vegetables, especially navy beans such that our table was always supplied in abundance. My mother could cook beans in so many ways that it seemed we had them for breakfast, lunch and supper. In addition, we, the young children in the family, had to be content with hand-me-down clothing and things that some of the more fortunate people in the community shared with us. We would have been right in style these days with our baggy pants and holey shirts.

The first and only bicycle that I owned as a boy was one of two that my brother George and I assembled from parts found in one or more of the three junk yards we visited every Saturday for weeks on end. We even patched the tires in order to have them remain inflated. I rode that bike all through my high school years delivering the Windsor Star on my paper route. My route, eight long blocks with the side streets, ran along McDougall Street from the Detroit River to Giles Boulevard. Before I could begin my deliveries I had to carry my paper bag, filled with over one hundred newspapers, five blocks from the Windsor Star building to McDougall Street. Before I learned to fold the papers in such a way that I could toss them to most of the front porches from my bicycle while riding on the sidewalk, it had taken me almost two hours to cover my route. With the bike I was able to cut the time almost in half.

Along that two mile, eight block stretch I never had more than 110 customers at any one time. On my route lived some of Windsor's poorest families and some who gave me real problems collecting the weekly paper money. Since I had to make deliveries immediately after four o'clock when the final edition of the paper came off the press, I had to forgo all of the after school extracurricular activities throughout my high school days. Then I had to make the collections on Saturday mornings, again forgoing any activities at that time. Nevertheless, I managed to fill my Saturday afternoons and my Christmas, Easter and summer holidays with all kinds of sports and other group endeavours.

During this period there was one very remarkable historical event connected to my newspaper experience. Just as I was finishing my deliveries one day, my friend Vern, my sister Luella's brother-in-law, met me and said that he had just heard on the radio that Charles Lindbergh's baby son had been kidnapped. Vern said that if we rushed down to the Windsor Star building right away, there would likely be an extra edition of the newspaper out that we could sell to the people getting off work at five o'clock. He was right. The extra did come off the press at about 4:45 p.m. The headline read, "LINDBERG BABY KIDNAPPED", in four-inch block letters, but when we folded the paper in half, all that showed was "LINDBERG BABY". Vern and I each sold our one hundred papers in less than fifteen minutes without moving away from the main intersection of Ouellette Avenue and Wyandotte Streets. In those days not many people had radios in their cars, so neither they nor those riding buses and streetcars would have heard the breaking news. I never sold an extra paper edition after that one. Since Vern had thought up the idea of selling the extra, we were the only ones selling it on the streets where we went. We had no competition.

I think that what our circumstances and limitations did for those of us who experienced those Roaring 20s and Hungry 30s was to instill in us a deep sense of the value of time, material, money, and I think, most of all, interpersonal relationships. Sure, you could buy a loaf of bread, a pound of butter, a quart of milk and a pound of hamburger, all for a dollar bill and get some change back, but who had a dollar bill? I was most fortunate to have had a newspaper route from 1927 until 1933, so unlike most of my companions I was relatively financially independent. When I was twelve years old I bought my first suit with two pairs of pants at Gray's Department Store on Ottawa Street for twelve dollars, and from that time on my parents never bought me an item of clothing. McCann shoes, the most stylish of men's shoes, sold in Detroit for $3.09, tax included, and Sam's department store, also in Detroit, had clothing and other things at discount prices.

Buying clothes in Detroit was more common for us in Windsor than buying them in Windsor. Shoes similar to Tom McCann's, but not nearly as stylish would be about double the price in Windsor. Also, nobody ever paid duty. We would wear our old things to the store in Detroit, change into our new things, scuff the soles of our new shoes up a bit and buy some peanuts and candy or other food that was duty-free. When the customs officer at the Canadian end of the Detroit Windsor Tunnel asked us if we had anything to declare, we didn't answer. We would just show him the food we had bought, and he would smile at us and wave us along. Call it smuggling if you will, but we called it surviving with very little resources.

As young children my friends and I did have the privilege of watching the building of the Ambassador Bridge, the longest single span suspension bridge in the world at that time. A year or so later we witnessed the construction of the Detroit Windsor Tunnel. A neighbour of ours, Mr. McCarthy, was the security guard on the tunnel site, and on Sunday afternoons he would take us down into the part under construction below the riverbed. It was cold and damp, but we three or four neighbourhood boys had the unique privilege of watching each phase of the project.

A black man named Lyndon Brooks operated the first electric streetcar in North America in Windsor in the early 1900s. At that time there were about five streetcar lines in the city. In 1928, when I started high school, Windsor Collegiate Institute (later named Central Collegiate Institute, then Patterson Collegiate Institute) was overcrowded, so we had to attend Grade 9 in the new John Campbell school about two miles south on Tecumseh Road. The board of education supplied us with tickets for the streetcar, and we rode on the Parent Avenue line. The streetcar on that line was a small one and like the one in the "Toonerville Trolley" comic strip of that period; it had just four wheels located in the middle of the car. Three or four of us boys would go to the back and make the car rock up and down until the trolley jumped off the power line. It was our way of enjoying the ride.

The first car I drove was a Gray Dort. When I was about fourteen years old a preacher friend of Dad's left his old Gray Dort in our shed (which later became our garage) while he went somewhere for a month. George and I figured out how to start the car without the key, so when Dad was as work we would push it out into the alley and take turns driving it up and down the length of the alleyway. We did this only a couple of times because we didn't want to burn too much of the preacher's gas.

As I reflect on those next five years I consider them the best of times in my life. I was happy in the Lord, happy at home, happy at school and happy at play. I enjoyed every aspect of church life: Sunday school, the Young People's Union and travelling with Dad on his regular Sunday trips to North Buxton, Dresden, Chatham Township and Shrewsbury. I made many friends, young and old, male and female, and I still relish the many old-fashioned country meals that we could expect each week as the dear women vied with each other to entertain their pastor and any members of his family travelling with him. It was an added thrill to receive my driver's license at the age of sixteen. I could then share the driving of the 1932 Model B Ford that Dad had acquired by then.

There has never been another vehicle like the Model B since that one. It had no starter and no gearshift. First you put the key in the ignition, turned it to spark (I think it was) gave the hand crank a quick jerk, being aware that the motor might kick the crank back if it backfired. Then after the motor started you ran around quickly and turned the key to run. But you weren't done yet. To get going you pressed the clutch pedal to the floor and released it slowly and evenly to allow the transmission to connect. There was no accelerator pedal; the throttle arm, which was the accelerator control, was attached to the steering column. To stop you pressed the clutch pedal halfway down and applied the brake pedal or the hand brake, whichever one was on the vehicle.

When Henry Ford came out with the Model A, with an electric starter, gearshift, manifold heater, balloon tires and high and low beam headlights, he revolutionized the auto industry. He would have revolutionized it even more if the story that dad told us was circulating around the plant had become a reality. According to the shop story Ford planned to give each of his employees a new Model A car and then sell them parts and service as required. The story I heard many years later when I worked at Ford's was that the Wall Street financiers threatened to bankrupt the company by cutting off its cash flow if he carried out his plan. Our second car was a new 1929 Model A four door sedan, which marked the beginning of a series of ownerships of many Ford vehicles by almost every one of Rev. Henry L. Talbot's descendants.

The Lord travelled with us throughout the years protecting us from harm and danger. Dad never had an accident driving the highways, country roads and city streets throughout the more than thirty five years of his preaching ministry. He didn't make much money though. There were weeks that I can remember when he would come home with less than five dollars after paying for his gasoline.

In high school, as I did in elementary school, I did well in those subjects that could be evaluated objectively such as math, science, French and Latin but not so well in English composition and literature. For the first four years I received the general proficiency school pins for the highest academic average in my class. However, in Grade 13 there were only subjects equivalent to first year university courses available. Consequently, usually only those students (almost all honour students) who intended to attend post-secondary institutions took the Grade13 courses. These were known as senior matriculation courses in Ontario.

Our family's financial situation made it virtually impossible for me to attend university, but jobs were scarce, and for non-white people like me those were practically unavailable. There was little else for me to do at seventeen years of age other than continuing in school as long as I could without cost to my parents. It would take thirty years for me to realize the material benefits of that fifth year in high school.

I could have quit and hung out with the other unemployed youths in the community, but I really enjoyed high school. During those five years I was part of the in-group on campus in a way that I had never experienced before. As I was an honour student, other boys, particularly athletes who were having difficulties with their schoolwork, sought me out to help them with math and science. Both the boys and girls who considered it a status symbol to be seen with the top athletes in the school therefore accepted me along with the big men on campus.

Among the boys with whom I associated on campus was Walter, the son of a member of one of the most prestigious law firms in the city. They were part owners of the second largest department store in town (Bartlet, MacDonald and Gow, commonly known as Bartlets'), where my wife, Marietta, worked from 1954 to

1965. There was also Hugh, the son of the pastor of the large downtown Presbyterian Church. Wilbert was the son of a prominent physician who was also a deacon in the big Temple Baptist Church, and whom we nicknamed Jake for some reason or other. Another Hugh became the city engineer for Philadelphia, Pennsylvania, in his adult years. Finally, there was Irving Toots Meretsky, son of one of the owners of the largest furniture store in town. He played on the Canadian Olympic basketball team in 1936 and established his own furniture store in the mid-1950s.

I was also able to make friends among the girls even though there were no black girls my age in the school. In Grade 10 a tall blonde girl named Velma insisted that I should attend the class sleigh ride party in spite of the fact that I was the only non-white in the class. Reluctantly I went and Velma and her friend Marie, a redheaded girl who later won the title of Miss Western Ontario, saw that I was made to feel accepted on the sleigh ride and for the serving of hot chocolate and donuts afterward. There were only four or five other black girls in high school during my years there, but they were either a couple of years older or a couple of years younger than I was and accordingly interested in boys of a suitable dating age for them.

When I was in Grade 13 I was assigned to sit in an all girls' Grade 11 class for a weekly study period. I was expected to assist any of the girls who requested help in those subjects in which I had excelled. In this way I came to know several of these girls personally. Two of them played a significant role in my teenage years and beyond. Ivy was a member of the school swimming team. One Friday night there was to be an intercollegiate swimming meet at Kennedy Collegiate, the only high school with a pool area large enough for spectators. Ivy asked me if I would walk with her to Kennedy C.I., about two miles from our school, Patterson C.I., and then see her to her home after the meet. I was aware that she could have taken the bus to the meet and home afterward, or that she could have gone with other members of the team, but being a reckless teenager I accepted her invitation.

After the meet I asked Ivy where she lived, and when she told me on Bruce Avenue down by the Detroit River, a distance of about five miles. I suggested that we should take the bus. She insisted on walking since it was only about 8:30 p.m. and she didn't have to be home until ten o'clock. As we walked we talked mostly about school things but also about our families. I learned that Ivy was an only child and lived with her mother. We arrived in front of her house at just about ten o'clock. Unsure of what to do at this point I stood there shifting from one foot to the other. After an awkward pause I reached to shake her hand and bid her goodnight, but Ivy pulled me to her and planted a kiss on my lips. I felt like running away as fast as I could, but at that moment Ivy's mother appeared in the front doorway and called out, "Ivy, don't stand out there. Bring the young man inside."

I wasn't prepared for the reception I received since at that point in time it was strictly taboo in that part of Canada for a black boy to be seen in public with a white girl. Mrs. Mason, however, was very gracious, serving us milk and cookies and holding a very pleasant conversation with us. Ivy never invited me to walk her home again although we remained friends throughout that school year until I graduated. About twenty years later I happened to be in the income tax office and guess who served me, Ivy Mason. After reminiscing about our school days she suggested that we should get together for coffee someday even though we were both married. She probably knew as I did that this was an unlikely possibility.

The other girl in that Grade 11 class who played a significant role in my teenage years and beyond was Margaret Power. Margaret had real difficulties fathoming the intricacies of Grade 11 algebra, so she asked me if I would come to her house after school on Fridays when we got out forty minutes early. She assured me that she had cleared it with her mom, and so the next Friday I accompanied her home. She also was an only daughter, and when we arrived at the family apartment her mother greeted me cordially, left some treats on the kitchen table and left the room. About an hour later when I was about to leave, Margaret's mother reappeared accompanied by her husband. Her mother introduced me explaining that I was the boy who had agreed to tutor Margaret in algebra. The father, however, was less than cordial when he saw who I was and mumbled something inaudible under his breath as he turned and left the kitchen.

That was the end of my tutoring sessions at Margaret's house, but they continued in the school study room. Margaret became a model after leaving high school, working in Detroit and Toronto. We would occasionally meet on the street during the next ten years or so, maintaining a friendly relationship. In the early 1950s I was heavily involved in the civil rights movement in Windsor. On several occasions I appeared on a local radio program entitled, "Labour Speaks". Margaret was a disc jockey at the station at that point in time, so we were able to renew our friendship. She became involved with our group called the Windsor Interracial Council (later called the Windsor Council on Group Relations) for a period of time acting as our recording secretary. This meant, of course, that she attended our executive meetings as well as some committee meetings, and on occasion accompanied us to after meeting coffee sessions at the home of one of our members.

I didn't own an automobile in those days, so both Margaret and I would receive a ride home with Bond, our publicity coordinator, and his wife. One night, after we had let Margaret off at her apartment, Bond stopped the car in front of my house, turned off the ignition and said, "Lyle, there's something I have to tell you." I had by this time suspected what that something was about, so I was not taken completely by surprise when Bond continued, "Margaret has confided in my wife that she is falling in love with you. She has told us about your long friendship since high school days, and she said that, for her, friendship has turned into love. We have explained to her that you are a happily married man and that she shouldn't get romantically involved with you. Margaret is prepared to continue seeing you even if it means putting your marriage in jeopardy. How do you feel about it?"

My response was as firm but as gentle as I could make it. "Listen, Bond, I have very deep feelings for Margaret, going back many years, but I'm not prepared to risk my marriage, now or at any time in the future. I'll tell Margaret that I would like to keep her only as a friend; my wife and my children mean too much to me."

I never got the chance to tell Margaret this. Bond and his wife must have convinced her of my decision, for she resigned immediately from our group and I never saw her again. Bond told me later that she had resumed her modeling career in Toronto. Who knows how my life would have evolved if, for instance, Ivy Mason's mother had invited me back or if Margaret's father had been friendlier. Suffice it to say, that in the years before the civil rights movement of the 1950s interracial relationships between males and females were taboo in Canadian society as well as in the United States.

My first real girlfriend, Harriett, nicknamed Hattie, was the youngest in a family of about four boys and three girls. We often gathered at one of the family homes in Buxton, and Hattie's niece, Gloria, an accomplished pianist, would play hymns and folk songs for us to sing along. Hattie remained my steady girlfriend in Buxton until I graduated from high school.

If there was ever a period in my life when being black was not a pressing problem, except for a few isolated unpleasant incidents, my high school time was it. One outstanding incident occurred one day when the class was reading aloud passages from a short story called "The Municipal Report", a tale of the American Old South. One of the characters was a black hack driver who was a caricature of just about every negative stereotype of black men held by white people. In that particular class there were three of us black students. I never did understand why the teacher chose that story to read aloud considering the kind of language the author used, but when she picked one of us, Lloyd, to read a passage containing the phrase "you old fool nigger", that was the last straw. Lloyd refused to say those words and the three of us got up spontaneously and left the room. A few of the white students came to us afterwards to express their sympathy, but most of the rest considered the matter a big joke. None joined us in the walkout. As for the teacher she did nothing except to ask another student to continue reading. In the next class she selected another story and treated the matter as though nothing unusual had occurred.

During my time at Patterson C.I. there were from fifteen to perhaps fifty other black students in attendance from year to year. The only times that we faced racial problems was when we had an overtly prejudiced teacher or at purely extracurricular activities such as school dances. There were a few white students who brought their prejudices and inhibitions into the high school world, but they were a very small minority.

The schools in places like Chatham, Dresden, London and Toronto were much like those in Windsor and Amherstburg. In other small communities like North Buxton and Harrow, where the population was almost all black, the facilities were far less adequate. However, they almost always had black teachers who took a personal interest in the children and who, in cases like that of Mr. Alexander in North Buxton, provided wise counseling, guidance and inspiration to their students.

For blacks in Nova Scotia the school situation was quite different from that in Ontario. It seems that in places like Africville and the black satellite communities on the fringes of white towns the education of black children was sorely neglected. As an illustration, on an occasion in 1972, it was necessary for me to interview a number of men involved in a racial problem on the Halifax dockyards. Three of these men were blacks in their late fifties or early sixties. All three of them were unable to read and comprehend a simple document; one of them could not even sign his name. All of these men would have been of normal school age at the same time as I, and they were all Nova Scotia born Canadians. I'm sure that one could not have found three black persons in that age group in Windsor as illiterate as any of those three men.

The lack of adequate facilities, the neglect, either benign or malignant by white teachers and the general poverty of the people did not deter some from acquiring as good an education as possible under the circumstances. In fact, for some, the apparent handicaps proved to be a challenge to meet, an impediment to overcome. Nevertheless, for many, the struggle was not worth the prize. My friend Alfred, for example, an above average student, made it to grade 12 before he gave up. When he started talking about quitting school I tried to persuade him to stick with it at least until he graduated, but Alfred's family was having a hard time during the Depression. His younger sister had tuberculosis and spent her entire life in and out of the sanitarium without the benefit of medicare in those days. Alfred tried. He studied. He did his homework. He attended Sunday school regularly, even acting as secretary. But he was very poor, very dark and very bitter. Who knows what potential was lost forever when Alfred dropped out. What I do know is that one who was capable of achieving much was found a few years later bumming drinks from one cheap Toronto bar to another after being fired from his job as a sleeping car porter for excessive drinking on the job.

Walter, the brother of James Watson, was another black student in my Grade 10 class. Two things stand out in my memory of Walt. One was his uniquely humourous style in delivering oral compositions. Once he gave a speech about hunting rabbits and another time one on repairing his car. Both were informative, well delivered and interspersed with humourous anecdote, all of which kept the class in rapt attention and gained the praise and an appropriately high grade from the teacher. Another situation concerned a mathematics exam. Walt finished the paper in less than half the allotted time and then whiled away the time waiting for the teacher to receive his paper by scribbling nonsense notes on every page. The next day the teacher returned his exam paper to him with instructions to recopy it without the scribbling. Well Walt went further than that. He changed all the answers. The teacher informed him that his first answers had all been correct and would have earned him a perfect 100 percent. She asked him why he had changed everything. Walt's excuse was that he was sure that the teacher would think that he had copied the correct answers from another student. No one was surprised when Walt dropped out of school as soon as he reached sixteen years of age.

Some may say that Walter didn't deserve to succeed, but who knows what went on in the mind of a very bright boy who saw himself as a victim of discrimination, a second-class member of his local community and even in his own family. What reward did the future hold for him for good effort? Since their father was employed as a common labourer, Walter knew that he would not be able to go beyond high school for financial reasons. He didn't receive the same kind of encouragement as Jim did and who was already in university when Walt was in high school.

There are many parallels to Alfred and Walt's stories. During the Depression of the 1930s many young people experienced feelings of frustration and hopelessness, and many, both white and black, gave up the struggle. On the one hand, white kids could have hopes of someday getting out of their deprived situation when times got better. On the other hand, for blacks there was no such hope. The black high school student of the 1930s had more obstacles than the Depression to overcome. He knew that even if he did finish school and even if times did get better, he would be hard-pressed to find a job in which he could utilize his educational achievements simply because he was black. In fact he would be lucky to get any job at all. A few of us did stay in school clinging to a slim hope that had little foundation in reality: some of us, because there was nothing else to do with our time with no job and no money. In

1933, the year in which I graduated from grade 13, there were no graduation ceremonies. This was to avoid embarrassing those students who had no decent clothes to wear.

VOICES IN THE WILDERNESS

How does a black person in Canada become involved in social action to combat racism in an organized way? What kinds of resources must mobilized and what skills are needed to conduct an effective program?

You may ask why social action groups or protest movements did not emerge in Toronto, Montreal, Halifax or other places where blacks were subjected to similar treatment. The answer is that they did, but efforts to combat discrimination were sporadic and diffuse. Several reasons for this included such issues as diversity of attitudes, the lack of consensus as to the best way to attack the problem and the fact that blacks as a group were poor and either could not or would not communicate over large distances. The exceptions were brief periods when local groups and individuals coordinated their efforts to achieve a common short range goal. When that goal was achieved or the cooperative effort became diffused through frustration, attrition or disagreement, it was common for most of the local leaders to drop out of the action as well.

Racial discrimination was practiced openly in all parts of Canada prior to World War II and it permeated every aspect of life — employment, housing, services, accommodations, education, and religion — wherever there was any form of social interaction between the races. A few individuals and small groups who had stood up to challenge the system in isolated instances had managed to break down small barriers here and there, primarily through protest, but the patterns of discrimination and the social arrangements which emanated therefrom did not noticeably change.

The first indication of an organized movement in Windsor began in the early days of the Depression when a group of concerned people formed the Central Citizens Association. Its primary purpose was to obtain jobs for black people and to take complaints about the administration of welfare and similar matters to the civil authorities. The Association flourished for about six years with monthly meetings attended by twenty-five to over one hundred people depending on the importance of the items on the agenda. Their method was one of pleading as opposed to demanding, or compromising rather than confronting. Whether or not it was one individual or fifty people who had the same complaint, the Association considered each complaint separately rather than as a common problem or as the basis for some sort of class action. For example if John Doe was refused a job or a house because of his colour, a committee would try to find him a job or a house somewhere else. Accordingly, the Association did not attack discrimination as a problem common to all blacks but as the problem of a particular individual.

Even when a problem arose that had an impact on the whole community, this mindset whereby the interests of the individual took precedence over the interests of the whole group as a racial entity persisted. This was exemplified in 1943 when Central Mortgage And Housing Corporation proposed building a block of about twenty wartime houses at the intersection of McDougall and Elliot streets, in the heart of the existing black residential district. CMHC had consistently refused to place black families in white neighborhoods. It had repeatedly relegated black families to the bottom of a waiting list. These new houses were intended for those families. When the announcement of this proposal was made, a meeting of concerned citizens was called. About 150 black residents of Windsor attended the meeting and passed a resolution objecting to the building of houses exclusively for blacks.

The resolution called for the assignment of black families to already existing vacant wartime houses throughout the city and to assign the new houses on a first come, first served basis without discrimination. I was one of a delegation of three property owners appointed to present the resolution to a joint meeting of CMHC officials and city council members. When we arrived at the city hall we found a group of three black applicants for housing already there. They were led by a well known Uncle Tom type leader with a record of collaborating with the establishment on racial matters. Our delegation was told that since these applicants were most directly concerned with the problem of housing and did not object to the segregated housing arrangement, we obviously did not represent the views of our people. Because of this meeting the twenty houses were built and for a quarter of a century they were occupied exclusively by blacks.

The efforts of that delegation were not entirely in vain. After this particular group of wartime houses was filled, black families were given houses in other parts of the city. Then after the war, under pressure from organizations like the Windsor Council on Group Relations and the labour unions, government subsidized housing was virtually accessible to all people without discrimination.

In spite of its aforementioned shortcomings the Central Citizens Association was responsible for the formation around 1933 of the very successful auxiliary for black youth, the Science Arts and Crafts Club. The club achieved a membership of well over one hundred, the largest organization of black youth ever to function in Windsor.

They raised money to finance their activities primarily by giving dances. As the name implies, the club had three subgroups for members interested in developing their knowledge and skills in a science, an art or a craft. I was in a group that studied the art of developing black and white film and I continued to develop my own snapshots until coloured pictures became the in thing. The two most active committees of the club were the social committee, which operated the dances, and the citizenship committee, which dealt with the serious socio-economic problems faced by black youths during that period of the Great Depression.

Most of the young people were active in their respective churches as well, but they realized the denominational traditions that limited the kinds of activities they could sponsor. They got around some of these limitations by supporting en masse the Parliament of Youth of the British Methodist Church, the Christian Endeavor Society of the African Methodist Episcopal Church and the Baptist Young People's Union of First Baptist Church. It was not unusual for a person to be on the executive of all three youth groups. Each year the young people conducted an ecumenical youth service in each of the three churches. Some of the largest congregations of any function held in any of the churches attended these services.

The black youth of Windsor received many benefits from these experiences: experiences which were to serve them well throughout their adult lives. They learned to work together in groups, to talk through differences, to organize for specific purposes, to conduct meetings in an orderly fashion, to settle disputes and solve common problems. They learned the importance of being consistent, persistent and dependable when they accepted responsibility. Virtually all of the black community leaders and successful blacks in the immediate post World War II era had been active in the Science Arts And Crafts Club as youths. Some of them will be mentioned in later stories of some of the black graduates of Windsor's high schools in the mid-1930s.

THE REAL WORLD

Among my generation it was a commonly accepted fact that, before there was such a thing as human rights legislation, blacks were the last hired and the first fired. There was no recourse for them to endeavor to change it no matter how unfair the situation may have appeared. As a member of the clergy my father was one of the more privileged men in the community. Even with eight children he managed to stay off welfare primarily because he was able to hold onto his job at the auto plant. The work was hard and the foreman demanded more and more production from him. Every night his hands and forearms would be livid with the irritation from the solutions used to wash the fine metal particles from the parts he machined. Moreover, his mind was never at ease; there was always the threat that he would be the next one laid off at the whim of his foreman. This was a situation which happened several times during the Depression, but he was always called back to work just in time, it seemed, to save him from applying for welfare. We managed to survive with the few dollars he received from the three-point pastorate that he held and the two or three days' work he got at the factory,

My own work experience began as a newspaper delivery boy. When I turned sixteen and had been a delivery boy for more than three years, an opening occurred for a jumper. The jumper's job was to help count and bale the bundles of papers for the various routes in the area, and then ride on the back of the truck and toss the bundles off at the corners where the route boys would be waiting to start their deliveries. I went to see my supervisor, Tom, to apply for the jumper's job. I was aware that Tom had chosen the previous route boy to be a jumper. Tom told me that I would have to speak to his brother Charlie, the circulation manager. When I approached Charlie he greeted me by asking how my dad was. Both Tom and Charlie were originally from Dresden, Ontario, where they had played on the town baseball team for which my dad was the catcher or in the town band in which my dad played the trombone.

When I asked Charlie about the jumper job he said, "Sorry, Lyle. As much as I would like to do something for my old friend Henry's boy, I can't put a coloured boy on one of our trucks." When I asked for a reason he replied, "That it is just the way things are." So much for nepotism when discrimination is a factor! As long as I lived in Windsor (until 1970), no black person was ever employed by the Windsor Star other than as a route boy, and that only because a route boy could sell or give his route to anyone he chose.

My second experience with racial discrimination in employment came during the summer of 1933, soon after my graduation from Grade 13. I received a letter from the Ford Motor Company inviting me to an interview with the prospect of employment as a trainee in a supervisory role or other related work. There was the potential for advancement in the office or factory. Enthusiastically I dressed in my Sunday best and arrived at the personnel office well before the appointed time of the interview. By the time of the appointment I was a bit surprised to see about seventeen boys including most of my classmates and others whom I had known from the other high schools in the city. They had all received the same letter as I had. While waiting in a large room we exchanged ideas about the purpose of the invitations.

Right on time a young man seated at a desk in the room began to call the names in alphabetical order: Andrews, Bellemer, Cook, etc. As his name was called each boy would stop at the desk for a minute and then proceed through a door into what I presumed was an inner office. When my name, Talbot, almost the last to be called, came up, I stepped up to the desk. The young man checked my address, telephone number and birthday. Then he excused himself and left the room. He returned in a couple of minutes, sat down and said, "I'm sorry, Lyle, but we don't have anything for you right now. We have your phone number; we'll call you if something comes up."

That was my first encounter with the "Don't call us; we'll call you" approach. It's interesting that in Canada whenever a person was about to commit an act of racial discrimination on a personal basis, they invariably prefaced their act with an apology: "I'm sorry, but . . . ." I never heard of that being the case in the southern United States or South Africa. I guess Canadians are just more polite in that regard. However, my curiosity was working overtime.

What was happening with the other young men, none of whom had come out of the inner office? I decided to wait and see. Andrews was the first to emerge. He had been offered a supervisory trainee position in the production office. Bellemer got a job as a foreman trainee in the machine shop. Norwood was offered a position in the parts and accessories division. Fisher was offered a trainee job but turned it down because he planned to work in his father's men's clothing store. As a matter of fact every single one of the other boys who had shown up for the interview was offered some kind of employment. I didn't get past the reception desk.

On the way back home something else dawned on me. I was the only non-white boy there. Why weren't the three or four other non-whites who had graduated present? Simmons, a black graduate in my class, was the son of an eccentric bearded preacher who blew his long, straight trumpet every morning at eight o'clock and who preached every Wednesday and Saturday at the open air farmers' market downtown. His name would no doubt have been known to the Ford personnel office. Besides, his address on Mercer Street was right in the center of the black section of town. I learned later that he had not received the invitation. On the other hand, no one could tell from my name, Talbot, whether I was white or black and our address on Lillian Street was well outside the center of the black community. Also missing from the boys assembled in that waiting room was Wing Chu, whose Chinese origin was obvious from his name, and Meretsky, whose family was prominent in the Jewish community. Fisher was also Jewish, but not so readily identifiable by his name.

Seven years later, in 1940, I did receive a job at Ford's, and during the thirty years that I worked for the company, I was at one time or another under the supervision of at least four of the young men who were hired on that day. Many years later I heard Rev. C.L. Wells, my pastor, say, "The problem is the black man doesn't present a problem until he presents himself." I have experienced the truth of that statement many times since that first time that I presented myself. Was racial discrimination that obvious in central Canada in the 1930s? Let me assure you that it was! The black community could draw a line on the map from the north end of Lake Huron due east across southern Ontario to Oshawa, a line known as the Mason-Dixon Line of Canada, named after the imaginary line that divided the northern United States from the southern states during the days of rigid racial discrimination and segregation.

I spent the rest of the summer of 1933 looking for work and taking whatever jobs I could find. Mr. Burman, a Jewish chicken dealer who lived several houses down the street from us, told my friend Saul that he needed someone to drive his truck for a few days because his son, who usually drove for him, had to go out of town. I agreed to drive him for two dollars a day plus food and lodging. We started out early the first morning, drove to Tilbury about thirty miles east of Windsor and started visiting farmers who might have chickens for sale. It was fascinating to watch Mr. Burman haggle with the farmers over the price and then over the size and health of the chickens to be bought. Finally we would load the crates of live chickens onto the pickup truck.

Lunchtime came and Mr. Burman offered to pay the farmer's wife for a meal. Interestingly enough, Mr. Burman ate whatever it was that was served, not even asking whether the food was kosher. When suppertime came, however, we were in

Dresden and he told me to drive to Inwood, a few miles further north, where a relative of his lived. Here the Jewish family had prepared a kosher meal whereby they served the milk foods separately from the meat foods. I didn't get a chance to taste the kosher foods. I was given some meat and potatoes and told to eat my meal outside in the truck. It was not at all an appetizing setting with the smell of chickens permeating the air. I slept in the truck too even though Mr. Burman's relatives lived in a large two story house.

Arriving home sometime late the next evening we unloaded the crates of chickens into his garage that was more like a barn. Then the haggling began over my pay. According to him the trip had been a bad one, and in that case he wouldn't be able to pay me the full two days' pay even though I had put in much more than the usual eight hours each day. I don't remember how much I finally got except that it was less than I had been promised. It wasn't that Mr. Burman was dishonest; he just hated to part with money.

Another job I had that summer was at Speedy Auto Wash. Eight of us fellows shared ten percent of the price of the wash, which in those days was about one dollar, with fifty cents extra for vacuuming the inside and three to five dollars for a wax job. The two guys who did the waxing shared in the wash money, but the rest of us didn't share in their portion of the waxing job. On an average day I probably made about a dollar, but on a Saturday with good weather I would make as much as three dollars. On the busiest Saturday during the few weeks that I worked there, we washed over 150 cars between 8:00 a.m. and 5:00 p.m. My job involved washing and scrubbing the wheels and undercarriages on one side of the vehicle. On rainy days and other slow days we just sat around and exchanged stories. I don't remember what I talked about; I think I mostly listened to the tales of sexual exploits and conquests of the other fellows. Judging from the way they tried to outdo one another with their tales it was my impression that the stories were largely exaggerations or perhaps even figments of their vivid imaginations.

After my experience in that summer of 1933 I began to think much about the injustices that I had observed in Canada and throughout the world. I resolved to do what I could to combat these injustices. I sat down one day, compiled a list of things, and gave them the title, "My Purpose in Life". I lost the original list that I made when I began to become involved in social action, but here is the list several years later as I recall it:

My Purpose in Life

To live so that other people with whom I come in contact may be constrained to live better.

To help establish coloured *(sic)* business enterprises built on a community stock basis wherever I may be located.

To strive to promote a classless society, devoid of all prejudices, jealousies and mental complexes.

To instill in the minds of all people a sense of equality.

To help to promote better housing projects for those in need.

To advocate a more humane and scientific treatment of criminals.

To advocate free education for youth based on publicly owned and operated universities, technical schools, secondary and elementary schools.

To advocate the elimination of all involuntary unemployment and the abolishment of the profiteering and exploiting classes

To aim for the implementation of employee profit sharing.

To advocate that the study or even the publication of all literature that tends to awaken racial prejudice or class distinction be abolished.

To uphold the beliefs and practices of Christianity as the only religion that makes men brothers.

To strive to eliminate mental, physical and economic slavery and all other forms of evil.

To teach that the true values of life are not the material elements: i.e. success is not the accumulation of vast monetary possessions but the accomplishment of a noble purpose.

To prove to humanity that true charity is not giving money to the poor but that charity means the opening up of the doors of opportunity so that the person toward whom the charity is directed may be able to exert his latent talents and abilities.

To prove by example that one finds true happiness in helping to improve the mental, spiritual and physical condition of those in distress.

To advocate that the privileges and rights of all citizens be equalized and exercised. That is, to advocate the freedom of the individual so long as the freedom of the community is not hampered.

To promote peace through a better understanding and a more tolerant love and respect for individuals, groups and nations.

To spread the gospel of Jesus Christ as the only ultimate hope for mankind.

When September came around I began to ponder my next move. Post-secondary education seemed to be impossible for me until one day when my former math teacher, Mr. Orr, who was also a deacon in Temple Baptist church, called me.

Mr. Orr told me that McMaster University was offering a scholarship in mathematics and that if I wanted to repeat my Grade 13 year the dean had agreed to let me compete even though I had already tried for a scholarship the previous year and had placed fourth in the province. I discussed the proposition with my parents, and my dad pointed out that even if I were to win the scholarship I would have to have money for room and board and clothing. We just couldn't afford those expenses.

When Mr. Orr was unable to assure me that I would find work in Hamilton, I decided that another year of academic work would be fruitless. On the advice of my elders, who were believers in the theory of Booker T. Washington that the best future for black youth was to learn a trade, I enrolled in the electrical course at Windsor Vocational School. Due to my age and my knowledge of elementary physics, learned in Grades 12 and 13, I was assigned to a third year class with the understanding that the other boys, who had had two years in electricity, would help me with any problems I encountered.

During the first two years the boys had been taught the basic principles of electricity and simple wiring methods. This third year class was beginning to learn about motors, dynamos, generators and other such things. The problem for me was that whenever I encountered difficulty in following a circuit, a schematic, an armature or a blue print, no one in the class seemed to be able to help me. I began to think that the guys in the class didn't know much more than I did, so they couldn't help me. Besides, I was told that even if I did get a diploma, I'd have to find an electrical company that would hire me as an apprentice. This too was an unlikely possibility since a master electrician had never taken on a black boy as an apprentice in Windsor. Unless I was prepared to go it on my own, as two black men had done in previous years, electricity wasn't the trade for me. I wouldn't even be able to join the union if I did manage to serve an apprenticeship. Neither of the two black electrical contractors had been able to obtain journeyman's papers; hence they could not take on an apprentice that would be recognized by the trade. Thus my career as an electrician came to an abrupt end after less than two months.

I was walking down Mercer Street one afternoon soon after I quit the course when I met my second cousin, Ted. He called me over and asked, "Hey! Cuz, how would you like a job?" I was sure that he was joking as he had often done, so I played along.

"Just where is this great job you were going to give me?"

"No!" he went on, "John Brown!" (Ted's favourite epithet) "I'm serious. If you want a job, be at the Norton Palmer where I work at eight o'clock tomorrow morning. You can tell your brother, George, and any of your buddies who want to work to come too. I knew that Ted was a bell captain at the hotel, but I didn't see how he could be offering several jobs to us.

With some misgivings I arrived at the rear entrance of the hotel the next morning along with my brother, my cousin Harold and two other friends. Ted met us along with another older man in a bellman's uniform with a badge designating him as the superintendent of service. Ted introduced him as Albert who explained that the hotel had been compelled to lay off all the female elevator operators, so they were replacing them with boys more than sixteen years of age.

There were four elevators in the building: two passenger elevators in the front lobby, a freight elevator at the back and a service elevator on the other side of the building used for room service from the kitchen. Someone had been selected to teach each of us how to operate the elevators; as a result I spent several hours going up and down, stopping at various floors, missing floors and having to go up and down, up and down until I could stop the elevator within four inches of each landing. In those days elevators didn't stop automatically at each floor. The operator had to do it manually using a crank-like control. Sometimes it took two or more tries to get the elevator floor within the four inch limit. At the end of the day Ted informed us that all five of us had been hired, and that there was still one opening. With a total of six operators there would be three operators for each watch or shift.

As we left the hotel that day we were still going up and down, up and down in our minds. We decided to celebrate our new jobs since each of us had received a week's pay of five dollars each in advance. As we made our way home someone suggested that we should stop at the home of an Italian family on McDougall Street, where we could buy a bottle of Dago Red wine for a quarter.

I don't remember how much Dago Red I drank that evening, but when I arrived home, still going up and down in my mind, I headed straight for my bed. I don't know where my brother George went. We usually slept in the same bed, but that evening he couldn't have gone to bed because the bed never stopped rolling repeatedly until I finally went to sleep.

In 1934, while working at the hotel as an elevator operator, I applied for a job as a meteorologist with the federal government. I received close to 90 percent on the written examination and was given an oral interview in the hotel where I worked. After the interview I returned to my elevator and in a short time the two men who had interviewed me got on my elevator. One of them commented, "Well, Lyle, why didn't you tell us you could run an elevator? It might have made a difference." Do I need to mention that I failed the oral examination? What did running an elevator have to do with reading a weather map?

For almost two years I held that elevator job at five dollars a week. The girls whom we had replaced had received some gratuities from guests, but we rarely did. The regular guests resented the fact that the girls, whom they had come to know and like, had been fired. I eventually learned that they had been replaced because the government of Ontario had passed a minimum wage law for women working a certain number of hours a week, and the hotel had decided to replace them with boys for whom there was no minimum wage. Interestingly, the other large hotel in the city retained the female elevator operators for many years until it was closed in the 1970s.

Sometime during the months that I worked in that hotel, my interest in spiritual things was reawakened. I used to carry a pocket New Testament in my uniform, and when the elevator traffic was slow I would read from it. My co-worker, Morris, was nicknamed Mutt, which was ironic, since Mutt was quite short in stature, while Mutt in the comic strip "Mutt and Jeff" was quite tall and Jeff was the short one. Mutt worked the same shift as I did on one of the passenger elevators and we had many conversations, sometimes arguments, about religion. His mother was a faithful member of the British Methodist Church, but Mutt and his two older brothers seldom if ever attended with her. Mutt used to refer to the "dirty foot Methodists" and the "kinky haired Baptists", an allusion to the different modes of baptism. The Methodists were dirty foot because they wouldn't go into the water and the Baptists were kinky haired because when they were immersed, their straightened or konked hair had a tendency to revert to its natural kinky texture.

One Saturday an electrical storm hit Windsor and a bolt of lightning tore a large hole in the side of the B.M.E. Church. During the next shift Mutt's comment was that the only way that the Lord could get into the church was to kick a hole in the wall. Referring to the trouble in the Baptist church a few years previously, he said that the preacher ought to be like another one he had heard about and hide a pistol behind the pulpit. His favourite way of ridiculing me was to say that I went around with the Bible in one hand and a glass of wine in the other. He had a valid excuse for his ridicule because he had seen me take a glass of beer or wine on two or three occasions. Partying guests would ring for the elevator, and when we arrived at their floor they would insist that we must join them in a drink. I regret to this day that I was such a weak Christian. I might have been a better witness to Mutt as well as to the other people I worked with in the two hotels in which I worked if I had been stronger.

Working in hotels was an extremely great challenge to a young Christian. The whole atmosphere in a hotel was one of pleasure seeking and immorality. The travelling public was largely out for a good time and they always had lots of money to spend. As an elevator operator I was not exposed as much to those influences as the bellmen and waiters were since I dealt only with the guests going and coming to and from their rooms.

In the summer of 1936, when I turned twenty-one, the other large hotel in Windsor, the Prince Edward, offered me a job as a bellhop. There I came into close contact with travelling sales people, tourists, convention attendees, business persons, politicians, professional people, spouses cheating on their mates and well to do alcoholics hiding out in the hotel. My duty as a bellhop was to cater to the desires and fancies of the guests because, in hotel parlance, the guest is always right. If a guest complained that a bellhop failed to give good service, the bellhop had no defense unless his reason was that he would be breaking the law by complying with the guest's demand. Even when it would have meant breaking the law, such as when the guest wanted the bellhop to procure a woman for immoral purposes, a situation which was frequently the case, the bellhop ran the risk of being disciplined if the guest chose to falsify the grounds for his complaint.

Let me give a couple of examples of this kind of situation during my five years as a bellhop. One involved an airplane pilot who had made a forced landing in Windsor and had checked into the hotel to await repair to his airplane. He stayed for three nights drinking heavily the whole time. He said he had a few hundred dollars when he registered, but when he went to check out he didn't have enough money to pay the bill. Only two bellhops had served him, my brother-in-law, who was on the other watch, and me. When he was ready to check out he alleged that someone must have stolen his money. My brother-in-law, who was on the shift when he was checking out, was not suspected in the theft.

I was summoned to come in and face the guest and I feared for my job as I made my way to the hotel because the pilot had been overly generous in his tips with me. For example, on one occasion he had given me a ten dollar bill to go and buy him a fifty cent tube of toothpaste. When I returned I proceeded to hand him his change, but he told me to keep it. Overall, in the two and a half days that he stayed in the hotel, he had given me about thirty dollars in tips. I must have prayed a prayer as I entered the manager's office. I told the manager that the guest had been very generous with tips to me and I was prepared to give all the money back. But when the pilot saw me enter the office he exclaimed, "Oh no! It wasn't Lyle. Whatever money he got from me I gave to him." The manager agreed to trust him to remit the amount of his bill by mail. After he left my brother-in-law explained to the manager that the guest had been drinking heavily and probably was not fully aware of the amount of the tips he gave us.

The other incident that I will recount was a little unusual since it involved the assistant manager who was a paraplegic. He was able to move about all day in his wheelchair, but when he was ready to go to bed at night he needed someone to assist him and then turn out the light in his room. It was the last boy's duty to answer this call. On the night in question I was the last boy, meaning that I was last to respond to a guest's request for service. I had never performed this task before, so, being aware of the assistant manager's brusque way of dealing with employees, I was a bit nervous when the call came to go to Room 202.

I did everything that I had been instructed to do. Then as I was about to leave I asked, "Will that be all, sir? "He grunted in the affirmative, and I opened the door to go. I had used the passkey to enter the room, and as I closed the door behind me I instinctively turned the key in the lock as we always did when leaving a room. In the hotel we worked alternate long and short days. On the long days we worked from 7:00 a.m. until noon and from 6:00 p.m. until 11:00 p.m. On our short days we worked only from noon until 6:00 p.m. It was on my long day that I had gone to the assistant manager's room at about 10:00 p.m. I was called in at nine o'clock the next morning by the manager. The manager, the house detective and the superintendent of service were there to meet me when I arrived.

The superintendent spoke. "I understand that you locked the assistant manager in his room last night. Is that true?" Suddenly I remembered turning the passkey in the lock. Mr. R. had heard the click of the key in the lock and was unable to rest; he had worried that something might happen and he wouldn't be able to get to his wheelchair get out of the room. I could think of several ways that he could have handled such an occurrence, use the telephone for one. But I had broken a strict rule of the house, and for that I was fired. I've always felt that I was suspected of breaking some other rule for which they didn't have any proof.

"CLIMBING THE MOLASSES MOUNTAIN"

"Blacks are climbing the molasses mountain wearing snowshoes while whites ride the ski lift to the top." Joe Drummond, New Brunswick Black Activist

Alton Parker was a black contemporary who had some remarkable experiences. On an athletic trip the members of the Lowe Vocational School football team stopped at a Chatham restaurant on the way home from London, Ontario. There was an argument between the coach and the manager of the dining room over whether or not the restaurant was going to serve Parker. In a few minutes the team themselves settled the argument. They got up from the table and left their meals untouched and unpaid for. About fifteen years later that same Alton Parker became Windsor's first fully recognized black police constable and a few years later he was still the only detective of black ancestry the city had ever had. In 1976 he received the Order of Canada medal for his outstanding police and community work.

Other blacks who graduated from Windsor's high schools in the 1930s included a chemist who became one of the leading specialists in foundry operations in North America, a manufacturing entrepreneur, an ophthalmologist, a medical doctor, a drafting engineer, an outstanding pianist, an organist music teacher, a nurse, two social workers, two clergymen, a hospital administrator and more. One of the social workers, Ken Jacobs, eventually joined the Canadian Air Force and became the first black to attain the rank of lieutenant colonel; the other became a senior parole officer with the Canadian correctional services commission. All of these managed to complete their post-secondary education and establish themselves in Canada. Another group went to the United States in search of career opportunities. Of these, there were two ophthalmologists, a superintendent of schools, a high school principal, a county prosecutor, a nurse and others of whom I have lost track as the years passed.

This is a very impressive list for a group that claims to have been disadvantaged by racism, discrimination and social segregation. To some extent I must agree. But lest one jumps to the conclusion that all was rosy in the garden or that these people didn't have to struggle harder than white youths raised in similar economic circumstances, we are going to take a closer look at the actual career paths of a few. All had to deal with the unique circumstance of being black in a white racist society.

First, consider the city solicitor, James Watson. His father had worked as a labourer in Detroit and was determined that at least one of his two sons would have the opportunity to get a college education. Jim was the elder son and it was probably for this reason that he seemed to receive more encouragement to pursue an academic career. This may not have been the case, but the fact is that the younger son, who was a very clever student, seemed to lack the motivation to follow an academic career as his brother had.

Jim completed Grade 13, went to university and completed his studies in law at Osgoode Hall. After he was admitted to the bar he tried unsuccessfully for almost two years to gain acceptance in a law firm as a junior partner. Finally, after a fruitless search, he took a job as a porter on the railroad until a black lawyer in Toronto took him on as a junior partner. In that position he handled all the low fee prostitution, vagrancy and drunk driving cases which nowadays would likely be handled by legal aid.

Jim also served in the armed forces during World War II. Sometime soon after that Windsor's city solicitor received an appointment with the Ontario government. Since the black community considered Mayor Art Reaume a friend, Jim Watson's name was suggested to him for the vacant position of assistant city solicitor. Reaume took it upon himself to see that Jim received the appointment, and after a bitter struggle within city hall, James Watson was named assistant city solicitor. He was the first black person to hold such a senior position in any city in Canada. A few years later, with much less of a struggle, Jim became the first black city solicitor in Canada. The way Mayor Reaume fought to have Jim appointed was an example of what one white person of good will could accomplish for the cause of human rights in Canada when he was in a position of power and influence.

Lloyd Watkins attended a school very much like Mercer Street, as far as facilities were concerned, but with a much smaller percentage of black students. At about thirteen years of age he was stricken with spinal meningitis, streptococcus and another serious disease simultaneously. For several weeks his life hung in the balance, but Lloyd had an indomitable will to live and he survived. When he had passed the crisis and begun to recuperate, his doctor told him there was a strong possibility he would never walk again. Lloyd refused to accept this prognosis and struggled to regain the use of his arms and legs. Although he recovered from the illness he did have some permanent negative effects from it. Lloyd was unable to turn his head freely in a normal way, one shoulder was partially paralyzed, his voice became deep and coarse and he always seemed to have difficulty in speaking.

He returned to school after his long illness, finished Grade 13 at Sandwich Collegiate (now E. L. Forster C.I.) and continued to develop his strengths and capabilities. Then came World War II and many of Lloyd's friends were volunteering for service. He got caught up in the enthusiasm of the hour and chose the air force. For him, however, there seemed to be several obstacles too impossible to overcome. Firstly he was black, and the air force recruiters were not accepting black volunteers in southwestern Ontario in the early days of the war. Neither was the navy. Blacks who wanted to join the navy were told to go to Halifax where they might be accepted as ordinary seamen if there was a need for galley hands or positions with similar classifications. Needless to say, no black from Windsor that I knew of ever enlisted in the navy during World War II.

The army had its own peculiarities. The Essex Scottish Regiment had been a unit of the regular army prior to the war and was recruiting volunteers for overseas service. When blacks first tried to enlist they were told that since they wouldn't look very good in kilts, the dress uniform of the regiment, they should go to Chatham or London to enlist.

When the air force recruiter refused to accept Lloyd, he joined forces with the committee that had been formed to put a stop to blatant discrimination against young black men and women who wanted to serve their country but whose country did not seem to want their services. After months of protests the racial barriers began to crack. In the Windsor area it was the air force that first began to accept black recruits but only as ground crew. Of course there were blacks who wanted to fly, so the protests continued. As a result, by the time World War II ended, two or three blacks from the Windsor area had attained officer rank as flight crew, but none became pilots.

No black recruit who enlisted in Windsor ever became a commissioned officer in the Canadian army or navy during World War II as far as I was aware, and I'm sure I would have known. In the air force, a Windsor native, Kenneth Jacobs became the first black Canadian to reach the rank of lieutenant colonel in about 1975, but only after a twenty year struggle, and not as a pilot but as a social worker.

Added to the racial obstacles Lloyd had the physical handicaps resulting from his illness, but somehow he managed to get past the medical examination and was admitted to the air force. How he did it is a mystery to me. It makes some of the stories that emerged during the critical days of the Battle of Britain seemed less fictional. One such story related how the doctor would feel the pulse of the recruit and place a stethoscope on his chest; if his heart was beating and he was breathing he was accepted. In Lloyd's case something like that must have happened no doubt aided by the actions of the ad hoc committee against discrimination in the armed forces.

Eventually someone must have discovered the blunder because Lloyd was never sent overseas. He was discharged sometime in 1941 and began looking for a job. He had studied drafting engineering at Wayne State University in Detroit so he applied as a draftsman at Ford's in Windsor. He was hired, but not as a draftsman, but as a machine operator probably on a punch press. Whatever it was it didn't have the faintest resemblance to a drafting table. On this machine the operator put the piece of metal to be pressed on the table, lowered the hand lever in order to place the piece in position, pressed the foot pedal that brought down the press and ejected the finished part. In order to meet his production quota Lloyd had to make an average of seventy-five motions a minute over his eight hour shift.

Lloyd's engineering mind could not accept this as an efficient way of working. First he tried to convince his supervisor that the quota was too high. When that didn't work he devised a contraption which was simply a piece of wire attached from the hand lever to the foot pedal adjusted so that, as he pressed the foot pedal, on its way down it would trip the hand lever. Then he found a metal stool on which he could pile a number of pieces to be punched, and with a steel rod he could flick a piece onto the table and, in time with the humming of a rhythmic tune, pat his foot as fast as he wanted to and perform his job. If Lloyd had been white, no doubt his ingenuity would have been rewarded and his engineering skill recognized and utilized. But that was not to be. First his supervisor became suspicious of Lloyd having too much free time and yet always being able to meet his quota, while the men on the other shifts were hard-pressed to make the quota. So the boss started watching Lloyd very closely from behind other machines. Eventually he found out Lloyd's secret.

Lloyd was told to report to the plant superintendent. He expected to be fired for working in an unsafe manner. When the superintendent learned that Lloyd was the son of a man who had worked in his division for many years, he did not fire Lloyd. Instead he was transferred to the parts and accessories department located in the same building. One day soon after his transfer, he was walking past his old machine and, low and behold, the engineers had installed a steel arm attached to the hand lever and the foot pedal of his old punch press! They had also made a metal stool for stacking the pieces to feed the press just as Lloyd's contraption had done. Lloyd learned that they had also increased the production quota and cut the operation to one shift. Lloyd's idea saved the company thousands of dollars and should have entitled him to some reward.

Lloyd's story does not end there. He later left the auto company and got a job as a draftsman with a large steel company where he worked for several years. When this company refused to give him a promotion to an engineer's position that had come open, he left and obtained a drafting engineer's job in Detroit. This was more than twenty years after he had qualified for his profession.

In 1958 Lloyd was in a position to purchase a new home. He selected a lot in a new development just a few blocks from his family's home in Sandwich. He submitted an offer to purchase and placed the required deposit with the developer's agent, but his offer was turned down. That lot was not to be sold to a black person. Lloyd brought the matter to the attention of members of the Council on Group Relations and after months of negotiations his offer was accepted and he eventually moved into his new home. Everything then appeared to be quite normal except for one detail that few people even noticed. The developer who built Lloyd's house never built a house on the two lots next to his. Those lots remained vacant for several years. Eventually Lloyd's niece, Janice, and her husband bought the house that a private individual had built next door. Would she and her husband have been able to buy their house if Lloyd had not persisted in his fight against tremendous odds a few years previously? There are those who argue that people who refuse to accept injustices and who create crisis situations do more to impede than to help their own people. Not so! Human nature being what it is someone always has to fight to change the status quo, especially when the status quo means unfair treatment for an identifiable social group.

Jim DeShields was a black graduate of the 1930s whose parents had migrated from Bermuda where his father had been trained as an electrical engineer. Jim was born while his family lived in Montreal. When they moved to Old Sandwich Jim attended the same school that Lloyd attended. In addition to being an above average student, he was a member of some of the school's athletic teams. Along with three or four other black caddies Jim became an excellent golfer. Blacks were not allowed to play on the course but the caddies managed to get in a few rounds on slow days and in the evenings. Jim didn't pursue his athletic career beyond high school apart from playing golf.

Jim chose chemistry as his profession and, after completing his university work, he applied for a job at Ford's since Ford's was the only big three auto company that hired blacks in any capacity. It was near the beginning of World War II when Canadian patriots were calling on all people to give their best skills and abilities to the war effort in either the armed forces or the industries that supplied them. Despite Jim's chemical qualifications it seems that the interviewer saw him only as big, strong and black, so he sent him to the foundry. There he was given one of the dirtiest, heaviest, hottest jobs on the molding line — the shakeout. After the molten iron or steel had been poured into sand molds at temperatures of from 2500°F to 3000°F, Jim's job was to hook the red hot cylinder block or transmission housing castings, pull them from the vibrating conveyor and transfer them to the cooling line conveyor.

Jim worked on this job for months without complaining. Then one day one of the black workers who knew about Jim's knowledge of chemistry pointed out to the plant manager the shame of wasting Jim's skills and knowledge on such a menial job. Soon Jim was taken off the shakeout and given a job in the foundry lab. In the lab he was allowed to use his chemical knowledge to develop fast and accurate methods of analyzing iron and steel to determine their percentages of such elements as carbon, chromium, silicon, manganese, and copper. He trained both present and new employees in the procedures so that when the union became established in the plant, Jim was classified as a leader and paid five or ten cents an hour premium pay. He inducted about thirty men in the procedures during the five war years. In the early 1950s when the company purchased new spectrographic equipment for analyzing metals, it was Jim who taught this procedure as well. Several men whom he had trained became foremen and two of them became plant managers over the years, but Jim remained the lab's specials man.

In 1953 with the assistance of the auto workers' union, I obtained a job in the lab. I had to engage the union because even though I possessed the seniority and the chemical knowledge required, the lab supervisor maintained that I was not sufficiently qualified. After working with Jim for a couple of years I was finally able to convince him that the company was taking unfair advantage of him. At the very least the company should have placed him on salary and given him a substantial increase if they chose not to promote him. Finally, following a series of incidents in which Jim had been called upon to solve some serious problems, not only in the foundry at Windsor but also in the company's foundry in Cleveland, Ohio, Jim got angry enough to demand an increase and a salary instead of his hourly wage. He had to threaten to resign before the company gave him his requests.

But that was it! Jim remained as the lab specialist until he retired sometime in the late 1970s, freely giving of his knowledge and skills while white men with far less on the ball, men whom he had taught and trained and men brought into the lab after him, were given promotions. Jim was under employed throughout his entire working career.

There are many stories which could be told that would parallel those I have recounted. There were scores of Jims, Alfreds and Walters. There were also the Mariettas, Helens and Dorothys. A handful of them eventually achieved limited degrees of success in the careers they chose for themselves. However, all of them faced barriers common to all young blacks of that era, and most fell far short of their potential. For example, my wife, Marietta, always wanted to be a teacher. She was above average as a student in Amherst High School, but she dropped out at Grade 11 because she didn't see any possibility of becoming a school teacher for several reasons. Firstly, she was black; there were no black teachers that she knew of except Mr. Alexander in the all black school in North Buxton. Secondly, she was a female; few females of any colour ever went beyond high school in Marietta's circle at any rate. Finally, her family was very poor; there were seven children, and her parents didn't see any benefit in her continuing in school.

Almost surely Marietta would have been successful as a teacher. After she had taken piano lessons up to Grade 7 in her early thirties, she continued studying music theory with excellent grades. She taught our two youngest daughters piano in the 1970s and was so good that neighbours and friends insisted that she teach their children. At one point she had eleven pupils, some of whom had quit taking lessons from regular teachers because to them their lessons had become boring. The unique thing about Marietta's students was that, after a few months of lessons, each of them could sight read music up to the level of their lessons and each could transpose a piece on sight into several different keys. What might she have been able to accomplish if she had started as a teenager to study to become a teacher?

Why is it that in 1971 reports from Windsor, Ontario; Halifax, Nova Scotia; St. Johns, New Brunswick, and Owen Sound, Ontario, all showed that more blacks than whites, proportionately, dropped out of school between Grades 10 and 12? There are many reasons why kids drop out of school, but the most common one given by black students was frustration over the lack of economic opportunities open to them. In spite of laws prohibiting discrimination, Canadian blacks have had to consider whether it was worth the effort and time to get a good education. The stories of the three professional men above, who graduated from high school in the 1930s, illustrate the following:

— All of them were attracted to professions that were highly competitive in nature: law, engineering, and chemical science.

— They all were obliged to accept menial jobs outside their professions at the outset of their working careers.

— As a result, they entered their chosen professions much later than the average white graduate.

— Advancement in their profession was slow, if realized at all.

— Advancement had to be fought for, sometimes involving activist forces.

— Once achieved, whites viewed their advancement as examples of Canada as a free society.

These observations support the hypothesis that blacks in Canada tended to enter highly competitive careers or remained in low-skill careers. Also they entered their professions at a later age and advanced more slowly than their white counterparts. Consequently, they seldom, if ever, reached the top of the organizations in which they worked.

LOVE AND MARRIAGE

Figure 4
18 year old Marietta

When first I saw those laughing eyes

That cold December day

Stealing a glimpse from behind the hearth

Of this strange creature entering on the scene

Little did I know, or even dream —

Or, yet that sunny Sabbath afternoon

When eyes met often, smiled and turned aside

And then a quick hello and a running away

Sweet girl, I thought, nor could I yet discern —

Who could have known, that night at festive frolic,

When some mischievous prank of youth

Together brought us face to face but for a moment

Or when young folk gathered on a Sunday e'en

The convention over, there to share

A passing kiss – Ah! 'Twas but a game!

To begin this chapter, let us go back to the year after I graduated from high school. I have written about the girls I knew in the places where I travelled as a teenager. When I was about nineteen years old, during the Christmas holidays I went to Amherstburg with three of my buddies. There were several nice looking girls in that town, three of whom were in one family, the Wilsons.

I had met the oldest, Alva, at a church convention the previous summer, but she had told me that she had a steady boyfriend; she wasn't interested in seeing anyone else. Alva was almost a year older than I, her sister Marguerite was about two years younger, Marietta was another two years younger than Marguerite, probably sixteen. There were two other girls, Isabel and Violet, and two boys, Arnold and Herman, all younger than Marietta.

When we arrived at the Wilson home that day, Norman, their dad, greeted us cordially and invited us in. The four of us sat in chairs around the room feeling rather awkward trying to make conversation with Mr. Wilson. Mrs. Wilson was somewhere else in the house for most of our time there. After a few minutes three girls came into the room. There was a huge base-burning Quebec heater near one corner of the room with two or three chairs placed behind it. One of the boys with us had met Marguerite, so he introduced us to her. Then Marguerite tried to introduce us to Marietta and her friend Violet Webb (Vi), but Marietta and Vi hid themselves behind the stove, tittering and giggling, probably through nervousness. They would take a quick glance at us and then retreat behind the stove. After about an hour we left. Those two pretty girls behind the stove intrigued me even more because I really didn't get a good look at them. What I did see revealed that both of them were very attractive but flighty.

The next summer the youth choir from First Baptist Church in Windsor presented a program at the Baptist church in Amherstburg. From my vantage point in the choir loft I was able to get a good look at both Marietta and her friend Vi, from Detroit, who was visiting in town for the summer. I exchanged glances with Marietta, but each time our eyes met she would look away. After the program I was talking to Al, an Amherstburg boy whom I had known for some time. We talked about the program for a while and when Marietta and Vi appeared in the church doorway, Al remarked that Marietta had a crush on me. I commented that she had a strange way of showing it. "Would you like to meet her?" Al asked.

I didn't consider our encounter at the Wilson home the previous winter to be a proper introduction, so I said, "Yes, I would." Al went back into the church vestibule and returned a couple of minutes later. He was practically dragging the two girls to where I was standing out on the sidewalk with some other members of our choir.

Al began the introduction with, "Lyle Talbot, this is Marietta Wilson and her friend Vi Webb."

I hardly got the words, "It's a pleasure to make your acquaintance," out of my mouth when Marietta and Vi took off running down George Street toward the Wilson house as if someone were chasing them to do something awful.

I didn't see Marietta again until the fall of 1936, when she came to Windsor to work for the pastor of Temple Baptist church, Rev. Dr. Harry Nobles, and his wife as a sort of mother's helper. One Sunday evening she came to First Baptist Church with my cousin Barbara (Babe), Ted's daughter, and after church a group of young people gathered at Babe's for fellowship. My cousin Ted Talbot, his wife Theresa and Babe lived across the street from the church. We played games in order to become better acquainted, one of which was spin-the-bottle. On one of my turns the bottle pointed to Marietta, and we exchanged a kiss that we both tried to make look as casual as possible. As the time approached for us to disperse Babe took me aside and suggested that I should ask Marietta if I could accompany her to the Nobles' residence. I quickly did that, and it was a good thing I did because Marietta told me later that three other fellows had asked to walk her home.

About a half block from the Nobles' house I looked back, and about twenty paces behind us there were three other guys. They stayed that distance behind us until we reached the corner of Elliott and Pelissier streets where the Nobles' house stood, on the southwest corner past a vacant lot. The three other fellows turned north on Pelissier and I continued to accompany Marietta right up to the front door. I wasn't afraid to face either Rev. or Mrs. Nobles since they had known me for a few years through our church's relationship with Temple Baptist.

On the way, Marietta had told me that Thursday was her afternoon off, so I invited her to go to a movie with me since Thursday was my long day at my bellhop job. That meant that I would be off all afternoon. After the movie I asked her if she liked hamburgers. She said that she liked them so much that someone in Amherstburg had nicknamed her Wimpy, after the character in the Popeye comic strip whose typical remark was, "Can you direct me to a respectable hamburger joint?" We went to the New Service Restaurant where I had frequently gone during my newspaper carrier days on my way to the Windsor Star building to pick up my papers. They served patties that were at least as large as the quarter pounders from a McDonalds or Burger King today. You could have your choice of toppings including mustard, relish, ketchup, onion, dill pickle, cheese and even chili or sauerkraut, all for the sum of ten cents. Marietta liked the burger so much that later on when I was dating her on a regular basis, she expected me to bring a New Service hamburger with mustard, onions, relish and dill pickle every time I went to see her.

It was only a couple of weeks after this first real meeting with Marietta that the hotel dismissed me from my job. The next Sunday evening, after seeing Marietta home and visiting with Mrs. Nobles and her for a while, I arrived home quite late. The front door of our house on Lillian Street was seldom locked, so I quietly opened it and stepped inside. The house was in total darkness. I stood there trying to picture in my mind where the various pieces of furniture were situated. Mother was one of those people who liked to change the furniture around, and I didn't want to stumble over anything and wake her and Dad up.

I recalled that the library table had been placed in the centre of the living room, so I cautiously moved in that direction. When I touched the table I remembered that there was a lamp in the middle of it, so I felt around for the chain to turn it on and get my bearings to proceed to my bedroom. As the light came on I saw the Bible under it. I had been feeling badly about losing my job, and having now become better acquainted with the lovely, demure, attractive young Marietta, my mood had become even more dejected. No job and a new girlfriend is an unpromising situation for a young man.

It was in this frame of mind that I found myself reaching to open the Book having no idea what I would see. The Bible opened at 2 Chronicles 26:5 (*King James Bible*), and my eyes fell on these words that seemed to stand out in bold print, "As long as he sought the Lord, God made him prosper." I turned off the lamp and made my way to my room, resolving that, come what may, I was going to continue to seek the Lord. Many years later I learned in a Bible study of the incident where Moses asked the Lord to show him his face and God told him that no man could see his face, but he would show Moses his back. I learned that to see God's face is to know the direction in which He is moving. To see God's back is to know where He has been. To seek the Lord, then, is to seek His will and purpose for your life. With these kinds of thoughts on my mind I went to sleep.

Two days later, I received a call from the superintendent of service at the hotel telling me that the manager had reconsidered his decision to fire me. I was to report back to work the next day on my regular watch. Not long after I returned to work a travelling sales representative named Phillips registered in the hotel. I was assigned to show Mr. Phillips to his room with his luggage which consisted of the usual suitcase and a large leather case unlike any I had handled before. When I checked the room to make sure everything was in order, I asked, as I usually did, "Will there be anything else?" Mr. Phillips requested large bottles of ginger ale, coca cola and a large bowl of ice cubes.

When I returned with his order Mr. Phillips had lined up several bottles of various types of whiskey on the dresser. He informed me that he was the representative for the Alberta Distillery and that he was expecting several tavern owners to come the next day to sample his wares. "Meanwhile," he said, "I've been away from home for a long time, staying in hotel rooms all the time. It gets very lonely, you know. Do you have time to sit and talk with me?" I informed him that I couldn't be away from the lobby for more than a few minutes at a time; other guests would be calling for service. He gave me a generous tip and I left. That was about 7:00 p.m.

In about half an hour the call came on the switchboard. "Number 8 boy to Room . . ." (Mr. Phillips' room). This time Mr. Phillips had an unusual request. He said, "If you will just sit here and have a drink with me and talk for fifteen minutes, I'll pay you two dollars."

A two dollar tip was at least eight times the normal tip in those days, and I thought one drink wouldn't hurt me. So I agreed, "One drink and fifteen minutes." After the fifteen minutes I returned to the lobby.

About a half hour later the call came again, "Number 8 boy to Room . . . ," A second drink and fifteen minutes later I was back on duty. Altogether, with Mr. Phillips' two dollar drinks and my other tips for the shift, I went home with more than ten dollars, four times the average day's earnings.

My mother was up when I arrived home that night. I don't know why because she usually retired shortly after ten o'clock. I entered the house by the back door which was located only a few steps from my bedroom, but Mom called me into the dining room where she was sitting. When she said, "Come here and blow out my eye," I knew that somehow she suspected that I had been drinking. I had eaten some

Sen-Sens candies to mask the smell of alcohol, and I thought that had worked, so when Mom merely said, "Okay, kiss me good night." I did so, on her cheek.

The next day was my short day, noon to six p.m. I was sitting eating my breakfast, which I had prepared myself as usual, when Mom came and sat down at the table. This too was not unusual since she would often do this shortly after I started working in hotels. One morning, early in my hotel days, I got up about nine o'clock. Mom was busy in the kitchen, and when I asked, "What's for breakfast?" she replied, "What's for breakfast? Whatever you fix! There's the stove, and there's the icebox. Help yourself."

This particular morning, however, was quite unusual. Mother waited until I had finished eating and was sipping my coffee. "Lyle," she began, "I've got something say to you. Before you were born, I promised God that, to the best of my ability, I would raise you to know the Lord. After you were born I presented you to him in dedication promising, along with your father, to raise you up in the "admonition of the Lord" (Ephesians 6:4, *American King James Version Bible*). I have tried to do this all your life. Moreover, I have prayed for you every day as I have prayed for all my children.

"You, Lyle, have been a special child. I have seen you consistently studying your Bible. I've watched you learning in Sunday school, and being active in the young people's group. Even when you have to work every other Sunday morning and evening, you don't miss church when you are off. I've listened many times as you discussed deep spiritual questions with your Dad. Now this is what I want to say to you. I pray that the Lord will never allow you to stray beyond the reach of his Holy Spirit. I know for a certainty that my prayer is answered, Lyle, so don't try to stray beyond the scope of God's grace, because you can't."

With that brief admonition Mom went about her chores and I got ready to go to work. To this very day my mother's words, "Don't try to stray beyond the scope of

God's grace, because you can't, are ingrained in my soul, as fresh as the day they were spoken those many years ago. I have strayed many times in my life since then, but the Hound of Heaven, as the poet Francis Thompson described him, has always been there to convict, to convince, to restore and to teach.

In May of 1937 I proposed to Marietta after six months of a torrid romance. During that time I had to endure her parents, my mom and Mrs. Nobles all coaching her on the fine points of courtship. On that eventful evening we were sitting in my dad's car down by the Detroit River. As I recall, it was raining that night, but when she said, "Yes, I'll marry you," it seemed that lights came on all around us.

Then began the tasks of setting a date and preparing for the wedding. Marietta had always wanted a June wedding, but June of that year was only a week or so away and the next June was over a year away. She wasn't prepared to get married in a month and I wasn't prepared to wait a year, so we seemed to be at an impasse. Finally we agreed on the month of October when the fall colours would provide an appropriate backdrop. Once we agreed on the date preparations began in earnest.

At every step along the way there seemed to be a conflict between Marietta's ideas of proper procedures and mine. Being the son of a preacher, I had witnessed scores of weddings of just about every type — from couples who had knocked on our door without warning

Figure 6
28 year old Lyle

and without witnesses, to elaborate church affairs with bridesmaids, ushers, flower girls, music, i.e. the works. I guess I thought that all those experiences made me an expert on planning weddings, but looking back I have to admit that my ignorance caused some serious problems.

First, there was the question of invitations. Marietta wanted to handwrite the invitations, primarily because of the cost of printed ones. I thought the printed ones were called for, so I offered to pay the cost of printed ones. Her parents reluctantly consented to let me get the invitations. There was a small printing shop operating in the alley next door to our house and Mr. Ringrose, the proprietor, gave me a discount on the price.

Then there was the question of what was to be printed on the invitations. This proved to be another issue. Marietta wanted the time of the wedding ceremony to be included. Now, many decades after the fact, I can't for the life of me think of the reason why I wanted only the time of the reception. I learned, also after the fact, that church weddings are public affairs. Only a number of seats should be reserved for the families and close friends of the bride and groom. I guess I thought that if the wedding time was included the small church in Amherstburg might not hold all the people who would want to attend. Once again my opinion prevailed and the invitations were printed with no time of the wedding. We must have written the time of the wedding on some of the invitations, because the church was filled to capacity when the scheduled time arrived.

This social faux pas on my part was brought home to me in a very forceful manner. Rev. and Mrs. Nobles appeared at the reception hall at the time indicated on their invitation. After greeting Marietta and offering their best wishes for our happiness, Mrs. Nobles took me aside and chastised me severely for my failure to let them know the time of the wedding. She rightfully felt that their close relationship with Marietta and me over the previous months entitled them to the privilege of witnessing our marriage ceremony.

Then there was the matter of the wedding gown. My oldest sister, Luella, offered to make the gowns for the bride and bridesmaids. Marietta preferred a gown with princess lines, but the pattern Luella had chosen was of a different style. Marietta gave in to Luella's choice, but she never got over her disappointment at not having the style of gown she wanted. The fact that everyone told her that she was one of the loveliest brides they had ever seen didn't fully compensate for her feelings of disappointment.

A dear woman in First Baptist Church, Mrs. Ethel Johnson, volunteered to make the wedding cake. We felt relieved at her offer because the cost of a commercially prepared cake would have added more to the already high financial cost of the wedding for the Wilson family. Then five days before the wedding date, the day when Mrs. Johnson had planned to bake the cake, she suffered a severe stroke or heart attack and died suddenly. Fortunately some other women from the church took over the project and the cake was prepared in time.

A few weeks before the wedding date on one Sunday evening to see Marietta, I had driven Dad's car to Amherstburg. My cousin Grant had gone with me. A little after 11:00 p.m. we were travelling home along a five mile straight stretch of a two lane highway. Suddenly the headlights of an oncoming vehicle appeared to be coming directly toward us on our side of the road. I was cruising along at about fifty-five miles per hour, and when the light beams stayed in my lane, I took my foot off the accelerator. As the vehicle approached I mentally debated whether I should pull to the right and risk the ditch, or pull to the left and risk the chance that the driver of the vehicle would suddenly realize what he was doing and swerve back into his proper lane. At the very last instant I chose to pull to the left, and at that moment the vehicle went past me on my right hand side. It took several seconds for me to regain control of our car which was rocking back and forth.

Grant and I immediately decided to try to catch the car and find out why he was driving on our side of the road. By the time I regained control and got the car turned around, the other vehicle was out of sight. We continued on our way to Windsor still trying to make sense of the incident. Grant wanted to know why I had swerved to the left; he would have swerved right into the ditch. The only answer I had then and have now is that the Lord was directing my reflex actions at the moment of decision.

On the eve of the wedding day my buddies insisted on giving me a bachelor party. About eight of us gathered at Ernie's house for the occasion. Someone had purchased a gallon of Dago Red wine that we consumed as we exchanged memories of our single lives shared together over the years. I had chosen my cousin Harold to be my best man, but at three o'clock on the morning of my wedding day, I was walking the streets with Harold who had consumed more than his share of the Dago Red. On that occasion, as on others later when I witnessed Harold in an intoxicated state, he would insist on reminiscing about his mother who had died when he was about six years old, and about his years with his stepmother with whom he had experienced unhappy times. The more Harold talked, the more emotional he got, eventually breaking out in deep uncontrollable sobs. It was after four o'clock in the morning when I finally got him to his rooming house and arrived home myself to get some sleep.

With the ceremony scheduled for five o'clock, I had a lot to do in those final hours. I was up at nine o'clock, and after six hectic hours I was able to bathe and dress. At four-thirty I arrived at the First Baptist Church in Amherstburg with my best man, Harold, who appeared to have recovered from the previous night's festivities, and my other male attendants. My dad, Rev. H.L. Talbot, was to perform the ceremony with the assistance of the Amherstburg pastor, Rev. I.H. Edwards, but

Dad had been obliged to officiate at the funeral of Mrs. Johnson. At the time Dad had again become pastor of First Baptist, Windsor, and as such he was Mrs. Johnson's pastor. The funeral was set for 1:00 p.m. at Queen Street Baptist Church in Dresden, the Johnson family's home church. Dresden was about eighty miles from Amherstburg by the most direct route through Chatham. With the funeral service lasting an hour and then the internment at the cemetery taking up another hour, it was after 3:00 p.m. before Dad was ready to leave Dresden.

The funeral director offered to drive Dad to Amherstburg assuring him that if he drove the hearse with the siren going as they passed through Chatham and three or four smaller towns, he could just about make it for the 4:45 deadline. To cover the eighty miles in one hour and thirty minutes he would have to average over fifty miles an hour. With a city like Chatham, population 25,000, and no four lane expressways, that would be quite an achievement.

The 4:45 time came. I was waiting in the anteroom with my party, the church was full of people and Marietta and her family were waiting nervously and anxiously at their house two blocks from the church. They were to leave for the church at five minutes to five, but by 4:45 there was no sign of Rev. Talbot. Marietta later told me that she was so nervous that she had to go to the bathroom several times during that last hour. I, too, was beginning to get nervous, when, at seven minutes to five the hearse drove up in front of the church and a very tense Rev. Talbot disembarked and rushed to the anteroom to get ready.

At 5:05 the ceremony got under way. It mostly went very smoothly considering the events that had preceded it. The hectic ride from Dresden must have unnerved Dad. Whenever he was supposed to say Marietta's name he said her sister's name, Margaret, instead. (Marguerite had adopted the name Margaret instead of Marguerite by that time). Throughout our marriage, whenever she would become peeved with me, Marietta would remind me that Dad hadn't married me to her; he had married me to her sister. Of course I would respond by drawing her attention to the name on the marriage certificate. Several people remarked after the ceremony that the only person who didn't seem to be nervous during the wedding was the groom. My explanation was that I had witnessed so many weddings that I had memorized the ritual. Somehow I just believed that Dad would arrive on time, and when he did I just relaxed and let the wedding happen.

Then there was our honeymoon. Prior to the wedding, I had been discussing some options with my co-workers at the hotel. One of them suggested Cleveland, Ohio, giving the name of a good hotel where we could stay. Marietta and I had agreed to go to Cleveland and Dad had agreed to let us take his car for the weekend. Since I had to be back at work on Tuesday we left Amherstburg about nine o'clock Saturday evening, drove across the Ambassador Bridge and headed for Toledo, Ohio, sixty miles south of Detroit.

Just before we reached Toledo I became very tired and sleepy. The events of the long night before the wedding with my experience with Harold, followed by the busy day of the wedding, were taking their toll on my energy. We decided to look for a place to stay overnight, and a gas station attendant directed us to go over the high level bridge into the residential section where we would find a black woman who ran a bed and breakfast place. I found the high level bridge without much trouble, but after I crossed it, it seemed that every street I took brought me right back to that bridge. Marietta was near the point of utter panic and frustration. Here we were in a very dark part of a strange American city, lost, tired and alone. The only choice we had, I thought, was to keep looking. There was no point in recrossing the bridge because there was only the highway on the other side and I was much too tired to drive any further. I had no idea which way to turn, but somehow I must have taken a different street from any of my previous attempts because in the block just ahead of us stood a large house with a spotlight shining on a sign that read,

"Rooms." A very friendly black woman answered the doorbell and welcomed us in. She did have a room available and we agreed to take it.

The room was at the top of the stairs. It was very bright, very clean and a welcome sight to two tired newlyweds. I got the impression that the woman recognized us as such from her offer to bring us refreshments, that is, unless we just preferred to go right to bed. I went to the bathroom first, washed, brushed my teeth and returned to our room across the hall. While Marietta was in the bathroom I got undressed, but when I went to put on my pajamas I found them tied in many tight little knots. It took several minutes to untangle the knots, but when I finally got into my pajamas, Marietta had not yet emerged from the bathroom. I sat on the side of the bed and waited, and waited. At last she came into the room clad in her nightgown; it also had been tied in knots. After snuggling up close to each other, in bed together for the first time, we agreed that we were both too exhausted to do anything but get some rest and sleep.

Sunday morning we said goodbye to the nice woman at the rooming house, had no difficulty finding the high level bridge in the daylight and were on our way to Cleveland. We had been on the highway but a few minutes when we began to see signs along the side of the road. "See the Blue Hole", "Don't Miss the Blue Hole", "10 miles to the Blue Hole", "5 miles to the Blue Hole", "Turn left here for the Blue Hole", "You have passed the Blue Hole." By this time our curiosity had taken over, so we decided to turn around and find out what this Blue Hole was all about.

A short distance off the highway we found a fenced in area with a sidewalk along one side. The sign there, of course, read, "The Blue Hole." As we looked down from the walkway we could see what appeared to be a bottomless well of water, a deep, deep blue in colour, with what appeared to be leafless trees and shrubs in a state of fossilization nearby. It was simply as the signs had said, a blue hole filled with blue water.

However, as we stood gazing down into the water, both Marietta and I remembered that a few weeks before our wedding we had visited Mrs. Conway, a lifelong friend of hers in Amherstburg. Mrs. Conway had served us a cup of tea and then had offered to interpret the leaves at the bottom of the cup. In my cup, according to Mrs. Conway, she saw Marietta and I looking down at something very blue and very deep. It was like water only darker in colour. "Isn't it strange that Mrs. Conway predicted this?" I remarked.

"And isn't strange," added Marietta, "that we went past this place and then decided to turn around and come back?"

"Do you think Mrs. Conway is some sort of clairvoyant?" I asked.

"I don't know what to make of it," said Marietta," but do you remember the other prediction she made?"

"What was that?" I asked.

"Remember, she gazed into my cup," continued Marietta, and said, "I see you with two children, both girls." Does that mean we're going to have two girls in our family?" I replied that I was skeptical about anyone being able to foretell the future but that it would be interesting to see what happened.

I knew Mrs. Conway to be a devout Christian and I believed that God had bestowed on her the gift of discernment. She saw things in the teacup that God had placed in her mind as she concentrated on the person whose cup she was examining. I have never heard of her charging a fee or otherwise accepting money for doing what she did. She was an extremely poor woman with a large family and she died still extremely poor.

We proceeded on our way to Cleveland, arriving there in mid-afternoon. The directions to the hotel that my co-workers had given me proved to be easy to follow. We made our way down Euclid Avenue until I came to the hotel, clearly visible as we approached. Marietta had never been in a hotel before, so the sight of so many people, mostly black males, in the lobby made her uneasy. She never got more than an arm's length from me during the time that I registered and we were shown to our room. We had eaten lunch shortly before we arrived, but when I suggested that we could go out for a walk just to look around, she would not hear of it. I was, however, able to get her to consent to go to visit a cousin who lived in Cleveland. We spent a very pleasant evening there. The next morning I almost had to drag her bodily to a restaurant across the street from the hotel for breakfast. It was either eat at the restaurant or eat in the hotel cafeteria where she felt sure everybody would be staring at her.

After breakfast we headed back to Detroit where we arrived in time to do some shopping. We were almost out of money when I saw a mantle radio that I really liked. I even remember the brand name, Marshall. The price was $25.98. I counted my money; I had exactly $27.05, which meant that if I bought the radio and paid the dollar tunnel toll to Windsor, I would have a balance of seven cents left. We bought the radio and with it, a bed, a dresser, a kitchen table, two chairs and a bank account of seven cents we started our married life. My salary as a bellhop was ten dollars a month; I had earmarked it to pay for having my white shirts with stiff collars laundered and for cleaning and pressing my uniforms. The rest of my income consisted entirely of tips I received.

The Monday a week after our wedding was Halloween night. That night the Science, Arts and Crafts Club, the group of young black people that I had helped to organize, held their regular meeting. Someone got the bright idea of calling on the newlyweds after the meeting. At about ten-thirty the doorbell rang. When I went downstairs from our two room upstairs flat and opened the door, fifteen or twenty of our friends just barged in. Marietta and I were subjected to a third degree interrogation lasting over an hour about the most intimate details of the honeymoon.

It didn't stop even when I told I them that our landlord downstairs had to go to work in the morning and needed to get some sleep.

Finally, in desperation, I took Marietta by the arm, started toward the bedroom door and spoke loudly enough for everyone to hear. "Come on, Marietta; let's go to bed so these people can go home!" I guess they heard the anger and frustration in my voice, for they began to get up and walk to the stairway claiming that they didn't mean to upset us; they just wanted to wish the newlyweds well.

Figure 7
70 th Wedding Anniversary, October 23, 2007

BLESS THIS HOUSE

Our first home was an upstairs flat with only a bedroom and a very large living room. Marietta was allowed to use the kitchen downstairs where our landlord, George, and his wife Gert lived with their three children. During the first few months of our marriage we developed such a good relationship with this couple that they often went beyond the requirements of landlords to make us comfortable. There was a second bedroom in the upstairs part at the head of the staircase that George explained had been his mother's room. He once told us that his mother had died in that room and that she had left this life screaming and yelling. George's sister, Ada, who lived in Detroit, had made it a part of the settlement of their mother's estate that her mother's room was to be kept available for her whenever she came to stay overnight in Windsor. Ada had two sons; the elder one was nicknamed Diggie and the younger one was Bobby. Diggie was my age, and when we were about fifteen we were inseparable buddies along with another boy whose nickname was Dee. The reason for their nicknames was that they both had real names that they didn't like; Dee's real name was Dasnold, but I don't remember Diggie's. Being the preacher's son, my nickname with the letter D was Deac. The three of us used to spend Sunday afternoons strolling around the community eyeing the girls. I walked with a slight limp as a result of what I have learned recently was a mild case of polio. The limp was more of a swagger that both Diggie and Dee copied. Could it be that our swagger was the forerunner of the swagger that young black fellows in the ghettos of Detroit and other large cities have made popular in recent years? The first real tragedy of my life occurred when Diggie drowned while on a picnic with his mother, brother and stepfather. As his friends we suspected foul play since he had said he didn't get along with his stepfather. In any case, his funeral was my first experience as a pallbearer.

During Ada's visits to stay at George's, she developed a liking for Marietta, and it wasn't long before George was able to get her to open her mother's old room for us by sharing a portion of the rent money with her. George made the room into a kitchen with a sink and gas stove for cooking.

One night soon after the sink had been installed, we heard scratching noises coming from the room. I got up to investigate. When I turned on the light the biggest black sewer rat I had ever seen, or have seen since, scurried into a hole about two and a half inches in diameter where the drainpipe entered the wall. My mind went back about twelve years to the time when an old small stable had burned down in the lot behind the parsonage of First Baptist Church. As the fire increased in intensity rats of all sizes began to run from the stable. The boys in the neighborhood had of course been attracted by the fire, and we had an exciting time chasing the rats with sticks, hats or whenever weapons of destruction we could find.

Regarding that rat in our kitchen Marietta insisted that I must close up the hole immediately. I thought that plaster of Paris would do the trick, so I proceeded to mix a little at a time with water and began to fill the hole. Marietta was watching and she suggested that I could fill the hole faster if I mixed a lot of the materials at a time. Without too much thought as to why I had been mixing a little at a time, I followed her suggestion. However, before I got the hole even half filled, my pan of plaster of Paris was as hard as a rock. To add to my frustration, Marietta broke out in laughter at my predicament. That was the last straw. I picked up the pan of plaster of Paris and threw it in the general direction in which she had been sitting. Marietta had heard the desperation in my voice when I shouted, "What in the world are you laughing at?" and as the can was flying across the room she had taken one jump out the door.

After I regained my composure I apologized for throwing the pan of plaster of Paris in her direction and assured her that I had not intended to hit her with it. After telling me that I should control my temper better, she offered to help me by mixing the plaster of Paris for me as I worked it into the hole. "You'll have to admit, though," she commented, "that it was funny watching you trying to make that lumpy stuff stick in the hole." I did have to agree with that.

A few weeks after we had moved into the flat following our wedding, we were lamenting the fact that no one had taken any photos of our wedding and how nice it would have been to have such photos to show to our children. One of the crafts that I had learned in the Science, Arts and Crafts Club was the process of developing and printing black and white snapshots. I suggested that we should dress up in our wedding clothes and I could take a self-portrait with our cheap little box camera. Marietta dressed in her wedding gown and I donned my dark blue suit that I had worn. The idea was to set the timer on the camera for a ten second exposure, get situated with Marietta seated in the easy chair that we had just purchased on credit, get myself in position beside her and switch on the one hundred watt bulb in the floor lamp beside me with a four bulb spotlight focused on us. We tried the procedure a few times; then I wanted to take Marietta's picture outside in the daylight, but she thought it would be too embarrassing for her to go outside in her wedding gown weeks after the wedding.

I developed the film in my own improvised dark room and found that one picture of the two of us and one picture of Marietta alone came out satisfactorily, but they were a little too dark from under exposure. They were truly black and white with shadows in places where there shouldn't have been any. We still have those prints in our first family album along with some other pictures that I developed myself.

One other evening, soon after we had occupied our new kitchen, I had to go out to the drug store two blocks away to get something. Marietta assured me that she would be all right, but after I had gone down the stairs and was about to open the door to the outside, I heard a commotion behind me. Marietta had bounded down the stairs like an antelope and almost knocked me down when I opened the door. Although she had stayed in the house many evenings when I had worked the long day, this was her first time alone after the opening of George's mother's room. In the few seconds that it took me to get down the steps, she had thought of all the weird things that could emanate from that room in which the old woman had died kicking and screaming.

***

The first year of our life together was one of blissful happiness. There were the usual problems of adjustment for two people who had come from somewhat different backgrounds. One minor example stemmed from my love of sports. My dad was an avid baseball fan who listened to the Detroit Tigers' games on the radio whenever they were broadcast on Saturdays. At few times he even took me to games in Detroit, preferably when the New York Yankees or the Philadelphia Athletics were the visiting teams.

Those were the days of Babe Ruth, Tony Lazzerie, Lou Gehrig, and Lefty Gomez for the Yankees; Lefty Grove, George Earnshaw, Jimmy Foxx, Al Simmons and Mickey Cochrane for the Athletics; and Charlie Gehringer, Billy Rogel and Tommy Bridges for the Tigers. One game was particularly memorable. The Athletics were in Detroit and Dad had decided to take my brother George and me to the game on a Saturday afternoon. On the way to the ballpark Dad remarked that all that the Athletics' manager, Connie Mack, had to do was to announce that Lefty Grove was going to pitch. He could then send the batboy to the mound and the Tigers would be beaten. They call that psyching your opponent out. At that point Grove had a record of eleven wins, one loss against the Tigers.

On that Saturday the Athletics were leading seven to zero after seven innings, so Dad said that we might as well leave and avoid the traffic in downtown Detroit.

When we got to our car and turned on the radio, the score was tied at eight runs and the Tigers went on to win with a score of nine to eight. We had missed the most exciting part of the game.

Unlike my dad, Marietta's dad showed no interest in sports of any kind. He would say, for example, that baseball was a waste of time. Thus, the first time that a game came on the radio I presumed that I would be listening to it. Marietta had other ideas, no doubt influenced by her dad's example, even though she had participated in some athletic activities in high school and had even been a member of the winning senior girls' relay team at the Western Ontario Secondary Schools Association track meet. I guess that's where she got the training and practice in running away from me so much when we first met. As I often jokingly told my friends later, I had chased her until she caught me. Over our years together I didn't watch sporting events on television whenever she wanted to watch something else. In our later years we had two television sets, so if a game was really important, like the World Series, the Grey or Stanley Cup, the Super Bowl or the Olympics, I could watch it on the second set.

Nine months after our wedding Marietta discovered that she was pregnant, and as the months passed we became more and more excited about the coming event. On one of her regular visits to Dr. Taylor's office late in the pregnancy, the doctor told her that the baby didn't seem to be in the right position, but hopefully that would change. Since all of the women in Marietta's experience had delivered their babies at home, she was apprehensive about having the birth in a hospital. Even the fact that her older sister, Alva, had experienced serious complications during childbirth at home did not deter her.

Accordingly, I proceeded to make blocks to put under the legs of the bed to raise it to hospital bed level, and we made thick paper mats to place on the bed for absorbing the fluids discharged during delivery. Then there was the choice of hospitals, just in case. Hotel Dieu was the nearest to where we lived, being just five blocks away. It was a Catholic hospital and there was a superstition that if there was a choice to be made between saving the baby or the mother, Catholics would save the baby. Therefore we chose Metropolitan Hospital which was about three miles away.

Two weeks before the anticipated date of delivery, Dr. Taylor told me that I could continue with preparations for a home delivery, but that I should be prepared to take Marietta to the hospital at the last moment because the baby continued to maintain its feet first position. Even when he manually turned it around it would revert to the feet first position.

On Friday, March 31, 1939, we called Dr. Taylor and learned that he had come down with an attack of influenza, and that if anything happened over the weekend I was to take her to the hospital and have the nurses call him. Sometime around 2:00 a.m. on Sunday morning it happened. Marietta woke up with severe pains about twenty minutes apart. We had no car and no telephone and I didn't want to awaken George and Gert because they didn't have a car either. I jumped into a pair of slacks, slipped on my shoes and hurried out the door, planning to go to the nearest phone booth and call a taxi. When I got down to the corner I saw an automobile approaching. I recognized it as Tom Taylor's (no relation to Dr. Taylor) and I waved him down. Tom readily agreed to drive us to the hospital.

Dr. Taylor was called and he instructed the nurses to contact an obstetrician to replace him as the attending physician. At about 5:00 a.m., on Palm Sunday, April 2, 1939, our daughter Marilyn came into this world backwards as a breech birth. Later that day when Marietta asked one of the attending nurses who had informed her of the breech delivery if she had had any stitches, the nurse replied that there were too many to count. When Dr. Taylor recovered enough to visit her he explained that in breech births it usually becomes necessary to get air to the baby's mouth as soon as its foot is exposed to the air, and so the doctor does this with his hand resulting in severe lacerations of the vaginal area.

We had arranged for Marietta's friend Vi to stay with her for a few days, but the few days became three weeks because of the complications. For more than a week after she came home from the hospital, Marietta had a lot of bleeding and clotting. This left her weak and nauseated each time a clot passed. One day when the clotting appeared to have stopped, Marietta said that she felt well enough to walk the three blocks to the grocery store with me. While we were standing at the meat counter waiting to be served, Marietta suddenly felt very weak. She held onto my arm and looking down I saw a large clot of blood on the floor between her feet. I motioned to the butcher, Bill, who immediately took the shovel that they kept for cleaning up the store and threw a shovel full of sawdust over the clot. Seeing the distress and embarrassment that Marietta was in, Bill insisted that I drive her home in his car. Marietta's good friend Vi Webb proved to be a strong source of support for her during those traumatic days. Her calmness and her droll sense of humour were a big help in facilitating Marietta's recovery.

Over the years Dr. Taylor continued to play an important role in our lives. As our family doctor he attended all of our family members for many years. When our second daughter, Carol, was born he was the attending physician; when Carol caught her arm in the wringer of our electric washing machine, we called him; when our son Gerald fell off our porch at three years old and broke his collarbone, it was Dr. Taylor who rushed to the hospital to set it. Then when Marietta's sister Isabel had an attack of what she claimed was appendicitis, Marietta ran down to the corner restaurant and called Dr. Taylor to hurry to our house. She must have sounded quite desperate because Dr. Taylor arrived in about ten minutes clad in his pajamas. Isabel's appendicitis turned out to be a miscarriage, a pregnancy for which she had given us no warning.

After Dr. Taylor became quite ill and retired from active practice, Marietta and I went to visit him at his home while we were in Windsor on a visit from Ottawa in the mid-1970s. When we arrived at his house Mrs. Taylor met us at the door and informed us that the doctor had not been able to recognize anyone but her for several weeks. While we were talking to her Dr. Taylor slowly came down the steps from his room upstairs. Halfway down the steps he stopped, pointed his finger at Marietta and said, "Talbot". Mrs. Taylor was amazed, and so were we, but we felt that Marietta had made such an impact on his mind that the sight of her brought a momentary recovery of recognition.

RESTRICTIVE COVENANTS

The months following Marilyn's birth were exciting ones. Neighbours, friends and even strangers admired the petite brown-skinned baby girl that we proud parents enjoyed showing to everyone that we met.

It was during those months that we began to look for larger living quarters. One evening as I was walking down Howard Avenue, I saw a For Rent sign on the upstairs of a brick duplex. The Guaranty Trust Company had put up the sign. The next afternoon I went to their office to inquire about renting the flat. A man named Mr. Thomson informed me that the place was indeed for rent, but that he was sorry he couldn't rent it to me. When I asked him why not he replied that there was a restrictive covenant in the title to the property.

I had never heard of restrictive covenants before that time, so Mr. Thomson explained that certain properties were not to be sold or rented to certain classes or groups of people. I asked him if it was similar to the signs that read, "No coloured People Allowed", or "No Jews", or "For Whites Only" that I had heard about in the southern United States and had seen at a couple of so called public beaches around Essex County. In those days there were many sandy beaches along the shores of Lake Erie and Lake St. Clair, a stretch of about seventy-five miles, but there were only three that allowed access to black people. A carload of young blacks were told by the caretaker of one beach on Lake Erie that they could swim in the lake, but they could not go on the beach or use the change house. Under those conditions how were they supposed to access the lake?

Mr. Thomson agreed that restrictive covenants were like that. "But," I observed, "there are coloured people living just two doors away and another family directly across the street."

"I know," he replied, "but the particular house you are interested in is restricted. Besides, it's an upstairs flat, and the tenants downstairs object to having coloured people upstairs."

I thought for a moment and then I asked, "Do you mind if I go and see the people downstairs?"

"You can, but it won't help you. They have already told me that they object to coloured people."

"I'd like to hear them tell me that themselves if you don't mind."

Mr. Thomson seemed quite confident when he consented, "Oh I don't mind, Mr. Talbot, but I'm sure it won't do you any good."

One thing I was sure of was that no law, covenant or rule could prevent me from speaking with the downstairs tenants; I didn't need Mr. Thomson's permission to do that.

So the next evening, Marietta and I took little Marilyn, by then about three months old, and walked the block straight through Broadhead Street to the large brick duplex ahead of us across the street on Howard Avenue. As we approached it Marietta remarked, "Wouldn't it be nice if we could rent that? Too bad we can't!" I felt somewhat as she did as we climbed the steps and rang the doorbell.

A rather coarse looking man answered the door followed closely by a woman with a very pleasant face. Little Marilyn caught the woman's attention, and before anyone else could say anything she exclaimed, "Oh! What a beautiful baby! Is it a boy or girl? How old?" As she continued to talk to Marietta about the baby, I noted that she spoke with a distinct French Canadian accent. She used expressions and gestures that I had observed with other French Canadians such as the Castonguay family across the street from my parents' house on Lillian Street.

I allowed both the woman and her husband to admire the baby for a while, at the same time making small talk about the weather and about some of their neighbours that we knew. Then I spoke, "I see by the sign that the place upstairs is for rent."

"Yes, it is," the man replied.

"Would you have any objection if we were to move in upstairs?"

"Object? Why should we object? You look like nice people. Oh no! We don't object."

"But Mr. Thomson told us that you objected to having coloured people upstairs," I said.

"Coloured people? We don't want those people who have noisy parties and fight all the time. But you? Mon Dieu! We don't object; you're nice people."

The next afternoon I returned to the trust company office to inform Mr. Thomson of our conversation with the downstairs tenants. "I'm sorry," he said, "but the restrictive covenant still applies. That place can't be rented to coloured people." I reported this to Marietta, and we reconciled ourselves to the fact that we would have to find a place somewhere in the "coloured" part of town.

One afternoon about two weeks later on my watch in the lobby of the hotel, I saw a man come in whom I recognized as Blake Winters, a former mayor of Windsor and the current president of the Guaranty Trust Company of Canada. He stopped at the desk to ask about messages, and then he walked toward the open elevator nearest to my station. In an instant I decided to step on to the elevator with him, not knowing exactly why, and when the elevator stopped at his floor I got off right behind him. I hesitated for a second as he turned to go down the hall to his room. Then I walked as casually as I could a few steps behind him. He was putting his key into the lock just as I would have passed him. I stopped there.

"Good afternoon, Mr. Winters! How are you this afternoon?"

He looked questioningly at me as he asked, "How is it that you know my name? Do I know you?"

"I don't think so, sir, "but I think you may know my father, Rev. Talbot. He was the pastor of First Baptist Church when you were mayor." Mr. Winters' countenance lit up.

"Oh yes! Rev. Talbot, a fine gentleman! And how is your dad?"

"He's very well, thank you."

Somehow I sensed that this was a once on a lifetime opportunity, a do or die situation. "By the way, Mr. Winters," I began, "I've got a bit of a problem with your office here in town. I wonder if you might be able to explain it for me."

"Come inside," he said as he entered the room.

"Now, what's the problem? Why should Rev. Talbot's son have a problem?"

He listened intently as I related the events of my encounter with Mr. Thomson.

"Where is this place you wanted to rent?" he asked. When I told him he showed no reaction. He simply said, "Can you go to the office tomorrow at two o'clock in the afternoon?"

"Yes, I'd be very pleased to, sir."

"Okay! Two o'clock."

I left his room not knowing what to anticipate. Would he really do anything? Was he just getting rid of me? When he found out about the restrictive covenant, would it make a difference?

I continued to have these apprehensive thoughts as I made my way to the trust company office the next day. I really expected Mr. Thomson to meet me and perhaps have him chastise me for going over his head to the company president. When I arrived at exactly two o'clock, I was not greeted by Mr. Thomson; in fact he was nowhere in sight. Instead, a young receptionist who apparently recognized me from my previous visits greeted me.

"Come in, Mr. Talbot," she said as she led me toward an open door, "Mr. Fisher is expecting you."

"Mr. Fisher?" I thought, "Why Mr. Fisher?"

I was led into a large office where a handsome blond gentleman got up from behind a huge desk, came up to me, extended his hand and said, " I'm . . . Fisher, the property manager for our company. Mr. Winters spoke to me about your problem this morning. Have a seat; let's see what we can do for you."

It was like walking into a different world. There was no mention of restrictive covenants, objecting neighbours or anything of a negative nature. Mr. Fisher told me that if we wished to see the inside of the flat on Howard Avenue, he would be happy to show it to us. We made an appointment to meet him at the location the next evening.

There were many unanswered questions in my mind as I walked home that afternoon anxious to break the news to Marietta. What had Mr. Winters said or done to change the situation so drastically? Why was Mr. Fisher handling the affair instead of Mr. Thomson? Did the company wish to save Mr. Thomson the embarrassment of having to eat crow? How much effect did my dad's superficial acquaintance with Mr. Winters have?

I learned later that Mr. Fisher was a fine Christian man, a member of an evangelical church. The events of the following eighteen or twenty months would convince me that he was indeed an example of a person who loved the Lord and who tried to demonstrate that love in good deeds toward his fellow man. That evening, following our meeting in his office, Mr. Fisher met Marietta and me at the duplex. He was about to introduce us to the downstairs tenants and advise them that he would be showing us the upstairs when the man informed him that we had met a week or two previously.

We followed Mr. Fisher up the stairs into the living room where Marietta began to comment, "This room will have to be . . .", when Mr. .Fisher interrupted her.

"Now, Mrs. Talbot, I know that the rooms need a coat of paint. I wouldn't want to live in it like it is, and I wouldn't ask you to live in it. You can choose the colours you want for each room. And, Oh yes! The floors will have to be sanded, the woodwork refinished, and after you move in if you find anything else that should be done, just let me know."

While he was making notes as we talked Marietta suggested that she would be happy to clean up the place before the painters came, but Mr. Fisher would not hear of it. It was then around the middle of the month so he suggested that we could move in on the first of the next month if we wished. We had already discussed the possibility of moving with our landlord, George, and he had agreed to waive the thirty days' notice. Marietta's concern, however, was how were they going to do all that work on the place in two weeks.

We agreed to meet Mr. Fisher on the evening before the first of the month to get the key. As soon as we entered the front door and turned on the stairway light, Marietta's face lit up with astonishment. Mr. Fisher seemed to be enjoying every second of it too, and I was so fascinated with the two of them that I almost missed seeing all of the changes. Every room had been given three coats of paint according to the colours that Marietta had selected. The floors had been sanded, the woodwork, doors, windows and archways had been sanded down and varnished, the back stairway had been painted and new rubber pads were on the steps. When we stepped outside the back door we saw a new white picket fence around the large yard.

"Your little girl will have a place to play," Mr. Fisher commented. It was only when we went out the front door to thank Mr. Fisher and leave that I noticed a hedge along the south side of the yard next to the vacant lot there, and shrubbery in a flower bed at the front and along the side of the house. Neither Marietta nor I had remembered seeing the hedge or the shrubbery before.

The upstairs flat had a large sun room (8'x12') at the front of the house with seven windows, a living room (12'x13'), a dining room (12'x12'), a kitchen (9'x14'), one bedroom (11' x12') with a walk-in closet, a second bedroom (10' x12') also with a long closet the length of the 10 ft. wall. The bathroom was also a good size. Outside the bathroom door there was a linen closet with a clothes chute inside to take dirty clothes to the basement. I mention all these features to show the kind of facility we were able to rent in 1939 for . . . fasten your seat belts . . . twenty dollars a month!

When we moved in the next day our furniture consisted of a table, two chairs, a bed, a dresser, a day bed that we had bought for Marietta's friend Vi to sleep on during Marietta's recovery from childbirth, Marilyn's crib, and the Kroehler easy chair that we had bought on credit at Harry's furniture store and had used for the wedding pictures that I took. I had come to know Harry from my days as a newspaper carrier. Later Harry changed his store from furniture sales to a man's clothing store and I continued to be his customer.

During those first months on Howard Avenue the second contentious issue of the early days of our marriage, my hunting, came to a head. I liked to hunt small game like rabbits, squirrels ducks and pheasants, but whenever I planned to go hunting with my old buddies, I would almost have to shoot my way out of the house. An incident having nothing to do with hunting, however, ended my hunting career very abruptly. One evening in 1939 we were sitting in the kitchen when Marietta thought she heard noises in the basement. She was not to be appeased until I made sure that it wasn't a burglar. Our duplex was just a half block away from two pubs, and we were naturally suspicious of some of the characters we saw coming and going past our house.

Without turning on the stairway light I crept slowly down the long flight to the landing at ground level. I paused for a moment and listened. Hearing nothing, I slowly descended the few remaining steps to the basement floor and felt my way along the wall to where I had hung my twenty gauge single barrel shotgun. I took the gun case from its hanger and as I was unzipping it, I suddenly realized that if there really was an intruder in the basement, long before I could assemble my gun I could be dead. I turned on the basement light, took a good look around and found that the hook that held the swinging window shut over the laundry tubs had not been fastened. The wind had probably caused the window to swing open and then fall back shut causing the noise that Marietta had heard.

I made two firm resolutions at that time. The first was to make sure that the window was always fastened since a person could crawl into the basement through it. The second was to get rid of my gun. On the one hand, going hunting involved too much of a hassle in our marriage. On the other hand, I learned from that experience that having a gun in the house offered no real protection unless one was expecting an intruder. Even then the intruder would have to be armed and threatening to justify the use of a gun.

The very next afternoon, as I was walking down Mercer Street, I met Robert Sims, the son of one of the men with whom I had gone hunting several times. I asked Robert if he wanted to buy my gun since I had loaned it to him once to go hunting with his dad. Of course he wanted the gun but he said he didn't have enough money to pay what it was worth.

"How much have you got?" I asked.

"About twenty dollars," he replied.

"Robert," I announced, "You've just bought yourself a nearly new twenty gauge single barrel shotgun for twenty dollars."

I'm sure he thought I was kidding until I took him to my house and handed the gun over to him. Having used the gun himself he knew that it had been fired only a few times. It was worth several times the twenty dollars he was paying.

As summer faded into fall that same year we got a call one day from Mr. Fisher. "Do you recall," he began, "that I said we would take care of any problems you found after you moved in?"

"Yes, I do, Mr. Fisher," I replied, "but we haven't found anything yet; everything seems to be perfect and Marietta is really pleased."

"Well," he continued, "the reason I called you is that when we were in the basement I noticed that the furnace needed a new grate. I'd like to send a man out to overhaul the furnace before the cold weather sets in. Is that okay?"

Of course it was okay, but when our downstairs neighbour saw the furnace man working on our furnace, he became upset. He called me down to his place and wanted to know what kind of pull I had with Mr. Fisher. He had been trying for two years to get his furnace repaired and here we move in and in a month or two they had come and overhauled ours. I explained to him that we didn't understand it either. Mr. Fisher was just being good to us. Then he asked me if I would speak to Mr. Fisher about his furnace; maybe it would help. I did mention his concern to Mr. Fisher and, lo and behold, as soon as the repairs were completed on our furnace, the work was started on his. During the next two years that they occupied the downstairs, my neighbour would come to me with his requests for things that he wanted done. Finally I had to tell him that it wasn't right for me to carry his complaints to the landlord; he'd have to do it himself.

About two years after we moved to Howard Avenue Mr. Fisher called me one day to come into the office; he had a proposition to make. I expected that perhaps our rent was about to be raised; after all, twenty dollars a month was a real bargain. The proposition that he had for me was one more astonishing event in the chain of events that began the day I saw the For Rent sign. He advised me that the widow who held the mortgage on our duplex wanted to cash in the mortgage. She would be willing to sell the duplex for the balance owing to her, an amount just over four thousand dollars. The trust company would refinance the mortgage for me if I would make a down payment of five hundred dollars, their commission for handling the transaction. I was being given the first right of refusal, i.e. the opportunity to buy before the property went on the open market. I had ten days to decide.

At that time I had been working at the Ford Motor Company for a little more than a year and had managed to save a mere two hundred dollars. We had also had our second child, Carol, born in December, 1940. I didn't know where I could get the three hundred dollars I needed. I was afraid of a second mortgage, and the only person I knew well enough to ask for a loan was our family doctor. When I approached him he expressed his regrets, but encouraged me to go ahead with the deal if I could scrape up the down payment. "You won't regret it," he assured me.

My younger brother Andrew was engaged to be married in the fall of that year, so I asked him what his plans were for a place to live. He said he was looking around. I presented my proposition to him. If he could put up the three hundred dollars, we could be joint owners of the duplex, and he could move in downstairs with his bride, Kathleen, right after the wedding. Andy recognized the solution to his problem. He and Kathleen had admired our upstairs flat, so we made an agreement that we would be joint owners; he would occupy the lower quarters, and we would try to pay off the mortgage as quickly as we could. I would keep records of our financial involvement, giving him monthly statements.

Together we were able to pay off the mortgage in six years.

BEYOND BELLHOP

On Friday, September 1, 1939, Canada declared war on Hitler's Germany. That day also proved to be important in my personal life. On that day, the head of a large business firm in Detroit entertained his staff in our hotel, and I happened to be the bellhop that showed him to his large corner suite. When he asked me if I would look after his party, I told him that since it was Friday and the beginning of the Labour Day weekend we were not very busy, and so I was sure that I could get permission to accommodate him.

For the rest of that afternoon, from about 1:30 p.m. until after six o'clock, when the party of about twelve men left to go to dinner, I tended bar, ran errands and kept the party supplied with refreshments, liquid and otherwise. I left work that day with forty-three dollars in tips, the most I ever made in one day in the four and half years I worked in the hotel. It was a welcome gift to use toward Marietta's twenty-first birthday on September fourth. I think that it might have been at that time that we went out and bought a set of dishes decorated with a replica of the bouquet of flowers presented to Queen Mary on the royal couple's visit to Windsor a few months previously. The pattern was called The Queen's Bouquet. Marietta caused quite a stir in our family some thirty years later when she gave the set, along with our first set of silverware, to our son Gerald and his wife Denise after they were married. Apparently the need of a newly married couple outweighed the potential sentimental value of the heirloom to our two daughters.

In early 1940 I applied for a job as a postal clerk and was hired. Three months later the government ordered the layoff of probationary and term employees as a war measure. I had hoped that becoming a civil servant would mean permanent employment since several black men that I knew had been letter carriers or postal clerks for many years. One of them had even risen to the position where his next promotion would have been to postmaster, but he remained at the lower level until he died. Meanwhile other white men gained appointments as postmasters.

When I left the hotel the manager had told me that if I ever needed a job to come and see him. I did as he had suggested but the only job he could offer was the next opening for a bellhop. I had resolved that I would never again work as a bellhop and I informed the manager of this. I stated that I had hoped that with my hotel experience, my educational background and my three months as a postal clerk, that he could offer me some kind of clerical work. A friend of mine named Gordon Burnette, (brother of Hugh Burnette whose role in "The Dresden Affair" is described in a later chapter) had worked as a bellhop at the other large hotel in Windsor. Then he had gone to Detroit while I was at the post office and had found a job as desk clerk in a large hotel. My manager was not prepared to consider such a position for me. In fact the management of the Detroit hotel where Gordon worked somehow learned that he was black and fired him even though he was fair skinned enough to pass for white.

When I left the manager's office that day and was walking across the lobby toward the front door (I could do that now that I wasn't a bellhop anymore), I met a man who came in regularly for Rotary Club luncheons and other things. When I greeted him he remarked that he had missed me around the hotel. When I explained the situation to him he told me that his company, a foundry making parts for the automobile industry, was hiring men. His son was the personnel manager, and he said that I should tell his son that he had sent me. Since his son turned out to be a former high school acquaintance of mine, I had hopes that he would recognize my scholastic record and give me an appropriate job.

After we had reminisced for a while about our school days while I filled out an application form, he was ready to discuss employment. He asked me what kind of work I would like. I replied that I would prefer some kind of clerical work. "That's fine, Lyle;" he responded, "I've got a job as a shipping clerk." I visualized a job at a desk doing some kind of paper work with invoices, bills of lading and such things. The job to which I was assigned involved counting cast iron castings as I put them into large shipping boxes, recording the number of castings on a card and sticking the card in a slot on the end of the box.

This so called clerical job lasted only two days. On the third day a man with a nametag that read Henry Armstrong tapped me on the shoulder and told me to follow him. He said he was the foreman of the core room and that I would be working for him. His name, Henry Armstrong, became imprinted in my mind because at that very time a black boxer named Henry Armstrong held three world championship titles simultaneously, the first boxer in history to do that. The core room job was anything but clerical. There was a pile of sharp sand beside a big hopper; it was my job to shovel the sand into the hopper where it was dried by circulating it in hot air. I then filled a wheelbarrow with the hot, dry sand and wheeled it along a ten inch plank to the core makers' bench where they always seemed to be out of dry sand.

At 11:00 a.m. and again at 3:00 p.m. the core room operation stopped and we all went out to the molding floor where the molten metal was poured into molds. My job here was shifting weights. As each mold was filled with molten cast iron I had to shift a block of cast iron onto the next mold. They were pouring cylinder blocks on that line, so the weights I had to shift weighed about fifty pounds. The blocks served to keep the sand mold from breaking down under the pressure from expansion when the molten metal was poured into it. When all the molds had been poured on our line, we each took a long hook and pulled the red hot casting from the sand and lifted them onto a cooling conveyor.

Each day I struggled along the mile and a half walk home after work, threw off my sweaty, soot-covered clothes, climbed into the tub of hot water that Marietta had prepared and promptly fell asleep. She had to wake me up to finish my bath and come to supper. On the eighth day, during the pouring of the 3:00 p.m. heat, as I was weak from the hard work which I had never done before combined with the sweltering 105 to 120 degree temperatures on the pouring floor, I dropped a weight about an inch as I was shifting it.

Henry, the foreman, yelled at me; the molder who had made the mold and was being paid by the piece only for finished castings, also yelled at me. About three molds down the line I dropped another weight, this time ruining the casting. Henry yelled, "You're fired!" with an added epithet, loud enough to be heard all over the pouring floor.

I yelled back at him, "Don't worry, I quit!" In exasperation I threw my gloves and goggles down, kicked off the foundry protective shoes, which resembled snow shoes, and headed for the office to tell the other Henry, the president's son, to make up my pay cheque. I'd be back the next day to pick it up.

When I returned the following day the foreman was waiting for me in the office. He apologized for yelling at me and said that I could come back and work for him. My reply was that I would like to speak with the personnel manager first.

"Henry," I began, "when I came to your office a few days ago I had hoped that you would consider my school record in giving me a job. Moreover, when you said that the job you had for me was a shipping clerk's job, I didn't expect it to be counting and loading castings. But even that job lasted only two days; then your namesake came along and took me off to the core room."

"I'm sorry about that," Henry replied, after a pause. "How about going back to the shipping department?"

Now I knew counting castings was going to be his best offer so I said, "You know, Henry, when your dad told me to come and see his son, I was hopeful that I would get a job. Then when I saw that you were the son that he was talking about, I thought maybe you would give me a break because of our high school friendship. But if the best job you can give me is counting castings, thanks, but no thanks!"

In the eight days that I had worked there at Auto Specialties my weight had dropped from 170 lbs. to 145 lbs. When I stopped by my parents' place on the way home that day, my weight loss was the first thing that my mother noticed. Dad happened to be home that day, and when he heard my story he encouraged me by reminding me that all the major factories were hiring men for the war effort. He added that the auto industry was gearing up for capacity production to supply vehicles for the armed forces. I should be able to find work very soon.

Dad had worked at Ford's for almost twenty years at that time and had gained the respect of both his coworkers and supervisors. Bearing these facts in mind, I wasn't surprised a couple of days later when I received a call from Mr. Hancock, supervisor of factory personnel employment, inviting me to an interview. I recalled the previous invitation to an interview that I had received from Ford's back in 1933, so I was somewhat apprehensive. I had rightly presumed that Dad had arranged for the interview with Mr. Hancock and that gave me some hope.

There were several dozen men waiting at the employment office when I arrived, and each of us was given a number. When my number was called I was directed to Mr. Hancock's office. I thought that since the boss himself was going to interview me there was hope of something good forthcoming. Mr. Hancock cordially acknowledged his long acquaintance with my dad. Besides being the Ford personnel man, he was also a member of Temple Baptist church. Then he began to leaf through a box of cards in front of him. He pulled one out. "Here's a good job, Lyle; it's in the heat treat."

I interrupted him. "I'm sorry, Mr. Hancock, but I just quit a job in a foundry. The heat treat is too close to the foundry for me. If that's the best you can do . . ."

"Just a minute," he said, "let's not be hasty. Let's see if there is anything else."

I was aware that the company employed several black men. All but one other light skinned man and my dad worked either in the foundry, the heat treat or in the tunnel between the coal yard and the power house monitoring the soft black coal as it travelled along the conveyor belt to the huge furnaces in the power house. That was in my mind as Mr. Hancock leafed through the cards again.

"Ah!" he smiled, "Here's a good job for you. It's an assembler's job in the rear axle department. How about it?"

"Frankly sir," I replied, "I had hoped that when you told my dad you would interview me personally that you would offer me something more in line with my education and experience. Production work is not really what I expected."

He hesitated a bit and then explained, "There's something you must understand. The fact is that there are only certain jobs that I can give your people."

"You mean like the foundry, the heat treat, the coal tunnel and the assembly line?" I interjected.

"Come now," he assured me, "this job is not all that bad. You'll be working on a line with about ten other men putting the crown gear and pinion and the axle shaft in the real axle housings and bolting the housings together. Now does that sound like hard work?"

I pictured the rear axle of a Ford car; it consisted of the axle shafts extending from a crown gear and pinion encased in a steel housing. It didn't appear to be too hard a job and I really did need the work.

"Okay, I conceded, "I'll give it a try."

The next morning, after getting lost a couple of times following the directions I'd been given that took me through a maze of machinery, conveyors and huge boxes and barrels of stock, I reported to my foreman. I was not put on the passenger car axle line, however. Those jobs, I later learned, were only for the boss's red apple boys. I was put on the army truck line from which eighteen men had just recently been fired because someone had put sand in a barrel of rear axle grease. No investigation had been conducted to determine which, if any, of the eighteen men had sabotaged the grease. It was no coincidence that all of those fired had either German or Italian sounding names. Many were even Canadian citizens, but that did not protect them. For the next eighteen months I handled housings weighing up to ninety pounds each as I assembled 190 axles a day. I dared not mention to anyone that I had a weak left hand and a trick knee; it would have meant my job. Moreover, if I had been dismissed because of my disability, my chances of obtaining other employment would have been dangerously impaired.

After I had been working for about six months at Ford's, the Auto Workers Union began to recruit members with enthusiasm. Because of the adverse experiences based on racial discrimination that I had encountered, I was among the first to join the union and soon became an organizer. It was against company rules to recruit members on company property so we had to be extremely cautious about when and where we talked to the men.

My supervisors soon learned that I was active in the union, and I received several threats and warnings, but they were very careful to avoid any confrontation that would give the union ammunition to find fault with their actions. Hence, when I insisted that the bell housings that we had to lift from the floor to the assembly bench weighed much more than the fifty pound safety limit, the foreman felt obliged to have a hoist installed for me. My fellow assemblers, who also benefitted from the hoist, knew that I had put the pressure on management to get it, and they expressed their appreciation to me for doing so.

It was around this time that Rev. C.L. Wells returned as our pastor. When I had been about to graduate from high school, Rev. Wells had written a letter to Dad suggesting that I could come to Charleston, West Virginia, and enroll in the state college there. He assured me that I would be accepted and that I could stay at his home. My dad felt that this would he good except that I would need money for tuition, room and board, and Rev. Wells had not mentioned the financial aspects of his invitation in his letter. Rev. Wells had said that if I could just get to Charleston he would help me in any way he could. My parents and I decided that there was still too much risk involved. We couldn't even afford the fifty dollars I would need for bus fare and pocket money.

One of the first things Rev. Wells did on his return to Windsor was to call me aside and ask me why I hadn't taken him up on his offer six or seven years previously. I restated how our situation at that time had made it impractical. His reaction was one of apparent indignation. "You should have gotten to Charleston any way you could, even hitch hiked, if necessary. I told you that you could stay at my house, and I had been assured that you would be given a job as a teacher of mathematics in the all black high school. Your senior matriculation would have qualified you for that."

"Why didn't you tell us that in your letter?" I asked.

"Don't you know that it is against the law for anyone in the United States to offer employment to anyone outside the country? But once you were in Charleston, we could have applied for a student work visa."

Since I had married Marietta and had two lovely daughters, whatever regrets I had were now overshadowed by the joy we were experiencing in our little family. Had I gone to Charleston, West Virginia, in 1933, it's almost certain that I would not have met and married Marietta.

After a year at Ford's I began to be bored with the monotony of assembly line work. In a discussion with Dad he promised to intercede with his former foreman, Norm, who was now the assistant plant superintendent of the machine shop, about getting me a transfer. Norm told him that he would be happy to do that for him, but he would have to speak to the plant superintendent. A few days later I was talking with my friend, Lloyd, whose father worked in the power house tunnel. Through his dad's boss Lloyd had initially received a job as a punch press operator in Plant 1 at Ford's in spite of the fact he was a graduate in drafting engineering from Wayne University in Detroit. Lloyd was able to arrange an interview for me with his plant superintendent who told me that if I could arrange for a transfer with my plant superintendent he would give me a job in parts and accessories, i.e. the stock room. Three months had passed since my last meeting with my superintendent, Tom Smith, but when I approached him with the request for a transfer, he became very angry and chastised me for bypassing him and going to another plant manager. However, he did sign my transfer slip.

The next morning I went to the office of Dale, the general foreman of parts and accessories, as I had been instructed. While I was waiting, a man approached me, and in a distinct English accent asked me what I was doing there. "I'm waiting to see Mr. Atkinson," I replied.

"Well," he said, "If you're looking for a job, you might as well go back where you came from. There's no job for you here."

I responded very firmly, "I've been instructed to see Mr. Atkinson, and if you don't mind, I'll just wait for him." He muttered something under his breath and took off down the hall.

Presently, Dale Atkinson appeared. "Are you Lyle Talbot?" he asked pleasantly.

"Yes, I am." I replied. He extended his hand as he smiled.

"Tom Groves has spoken to me about you. He tells me that you have your senior matriculation diploma. Is that correct?".

"Yes it is."

"Good! I have a job for you as a stock picker. Report to Jack Hobbs on the third floor at the center desk."

I followed his directions and when I arrived at the center desk, third floor, guess who was there to meet me: yes, Jack Hobbs, the man who had just told me to go back where I came from. This is the man who was to be my supervisor for six of the next ten years. Jack found it difficult even to be politely civil to me and sometimes I reacted to his abrupt manner in a similar vein.

Jack didn't give me the job I was supposed to get picking stock. Instead he assigned me to take stock off the conveyor. A few days later, Superintendent Tom happened to be walking past where I was working. He stopped to ask me how I liked my stock picking job. I had to tell him that I wasn't picking stock; I was working on the conveyor. Tom muttered a profanity and hastened toward the center desk. Fifteen minutes later I was assigned to a section of the stock room which included all the exhaust parts for all Ford vehicles dating back to the Model A. Since I had been blessed with a photographic memory, in the job of picking stock, that ability enabled me to recall whether there was stock of a particular part anywhere in our area. Thus, I was able to fill orders faster than others who often had to search the entire section to ascertain whether or not we had stock.

With the exception of three war years during which I was an expediter of parts for army Bren gun carriers, I worked under the direct supervision of Jack Hobbs. During that time I found it necessary to file several grievances against him, usually on the grounds of racial discrimination. Senior management upheld each of those grievances. My personal relationship with Jack was a bit strained, but I enjoyed my work in the stock room. It gave me time for personal activities like reading my pocket New Testament while the other stock pickers would read mostly pocket novels or detective stories n their free time.

In 1943 a position of clerical stock expediter became open. It was quite a responsible position whereby I would ensure that the spare parts for the armed force's Bren gun carriers reached the appropriate destination for shipment overseas.

After consulting with the plant chairman of the union, I applied for the position. Along with the shop steward he accompanied me to Harold Johnson's office. He was the division superintendent who had claimed that I wasn't qualified to do the job. The union representatives insisted that I was the most qualified of all the applicants, but the superintendent stated that he couldn't agree to have me working at a desk in the front office where the person chosen would be located.

"Is it because of Lyle Talbot's colour?" demanded the plant chairman.

"Well . . ." The superintendent stammered.

"Well nothing!" the chairman retorted. "I'll give you just fifteen minutes to agree to give Talbot that job. If your answer is not yes, we're going out to the stockroom and take every man out on the street."

I should explain that in those days a plant chairman could stand behind such a threat. After a fifteen minute recess we were back in the office. Management offered a compromise. I could have the job but we must agree to have a desk put in a small cubicle in the craneway for me. This was done in spite of the fact that I perceived the compromise as still discriminatory and the union reps agreed with me.

In a few months my job had grown to the point where I needed more help, and over the next few months I trained three other men to look after portions of the responsibility. Now we had another problem. The office in the craneway was much too small for four desks, but the superintendent remained adamant about not bringing me into the main office. The reason for this was that I would then have been located in the same large open office as a number of female office workers. To get around that perceived problem they cleared a large section of the stock room for our four desks. The irony of this situation was that the four of us men had to spend about half of our time in the main office engaging the help of female workers much of the time in order to perform our duties. If I required a clerk to work overtime with me, a situation that happened several times, one of the women would stay. The one who helped me on most of these occasions lived within walking distance to the office, and I would walk her home whatever the hour.

Often I would need to go into the vault to verify a shipment. Security rules required that a bonded employee from the cashiers' department had to be in the vault whenever anyone else was there. One of the female employees would get the key from the security office, and then together we would go into the vault that was in a tunnel under the street in front of the administration building. Once inside the cashier employee would lock the door; then no one else could get in except a security officer in the case of an emergency. There was a telephone in the vault as well.

I have described the foregoing in some detail because it is directly related to the next significant experience of racism in my employment career. When World War II ended my job as stock expediter was phased out. The company was returning to civilian production. Follow-up clerks were needed with duties identical to those I had been performing for three years except that the positions were located in the service department instead of in parts and accessories.

Two of the men whom I had trained were placed in these new positions as the army supply operations were closed out. The third man left the company to return to his insurance business. When I applied for one of the positions, the department head, John Norwood, who had been one of the sixteen high school graduates hired on that day in the summer of 1933 when I wasn't even interviewed, informed me that I could not be given a job in the service office because it would necessitate my working with white women. He insisted that it wasn't his decision; it was company policy. I was transferred back to the stock room and demoted to the rank of stock handler since my former job as stock picker was occupied. The union was unable to help me in this situation because the new follow-up positions were in a salaried occupational group not covered by our collective agreement.

I requested interviews with each level of management up to the office employment manager but I was not given a reason for the differential treatment. One manager told me that by simply applying for the job I had spoiled my chances of becoming a supervisor in his division.

I was finally able to get an appointment with the president partly, I think, because my name was known throughout the company as the writer of a column in the local union's weekly newsletter, "Ford Facts" which dealt with issues related to fair practices in employment. When I arrived at the executive office at the appointed time, I was told that the president was not well; I was to see the vice president in charge of personnel.

I was a bit disappointed at not being able to speak with the president. I was shown into the vice president's office who greeted me quite cordially, noting that he had read every one of my columns in "Ford Facts". He had been told the reason for my request for a meeting, so he went immediately to that matter.

"I understand that you have applied for a position in the service department. Is that correct?"

"Yes sir. I have applied, but I have been denied the job because I'm coloured."

"Oh no, Lyle! It's not because you're coloured. It's because you would have to be working in the same office as white women. The company can't allow that."

"Who made that rule?' I asked.

"Nobody made it. That's just the way it is."

"If there is no written rule why can't you give me the job?"

"Because the decision has been made by the division superintendent and I'm not prepared to override his decision."

I started to tell him of my experience during the war when I had worked with white women, but he cut me off. "Oh, we know all about your job during the war, but that was wartime."

I asked, "Did anyone complain? Did any of the women complain about my conduct with them?"

"No, I'm told that you did a good job and that you acted as a gentleman at all times; however,

we can't give you the job in the service department. I'm sorry!"

I thanked him for seeing me and left disappointed but determined to become even more active than I had been in fighting racial discrimination in all its expressions. The vice president had advised me that it was only because of the union that I had been allowed to work on the wartime jobs and he assured me that the company would make sure that it didn't happen again. His assurance was well founded. Up to the year 1970, when I left Windsor, the Ford Motor Company never employed a black person, male or female, in any office area where both sexes worked together.

CHAPTER 13

THE BIRTH OF A MOVEMENT

One wonders what black visitors to the cities and towns of Canada did for accommodations, food and services, much less for entertainment, before the passage of human rights laws. A simple thing like getting a haircut gave us a bit of a problem. The local black barbers and beauticians had a captive clientele because whites either would refuse to cut back people's hair, or else they would mess up the job so badly that the black person would never come back. I always admired Willie, a German Canadian barber, who opened his shop on the edge of the black belt during World War II. Willie wanted all of the business he could get, maybe because his business had suffered during the war. Whatever his reason he had no desire to exclude anyone from his shop.

I got to know Willie very well because he was my neighbor as well as my barber for almost ten years. When he encountered difficulty in trimming the hair of some blacks due to its texture, he got a black barber who was employed at the post office to work part-time in his shop. Willie soon learned how to handle the peculiarities of the many textures of blacks' hair and became an expert at grooming them all. He taught his son these techniques and it wasn't long before Willie's barbershop was one of the busiest in the city with about half of his clientele drawn from the black community.

Willie learned what every black Canadian has to learn — if you want to be competitive in a racist society you have to excel in your chosen field. Being good is not enough; you have to be better than your competitors are in order for the dominant race to accept you. Harry, the black barber, whose shop was on one of the busiest streets in town had few white customers for two reasons neither of which was because he was not as good a barber as any of the other barbers in town. Firstly, racial prejudice kept most of them away. Secondly, they were often so many customers waiting for one of his chairs that whites would pass by to another shop down the street where they wouldn't have to wait as long for a haircut. But getting a haircut was a minor problem compared to some of the other issues facing blacks in Canada.

World War II marked a major turning point in the history of blacks in Canada in many aspects of societal life. Historians writing about blacks in Canada have generally failed to appreciate this most significant factor. For instance, after the war the racial barriers to entry into the armed forces were broken. However, even during the war, these barriers were as strong as in civilian life.

George McCurdy was a native of Amherstburg and a graduate of Amherst Secondary School. He was an outstanding athlete excelling in track, baseball, football and boxing. One of his feats was to run one on one in an exhibition one hundred yard dash against Jesse Owen, winner of four gold medals in the 1936 Olympics. McCurdy enlisted in the army and was stationed in Chatham, Ontario. A second remarkable feat was becoming the light heavyweight boxing champion of the army while stationed with what I think was the Kent regiment. His commanding officer noted his outstanding achievements and chose George to be his bat man, making him a corporal. After a time the officer recommended George for officer training. George was accepted and completed the training at the top of his class. He was then eligible for a commission but he never became an officer. Instead he was given a compassionate discharge when his wife had some minor complications. George had not requested a discharge. He had fully expected to become an officer when he completed the officer training. As a matter of fact, no black member of the Canadian Army from Essex or Kent County ever became a commissioned officer before 1970, when we moved from Windsor.

A second related incident involved two black soldiers home on leave in about 1944. They were refused service in a downtown Windsor restaurant. When they insisted on being served the police were called and the soldiers left. The incident was reported in the newspaper and political leaders publicly deplored the fact that soldiers in uniform who had served their country in battle could not get a meal in a restaurant in their own hometown. The proprietor of the restaurant, however, remained anonymous, as did many others who continued to deny service to black soldiers, veterans and civilians alike until Windsor's city council passed an anti-discrimination bylaw in 1947. The bylaw stated that any restaurant, store, recreation center or other establishment providing a service to the public and licensed by the city would have its license suspended if found guilty of refusing service to any person because of that person's race, color, religion or national origin.

The bylaw was a major first step in the achievement of antidiscrimination legislation in the province of Ontario. However, it had several limitations. The majority of potential black clients in a border city like Windsor were visitors either from the United States or from elsewhere in Canada. Such people would not be inclined to call the police to report a refusal. They would just move on to somewhere else. Black Windsorites were also reluctant to call the police; they would rather go to one of the few restaurants that served everyone. Restaurant owners who wanted to continue practicing discrimination could do so with virtual impunity.

The bylaw had other limitations as well. Hotels, licensed taverns and pubs were under the supervision of the Liquor Control Board of Ontario and accordingly were not subject to municipal bylaws. Except for the Walker House, a small hotel/tavern owned by a black family, even the few licensed places that did serve blacks allowed them only in the men's beverage rooms. Those located in or near black neighborhoods had what were termed Jungle Rooms in which black couples and women were served. Up until 1955, other than the Walker House, there was no other tavern with meals and entertainment where a black couple, black group or a mixed black and white group could go for an evening out unless someone in the group personally knew the proprietor. Even after reservations had been made and confirmed over the telephone, when the party arrived on the scene they would be told there must have been some mistake; there would be no record of a call or reservation.

As mentioned in the previous chapter 1947 was a pivotal year in my life. One evening in that year I received a phone call from a man whom I had only known as a chiropractor in town. He told me that he was a pacifist and a member of the Fellowship of Reconciliation, an international group committed to promoting peace and goodwill among people. He had read the writings of a black pacifist named Bayard Rustin who advocated nonviolent resistance to racial discrimination. Rustin had conceived the idea of peaceful resistance to combat racism and he later helped to organize the famous freedom rides and sit-ins of the late 1950s and early 1960s in the southern United States.

Doc Harrison, as we knew him, invited me to a meeting held in the YMCA during which the attendees were to discuss how to deal with incidents of racial discrimination such as the denial of service to black soldiers. I accepted Doc's invitation and at that meeting the Windsor Interracial Council was born. Doc was selected as chairperson and I became secretary. In 1949 the Council was renamed the Windsor Council on Group Relations as we were unable to recruit enough non-white people such as African Canadians, Asian Canadians and First Nations citizens in order to make it truly interracial.

Unlike the Central Citizens Association (active from around 1935 to 1939), which was formed to assist individual blacks in finding employment at the height of the Depression, the Windsor Council on Group Relations was intended to combat racism in every aspect of life. The members were primarily young CCF/NDP supporters, UAW activists, Roman Catholic priests and laypeople, a Jewish rabbi and community leaders. Our primary focus was in three areas — education, legislation and direct action.

We decided to approach some of Windsor's prominent citizens to be on our advisory board. First we approached leading citizens, starting with the mayor, who had publicly indicated a degree of commitment to the cause of equal rights. These we felt would readily allow us to use their names. Then we selected those whose names on our letterhead would give us the status we would need. We felt that this second group would consent for one of several reasons. Firstly, they would not want to be seen as opposed to our objective to promote a better understanding among all people. Secondly, they would not want to be considered any less supportive than those who had already agreed to be on the board. If they were apprehensive about our methodology, they would at least agree in principle with our objectives. Finally, they might not be concerned with either our objective one way or the other, but they would accept the publicity of having their name on our letterhead.

As far as we were able to determine our advisory board members appeared to be satisfied with the arrangement. For most of them it meant being identified with a worthy cause without having to take an active part in it. For the Council it facilitated the acceptance of many of our activist projects. The board was kept well informed of all the activities of the Council and acted as a sort of buffer against the adverse publicity to which we were subjected. Every piece of correspondence issued by the Council was printed on the letterhead listing the advisory board members down one side of the paper.

With strong support from Doc Harrison and a few members of the youth division of the Cooperative Commonwealth Federation (later the New Democratic Party), we launched an aggressive, comprehensive and persistent campaign to combat discrimination in Windsor. One of the first projects was the Community

Audit in 1947 patterned after one that had been conducted in Montclair, New Jersey. It was factual, well documented and fair. It showed the positive as well as negative aspects of race relations in Windsor at that time. The survey indicated that there was more negative than positive to report.

Highlights of the Community Audit Report of 1947 entitled "How Does Our Town Add Up?"

Employment

Some factories hired men of all races and nationalities. Those with strong labour unions were relatively fair in upgrading blacks within the bargaining unit on regular production jobs. Seniority rights in these factories protected the jobs of employees covered by the contract on a relatively equal basis.

There had never been an incident of strife between employees of different racial or ethnic backgrounds. This meant that at the working level people of all races were able to get along together.

During World War II one large factory had promoted three blacks to supervisory positions without any backlash. However, none of those who had been promoted were in supervisory positions at the time of the Community Audit.

No industry employed black women and those men whom they did employ were concentrated in a very small number of factories.

Unions generally had no say in the hiring or promoting policies of factories, and apart from their union, employees had no recourse against discriminatory treatment in employment.

Although 10 percent of employable blacks were qualified to work at so-called better jobs, 97.8 percent of those employed were working at menial labour.

White collar positions were almost exclusively denied to persons who were not white under the collar. In a few isolated cases where blacks were given office employment, the quality of their work was reported to be from satisfactory to excellent, i.e. similar to that of the general population. Even those factories who hired blacks in the shop denied office employment to qualified blacks.

Stores, as a rule, did not hire blacks except as janitors, elevator operators and for other menial types of work. The fact that one store owner reported that the "Negro girls" *(sic)* that he hired were good workers and his business had grown, should have debunked the old excuse that the public would object to being served by black clerks and salespeople.

There was no overt or official racial discrimination. However, oral examinations were found to be an effective means of disqualifying blacks from government jobs (just as I had been disqualified back in the 1930s in spite of having passed the written test with 85 percent). Customs and immigration officer candidates were given these types of oral examinations so there were no black employees at the Windsor/Detroit border crossing. Six percent of all employed blacks worked for the municipality in the public works department and the parks department. One worked for the hydro and one for the water division. The board of education employed three men, but not as teachers. Three light complexioned black women had previously been employed as teachers, but none was working at the time of the survey. There were two police constables and two other blacks worked for the department in the garage.

The situation in the fire department provides an interesting commentary on the racial situation in Windsor at that time. Windsor's two largest hotels employed blacks only as bellhops, porters and elevator operators. Restaurants and small hotels generally refused blacks when hiring cooks or waiters.

There were a few self-employed tradesmen, three medical doctors and two dentists. The public did not noticeably differentiate on racial grounds in obtaining their services.

Housing and Accommodations

A direct quote from the Community Audit stated, "It is in this phase of community relations that discrimination, segregation and other forms of injustice and intolerance are most flagrantly exposed in this city," although it was noted that Windsor had no slum areas that could be attributed to any racial group. Half a dozen or so black families had crossed the segregation barriers but with considerable difficulty in many cases. Also, government sponsored housing projects had eased the housing problems for many people including blacks, but segregated housing was still quite common.

Practically all real estate agents recognized restricted geographical areas in renting, selling and servicing property in 1947. It was generally thought that property values would be adversely affected by the integration of blacks. What does affect property values is forcing people to live in substandard, overcrowded or otherwise in inadequate living accommodations in which the occupant has little or no economic stake.

The final observation above provides one reason why no black ghetto has ever developed in Canadian cities like Windsor. In the second survey done in 1957, it was reported that over 30 percent of blacks owned their own homes. Job security, gained as a direct result of union negotiations, had made it possible for many black workers to purchase their own homes.

D-Day 1946

It's all over now so I see no reason why the truth can't be told
About certain aspects of our effort to win the war.
I hope by this that some of the little people in our country
May be aroused to see through a lot of the tinsel show an' a' that.

In September of 1939 our government made war on Hitler's Germany,
And we, the people, were called upon, as loyal subjects of his Majesty,
To take up arms or work on the production lines
Making materials to supply our boys
Or labouring on farms to feed our men of war.

Gratifying, to say the least, was our response as little people.
Our combined volunteer army, navy and air force
Grew to be the largest per capita in the world.
Veritable arsenals our factories became,
And our farms were exploited to capacity.

The little people, inspired by the call to defend our way of life,
Pitched in with a will to win this war —
A war we did not want and did not cause,
A war which, for a great many after the depression years,
Meant only a means of livelihood, the thrill of adventure
Or a chance to travel to countries far and wide which otherwise they'd never see.

Nevertheless, they fought, worked, suffered
And many died or were left forever maimed
For a cause which was for them only a promise . . .
But let us look at another side —

At the start of war our boys were in dire need of supplies,
Transport, ammunition, tanks and guns.
England had her back to the wall drilling with broomsticks;
She was virtually at the mercy of the Nazi hordes.

Here are but some of the dastardly deeds done
In the name of the war effort
Against which there is no retribution.
But there was reward!
Industrialists, not just a few,
Refused to sign contracts for materials much in need
Until the margin of profit was raised to meet their demands.

When the cry was sounded for conscription in the House,
M. J. Coldwell positively declared,
In order to insure the steady flow of supplies to our forces,
That the liquid wealth of our nation, as well as the manpower,
conscripted must be.

The lovers of money more than lovers of country
Decreed that reserve funds, dividends and profits
Meant more to them than the lives of people,
youths in their prime of life.

The Prime Minister was given power
To conscript life but not wealth,
And we squawked when he hesitated.

Ford workers struck for equal pay for equal work.
Athough railroad sidings from Windsor to Montreal
Were filled with materials of war,
The cry went out to the men in the field
That Ford workers had cut off the flow of supplies.
But Ford workers' sons and brothers were fighting too, you know.

And in a land called Canada,
Where freedom of expression and religion were deemed to be a right,
Seventy men of the cloth were told not to expound on some aspects and attitudes.
Black soldiers and airmen were refused a cup of coffee in restaurants,
Beer in bars, rooms in hotels and even houses to live in —
Often by the very people whose lands they were protecting.

One famous industry received twenty million dollars in profits — tax free.
The president was honoured with a medal and cross
For services given to the war effort.

What war effort?
When the government decreed that no more chrome could be made or sold,
One company took countless tons of this vital metal
And painted it matte green and other civilian coloured paints
and sold them anyhow.

The little man was forced to save, compulsory savings plan 'twas called,
And all must save, though some could ill afford it, kids and all.

He paid the shot, this little man,
In battle, taxes forced and savings too,
And, what a lot of people easily forget
In buying the goods that he produced,
To pay the corporate taxes as well.
He fought the war counting his own life cheap
In the cause of his country.
Now who cares if he has place to lay his head?

Did he really win the war?
Business boomed,

Industries mushroomed

Millions were made,

But what had he to show?

Debts

Broken bodies

Broken families

No houses —

Or death

And they tell us . . .

We won the war!

GROWING PAINS

The Windsor Interracial Council (renamed the Windsor Council on Group Relations) was funded primarily by an annual grant from the city of Windsor, by contributions from Local 200 of the United Auto Workers Union, by other smaller donations and by membership fees. The few people who volunteered their services, about fifteen in number, kept the Council going at a steady pace for about ten years.

A series of sit-ins at several licensed hotels and taverns in the area in 1949 followed the survey, "How Does Our Town Add Up?" These sit-ins were the first of this type of civil rights protest ever held in North America; they predated the famous sit-ins conducted in the southern United States by almost a decade. During the years 1949-1950, the Council compiled documentary evidence of discriminatory practices against nineteen establishments licensed under the Liquor Control Board of Ontario.

The following account is an illustration of what happens when the strategies of the social action group conflicts with those of an appeasement oriented Uncle Tom. First, note the excerpt from an article from the files of the Windsor Daily Star, November 21, 1949, as it reported on one of the sit-ins and stand-ins conducted by members of the Council on Group Relations. The incident being reported occurred almost ten years before the famous sit-ins in the southern United States.

From the Windsor Daily Star, November 21, 1949:

Saturday night in Windsor saw what clearly looked to be an organized attempt on the part of Negro groups — believed to be mostly from Detroit — to force their way into several Windsor restaurants and hotels which have maintained a colour bar.

Their tactics amounted to indoor picketing and intimidation — antics that will do their cause no good, nothing but harm.

The campaign against racial discrimination, however well justified, cannot be furthered by antagonizing hotel and restaurant operators and the public alike. Bulldozing will get them nowhere but farther back.

As outstanding members of their race in Windsor, Dr. Roy Perry, candidate for alderman in Ward 3 at the coming municipal election, and his brother, Walter, leader of the Canadian-American Coloured Brotherhood, should be — and it's believed they will be the first to frown on such action — the first to condemn it.

A more accurate description would have read more like the following: Saturday night in Windsor . . . The campaign against discrimination was well justified . . . Dr. Perry, candidate for alderman etc. . . . .and his brother Walter . . . will be . . . the first to frown on this method . . .the first to condemn it.

As well as the above observations, there were other blatant inaccuracies in the newspaper account. The "Negro groups . . . from Detroit" was in fact a group of both black and white individuals, all Windsor residents, who did not attempt "to force their way", but instead they simply entered the tavern and waited to be seated. Such tactics did do good, eventually resulting in anti-discrimination legislation and certainly never involved any form of bulldozing!

As for the British-American Association of Coloured Brothers (incorrectly labelled in the newspaper article), here is the response from that organization:

> To say that I was deeply shocked by the display of ill manners reported in the "Now" column of Monday, is putting it very mildly. To our way of thinking, no moral battle has ever been won, nor have any appreciable gains ever been made, by rudeness and a chip-on-the-shoulder attitude. As a matter of fact, we feel that

our lifelong crusade against interracial intolerance has been set back many years by the coloured people who forced their way into a local dining place and demanded service.

May we of the British-American Association of Coloured Brothers offer an apology to our white friends for this action, and point out that it was not sanctioned by our organization, nor [done] with any knowledge on our part.

A little more than a hundred years ago our people were animals. Today many of the world's foremost educators, scientists, religious leaders, entertainers, doctors, lawyers, publishers, are coloured. This is a record of which we are proud.

When evidence of interracial discord appear, we would appreciate it very much if they could be referred to our organization which has the machinery to deal with them effectively and diplomatically.

W. L. Perry,

Secretary-Treasurer,

British-American Association of Coloured Brothers

This letter and the news report that preceded it illustrate how the media, anticipating the kind of response that will defuse action to correct a racial injustice, can distort the problems faced by blacks. Mr. Perry responded exactly as the press had predicted. He apologized for something that he knew nothing about and then pointed out the geniuses who in any race would be considered exceptional. Blacks are entitled to their just plain folks as well as their heroes. To attempt to show that blacks are human by extolling the celebrities is to disdain blackness itself. Notice how Perry tried to divert attention to his own group that, in fact, had no intention much less the organizational means of dealing with discrimination. Ironically, his brother Roy was an executive member of the Windsor Interracial Council.

On November 23, 1949, the Windsor Star published the verbatim press release of the Council after a committee had met with the editor. The release tells exactly what happened, whereas Perry was so anxious to jump to the white man's whistle that he didn't think it was necessary to investigate for himself what had actually occurred. The Man had said it, and for him, so it was.

Here is the Council's press release which reveals the inaccuracies of the newspaper article in more detail:

> A few days ago, complaints were presented before the Interracial Council against several taverns and restaurants alleging racial discrimination and segregation.
>
> The Committee on Specific Cases of Discrimination decided to investigate, and on two separate occasions, including last Saturday night, November 19, a mixed group of Interracial Council members, accompanied a group of coloured citizens of Windsor, including two veterans of the last war and their wives, on a visit to some of those places against which complaints had been received.
>
> The sole purpose of the Committee's action was to ascertain whether or not discrimination was being practiced. In the establishment visited on Saturday night, the entire group, including the members of the Interracial Council was denied service. In fact they were denied a seat, although they waited patiently for two hours.
>
> Although the group had made confirmed reservations, they were told that there were none. They replied that they were willing to wait until

unreserved tables were available. However, none became available during the two-hour period that the group stood waiting, even though tables were provided for many parties who volunteered the information that they had no reservations.

There was no evidence of "intimidation", "bulldozing" or "picketing" by any member of the group, either white or coloured, throughout the entire evening.

The Council regrets that it has been necessary to make these investigations and is working toward the day when such action will no longer be required.

One other example of distorted or misrepresented facts by the press was in a feature article in the Toronto Star Weekly dated November 29, 1952, under the caption "Windsor's Outstanding Negroes":

Windsor, a city composed largely of minorities in language, nationality and religion, has never known many of the barriers of intolerance which have marked other places. People are accepted for what they are rather than who they are. Beyond this, however, there has always existed a soft spot for the Negro...

The tradition that began in those days of perils for the coloured people (the Underground Railway) has grown stronger, if anything. James Watson is the grandson of a Negro slave. It is true that his ability is unusual, but if it were only the equal of that of others opposable for the position, Windsor's city council probably would have bent over backwards to see that he had the chance.

This conclusion is a flagrant untruth. The struggle of Mayor Art Reaume and a small group of citizens to achieve the appointment of Watson is a matter of record in the minutes of the city council. The article continues:

> ... There are those unpleasant occasions when an individual proprietor may refuse to serve colored patrons in his tavern. But Lyle Talbot, president of the Negro Community Council, says things are improving all the time. Like Mr. Watson and Dr. Perry, he agreed that one important thing is to be recognized in Windsor: any Negro who prepares himself for a better position will have little trouble in the labour market. ...

Watson didn't mention it, but some of his friends noticed that he, unlike other civic officials, had never been invited to join a service club. No blacks in Windsor belonged to these organizations.

The following is also close but there is still a misconception:

> Hundreds of Negroes work in the huge Ford plant in Windsor and other industries, but few are in offices and stores. Lyle Talbot thinks more would be employed if they demonstrated their competence and went looking for a job. He feels that too many Negroes have accepted a situation they thought existed and have never done anything about it.

In fact, I said nothing of the kind. What I actually said was that now that we have a Fair Employment Practices Act in Ontario more people should apply for jobs for which they are qualified and use the Act to report refusals to be hired. Too many were accepting the situation as if there were no such law. How easy it is to report an interview with only slight alterations in order to leave an entirely different impression with the reader.

The Windsor Council on Group Relations employed three basic strategies for achieving social change. These were, in order of priority, legislation, direct action and education. Before any appreciable changes could take place in the existing situation, legislation making acts of discrimination illegal had to be enacted. There were those who argued that the public must first be educated with respect to the need for such legislation in order to gain political support. The Council reasoned that true believers in the dignity of man and the rights of all people to the benefits of society need no such education. The bigots at the other end of the continuum would be immune to educational human rights programs. Those on the fence might be intellectually persuaded by education but they would be more likely to change behavior patterns if there were laws against discrimination. It was further reasoned that legislation is one of the most effective forms of education. People often learn that they should do by doing what the law says they must do.

The Council adopted direct action in the form of peaceful resistance to expose specific discriminatory actions and practices. Many Canadians have always believed that discrimination was not a serious problem in this country. They would compare Canada with South Africa or the southern United States and conclude like the nursery rhyme character, little Jack Horner, "What good boys we are!" Most Canadians fail to recognize that not only bigots practice racial discrimination, but good, respectable and mannerly people as well. In many situations it is considered right to conform to existing social protocol and norms. Also such people do not understand that, unless challenged, such subtle forms of discrimination will remain acceptable forms of behavior in white society. Finally, they fail to see that the smaller, politically weaker and economically poorer the minority group is, the easier it is to discriminate against them with impunity. Since blacks have never accounted for as much as 2 percent of the population in this country, not even in municipalities where they are most concentrated, they have been powerless as a political or economic force.

The Council decided that Canadians needed well documented proof of the extent of discrimination before any legislation could be expected. To those who contended for less legislation and more education, the Council's viewpoint was to let the evidence speak for itself. Direct action to deal with specific cases of discrimination was another educational vehicle "toward a better understanding and good will among all people", the express purpose of the Windsor Council on Group Relations as stated in their constitution.

The Council did not stress the need for legislation and direct action as a substitute for public education. In fact, without a vigorous program of promotion and the dissemination of information, legislation and direct action would have had even less positive results than they did. For example, the Canada Labour Code, Part I, Fair Employment Practices was little known and rarely invoked. There were less than fifty complaints filed in the first fourteen years and less than three hundred formal complaints in twenty-five years compared with four thousand complaints addressed to the Ontario Human Rights Commission in each of the years from 1973–1978.

In retrospect there is every reason to believe that the lack of sustained advertising and promotion led the federal government officials and Parliament as well to conclude that there had been very little discrimination in federal jurisdiction employment from 1952–1970. However, the experience of the Canadian Human Rights Commission since its establishment in 1978 combined with that of the Anti-discrimination Directorate of the Public Service Commission has been that allegations on the grounds of race and colour are the most frequently perceived forms of discrimination. These facts show that racial discrimination has been very much alive in this country.

The Council launched an energetic program of public education to coincide with their demands for legislation and their exposure of racist practices. They strategically distributed the Community Audit pamphlet that they produced to five thousand people. These locally and nationally selected people were persons considered to have some power and influence and who might help to bring about the desired social change. The Council used every available form of media to keep the public informed about its aims and activities. As an example, for five years the Council held its monthly meetings in the city hall council chambers and the local press reported the proceedings of each meeting.

During the dozen years or so that I was an activist in the union, the credit union, the civil rights movement and child welfare, not one prominent black person ever spoke out in support of what we were doing. This was the situation even though some of them had consented to having their names on the list of advisory board members of the Council on Group Relations. In fact I received phone calls from other blacks telling me that I should back off in the campaign against discrimination. They claimed that the strategy employed by the Council on Group Relations would do more harm than good. Pastors of black churches claimed that we were undermining the good relationships that they had established in the white community over the years. Even when the legislation banning discrimination was enacted, some pastors still viewed me as a troublemaker in the city.

A very close friend of mine who had been involved in the organization and operation of the credit union and who was himself an official of his local union of the UAW, once said to me, "You know, Lyle, you're climbing farther and farther out on a limb. One of these days someone is going to cut off that limb. Where will you be then? Don't you think you need the support of the leaders of our own community?"

"Yes," I replied, "I'd like very much to have their support. There's a job to be done, and if I wait for our leaders to support me, you and I both know that another generation will pass before anything is done to correct these injustices."

While both the Windsor Star and Dr. Perry predicted that the actions of the Council on Group Relations would have no positive effects, subsequent events in Windsor and throughout the province of Ontario indicate quite the contrary. In spite of the erratic reporting and commentary cited earlier, they served a useful purpose: the tactics employed by the Council proved to be effective. The Windsor Council on Group Relations was making news. In fact it was making history. The city bylaw against discrimination in 1950, the Fair Employment Practices Act of Ontario in 1951 and of Canada in 1953, the Fair Accommodations Act of Ontario in 1955 and the Canadian Bill of Rights in 1965 were all the direct results of actions taken by the Council and other similar groups across Canada.

As for personal support from the leaders in the black community, it was not until the mid-1970s that the National Black Coalition of Canada awarded me a plaque in recognition of years of service to the black community of Canada. Not until then and after I had been employed as a human rights administrator for several years, did the pastor of First Baptist Church in Windsor invite me to appear on the platform along with two or three other former members of the church who had gained national recognition in their areas of expertise.

BY THEIR FRUITS

"By their fruits shall they be known." Matthew 7:18, *King James Bible*

As stated in the previous chapter, peaceful protest, accompanied by a consistent program of public education and by representations to the municipal, provincial and federal governments, did prove effective.

In 1950 the Senate of Canada appointed a committee under the chairmanship of Senator Arthur Roebuck to consider the advisability of a Bill of Rights (not to be confused with the Charter of Rights drafted by the Trudeau administration). The committee recommended the enactment of the Canadian Bill of Rights, but the federal government was not able to pass the bill until 1965. One of the problems was that many of the provinces were not ready in 1950 to ensure equal rights to all their minority groups.

The Windsor Council on Group Relations selected me in May 1950 to present a brief in person to the senate committee. The Council voted to allow me fifty dollars expense money, including airfare, for the trip to Ottawa. The treasurer was an accountant in one of the downtown banks and some of our members suspected he had been persuaded to take the position in order to keep a close watch on the five hundred dollar annual grant which we received from the city. This was the kind of patronizing attitude that was common among whites at that time. Such an attitude was prevalent even among those who expressed their support for what we were trying to accomplish.

For about three years the Council on Group Relations held its monthly meetings in the of city hall council chambers. No other private or volunteer group had been allowed this privilege on a regular basis. The privilege was the direct result of the stand taken by the mayor and three members of the city's board of control who were members of our advisory board.

Extracts from Hansard, The Senate of Canada, Proceedings of the Special Committee on Human Rights and Fundamental Freedoms, No.7, The King's Printer, Ottawa, May 7, 1950, pp.254–258.

Mr. Talbot: Many people from our city would have you believe that there is no racial or religious discrimination being practiced here. They cite the fact that we have on occasion even elected a Jew as Mayor, that our present Mayor is a Roman Catholic of French Canadian origin, and that we have a coloured alderman, and a coloured member of the Board of Education, and that we have just appointed a coloured City Solicitor as conclusive evidence that there is no discrimination.

But are you told that if our coloured alderman, board member or city solicitor with their wives were to enter certain restaurants or almost any tavern in the Windsor area where the proprietor was not aware of their identity, they would find themselves denied the services of that establishment? The technique being used to exercise discrimination in our community is very intriguing. For instance, in employment, if a young Negro applies for a 'White collar' position he is invariably told that the firm hires only experienced help. If an older, more experienced Negro applies for a similar position, he is told that the firm is looking for younger people who can be trained to specialize in the firm's methods.

Seldom will an employer openly admit racial discrimination is being practiced when he refuses a Negro . . .

Hon. Mr. David: But would not, probably, the same answers be given to anybody? . . . I do not think that situation applies only to coloured people . . .

Mr. Talbot: It is true that possibly everyone might receive the same type of answer, but the fact remains that in those places where such answers are given they deny employment to people of minority groups. The practice, as I said in the beginning is very subtle. It is one which we could not bring before the courts of law. In the first place we have no law which says that a man cannot refuse employment to anyone because of his race . . .

Hon. Mr. David: My other question is: You say that these different people are refused service in restaurants. That is against the provincial law of Ontario, is it not?

Mr. Talbot: No, it is not. The provincial law grants to a municipality the power to grant licenses and the power to revoke licenses.

Hon. Mr. David: No, but did not the provincial government two or three years ago passed a law that there should be no racial discrimination in hotels and restaurants?

Mr. Talbot: No, they passed a law that there would be no signs exhibited which stated that an establishment was . . . For white people or Gentiles. These signs are prohibited in Ontario. But there is no law prohibiting the practice I have mentioned.

Hon. Mr. Doone: Have you not under the common law the right to enter that building? When a man opens a business is not a general contract with the public that the owner must serve customers?

Hon. Mr. David: I don't think so.

Mr. Talbot: They reserve the right to refuse anybody they deem undesirable.

Hon. Mr. David: Why did the town of Dresden have to pass a bylaw to put this in effect?

Mr. Talbot: The town of Dresden didn't have a licensing bylaw. People who work in the same field as I do, the field of group relations, asked the Council of the town of Dresden to pass a bylaw licensing restaurants. The Town Council did not wish to take that upon their shoulders so they asked for a referendum vote on the question of passing a bylaw, and the referendum was turned down by the people, so there is still no licensing bylaw in Dresden, and the town Council has no jurisdiction over the practice of discrimination.

Hon. Mr. David: Do you not get some satisfaction from the fact that in the United States, after years of objecting to it, negro players are now playing on the big league baseball teams; some of them are heroes and are the best players on their teams. I could mention some of them that you know: Jack Robinson, Sam Jethroe, and Roy Campanella. Do you not think that there is a move in the United States to decrease racial discrimination and that it will move into Canada in the same way?

Mr. Talbot: It is a contributing factor.

Hon. Mr. Grant: How could a Bill of Rights force a man who is employing people not to use his own judgment?

Mr. Talbot: We are asking that a statement of policy be issued by the Canadian Government on the question of racial discrimination. We feel that it would have a moral effect on employers...

I am not here to speak on behalf of the coloured race alone. I happen to be the Chairman of the Interracial Council. The Coloured community just happens to be mentioned first in the list of organizations belonging to the Council on Group Relations . . . All minority groups have suffered . . . We feel that a statement by the federal government . . . would have a tremendous effect on the people of our country . . . Legislation is one of the most effective means of education.

Hon. Mr. David: I see you mention sanctions. Do you believe this Bill of Rights should have sanctions?

Mr. Talbot: Yes I think it should . . . We studied cases of fair employment practices in certain states in the U.S., and we found that where there is no sanction the law is ineffective.

The Chairman, Hon. Mr. Roebuck: Thank you, Mr. Talbot. That was a very fine statement.

Senators were all people who had been appointed to their positions because, among other things, they were presumed to have a good knowledge of Canadian affairs. Some of the questions and comments made by the senators on this committee betrayed a naiveté that one would not expect in people of such stature in Canada, not even in early 1950.

I have stated that all blacks in Canada share common problems peculiar to their race. Among these problems are:

-The experience of some form of discrimination, either overt or covert in one or more aspects of living in Canada;

-The problem of being forced to depend on white decision makers for whatever social or economic mobility they may enjoy;

-The problem of group identity resulting from geographic distance, insularity, varied social and cultural backgrounds;

-Problems emanating from ideas and myths about blacks which are held by many whites;

-Constant awareness that racism in one of its insidious forms may surface in almost any type of interaction with whites any time.

Whites, on their part, generally lack a clearly defined perception of what individual blacks are really like partly due to the stereotypes created by the media and educational system. Informal, intimate, personal relationships between blacks and whites in my experience have been infrequent. Too often both parties find it difficult to see each other as individuals rather than as members of the other race; as a result, they behave in an unnatural affected manner toward one another rather than just being themselves. Most white people, moreover, deny that there is a serious race problem and insist that any alleged acts of discrimination are fortuitous, deviant or the perceptions of over sensitivity.

THE DRESDEN AFFAIR

Around 1948 a young Dresdenite carpenter named Hugh Burnette decided to move back home from Windsor where he had worked during the war years. While in Windsor Hugh had been active in the Auto Workers' Union, was the first black admitted to the Carpenters' Union, a founding member and first president of the Eastside Credit Union and active in the Windsor Council on Group Relations. When he decided to move back to Dresden he realized that things would have to change in the interracial relations there if he were to be content.

Hugh was a fifth generation Canadian whose ancestors were so intermingled with whites that many of his relatives would not be recognized as black by anyone who didn't know them. For example, Hugh's brother, Gordon, worked as assistant manager of a large downtown Detroit hotel at a time when hotels were hiring blacks only as bellhops and porters. When the owner of the hotel found out after several months that Gordon was black, he fired him. The townspeople of Dresden, however, knew the Burnettes, the Carters and the Davises and there was unconcealed jealousy and envy on the part of many whites over the prosperity that these families enjoyed.

When Hugh returned to Dresden one of his first projects was to organize a group to combat the racism there. They called themselves the National Unity Association. One day around 1949 Hugh walked into Kay's Café on the main street, sat down at the counter to order a sandwich and a cup of coffee. Hugh thought that since the restaurant attracted tourists with an ad depicting the town as the home of Uncle Tom, whom Harriet Beecher Stowe had immortalized in her novel, *Uncle Tom's Cabin,* surely the proprietor or would not refuse service to the great grandson of Rev. Josiah Henson, believed to have been the original Uncle Tom.

Seated facing a large portrait of Josiah Henson and a picture of his house, a site which had become a national landmark, Hugh insisted on being served. Morley McKay, the proprietor, faced Hugh from behind the counter.

"Coffee and a sandwich, please," Hugh said.

"Now you know very well, Hugh, that we don't serve your people here," Morley responded.

"Maybe that's been true up to now," Hugh replied, "but you're going to serve me."

"If you don't want to cause trouble why don't you just go out quietly," suggested McKay.

Hugh Burnette didn't get his coffee that day, but thus began what became known as the Dresden Affair. Subsequently Hugh Burnette and the National Unity Association were involved in a series of municipal hassles, public inquiries and court battles.

Under the caption "The Dresden Council in Stormy Session", the Windsor Star of April 5, 1949, described the council meeting that preceded the taking of a referendum on the issue of discrimination. The National Unity Association asked that the referendum should ask the simple question, "Should the town council pass a bylaw giving it the authority to license certain business establishments?" This would be a bylaw similar to the one passed by Windsor's city council.

This "stormy session" reported in the Star the issue became quite distorted resulting in a question entirely different from the one proposed by the National Unity Association. The actual question read, "Do you approve of the passing of a bylaw restraining restaurants from refusing service, regardless of race, creed or religion?" In an emotionally charged atmosphere, arguments about the civil rights of proprietors obscured a licensing issue. The vote of approximately five to one against the question on the ballot reflected the confusion caused by the arguments and distortions at the council meeting. The vote result also supports the hypothesis that, given the opportunity to express their prejudice in a closed ballot, 80 percent of this group of Canadians would do just that.

The referendum dealt a serious blow to the National Unity Association, but it did not stop their efforts. Groups in Toronto and Windsor joined them, and together they engaged in five years of persistent campaigning for human rights legislation against discrimination. In 1954 Premier Leslie Frost of Ontario agreed to meet a delegation of citizens demanding the enactment of a provincial Fair Accommodations Act as a consequence of the notorious Dresden Affair. He had expected a dozen or so people and had planned to meet them in his office. When more than a hundred and fifty people representing a broad cross section of the population appeared for the meeting, arrangements had to be made to hold the meeting in a large conference room. The premier could not ignore the wishes of such an impressive representation. He assured them that he would introduce the requested legislation at the next session of the legislature. I believe that is the largest delegation ever to appear before a government leader on a matter related to human rights legislation in Canada's history. Finally the Ontario government responded to those years of effort and passed the Fair Accommodations Act of Ontario in 1954.

The passing of this law did not resolve the Dresden situation nor alleviate the task of Hugh Burnette and his colleagues. Eight complaints under the Act were filed against two restaurant owners, and after investigations by an officer of the Ontario Department of Labour, Judge William Schwenger was named to conduct a public inquiry. Liberty Magazine, December 1955, ran a feature article entitled, "I Lived Through Hatred in a Canadian Town," by Gordon Donaldson. The article described the one-day hearing, in part, as follows:

About three hundred Dresden people crowded the barn like Dresden Arena to watch the proceedings. White and Black sat, side by side, on the wooden benches.

The judge selected two complaints for hearing — one by Hugh Burnette and one by Lyle Talbot, one of the three members of a Negro church choir from Windsor, Ontario who were refused service.

The owners hired a lawyer, R. A. Cascallen to present their case. The Negroes were represented by David Lewis, of Toronto, well-known for his work on labour cases.

The evidence was straightforward. I watched one man state blankly he refused to serve Negroes because it would be 'bad for business'. He said white customers had threatened to boycott his business, if he allowed coloured people to eat there.

Asked if he knew he was breaking the law he replied: "Yes, that's right, I protect the business, and that's why I broke the law."

The hearing had humourous moments. Talbot said a woman drove him and his friends out of the café with a broom. The woman, tightlipped, denied this vehemently.

In his final speech, Mr. Cascallen said education, not prosecution, was the answer to the Dresden problem. Making martyrs of the restaurant owners would solve nothing.

In a press statement October 20, Minister Daley announced he had read the report and decided to take no further action on the Dresden affair. The situation appeared to the Minister to have cured itself. Education, not prosecution, was the answer. Wide public interest aroused by press coverage of the hearing would have a 'salutary effect' . . .

Two Dresden restaurant owners appeared in court at Chatham, Ontario, and were fined $50 each by Magistrate Ivan B. Craig. He found them guilty of practicing racial discrimination, and dismissed a defense argument that Ontario's Fair Accommodations Act was unconstitutional.

The owners appealed and their appeal was heard in Chatham County Court in April this year by Judge Henry E. Groach . . . In September, Judge Groach handed down his decision — the convictions were quashed. He found the prosecution had not proved that denial of service, if this occurred, was because of race. He said 'quite possibly' there were other reasons.

So the Dresden affair dragged on . . . When prejudice is flaunted blatantly, in defiance of the law, it becomes infectious and dangerous. That is what happened in Dresden.

The Crown appealed Judge Groach's decision in the case against Morley McKay to the Supreme Court of Canada. The appeal was allowed, the court ruling that the Fair Accommodations Act had been violated, and McKay was ordered to pay court costs plus the fifty dollar fine that had been ordered by Magistrate Craig. The seven year struggle of Hugh Burnette and his associates was finally legally vindicated. Open and flagrant racial discrimination was now a violation of the law.

But what happened to Hugh Burnette? Hugh paid a high price for his refusal to acquiesce to the traditional pattern of racial discrimination in his hometown. After the Dresden Affair, Hugh could not get enough carpenter work in town to support his family even though there was a housing boom in progress. He commuted back and forth to Chatham, Wallaceburg and London for a while and then was forced to move out of the house he had built in Dresden and go to London where he was able to find steady work. Unfortunately his family was not happy in London; his wife didn't want to move away from her hometown a second time. Eventually he left London to seek his livelihood elsewhere. What happened to Hugh Burnette after his case was settled indicates how deep rooted and insidious racism in Canada was. But who cared?

Hugh Burnette's struggles for common human dignity for himself and his black friends cost him his job, and in many ways, his life. How many Canadians, black or white even know who Hugh Burnette was? That is the real Dresden story. It belongs in the record of human rights and black history in Canada because it is Canada's story too.

THE CREDIT UNION AFFAIR

From the *Windsor Star,* July 15, 1944:

Three Credit Unions Formed

New Organizations Set Up

in City and Ojibway

Organization of three new credit unions in Windsor was announced this week by Windsor and District Credit Union Chapter.

At an enthusiastic meeting held at the home of Mr. And Mrs. Hugh R. Burnett, 480 Broadhead Street, a committee was appointed to proceed with organization of a group which will serve the coloured community of the city. Arrangements are under way to hold a series of educational meetings in the various churches of the district.

COMMITTEE NAMED

The committee consists of Rev. F.O. Stewart, chairman; Carl W. Robbins, Andrew Talbot and Lyle E. Talbot, who is acting as treasurer protem. They have adopted the tentative name of the Fellowship (Windsor) Credit Union.

The first of the meetings was announced for Friday, July 28th at 8 p.m. in the B.M.E. Church, 363 McDougalll Street. This group is organizing under the direction of Harry Lee, vice-president of the chapter, assisted by Harry Finch . . . .

Early in 1944 I heard about the credit union that a group of Ford workers had just organized. I studied the material on credit unions and decided that the black community of Windsor could benefit from such an organization. In those days it was almost impossible for a black person to get a mortgage or to borrow money from a bank or trust company due to the stereotype that blacks were a poor risk. Prior to the achievement of seniority rights by the union, one of the factors enhancing this stereotype was that, if blacks were hired at all, they were the last hired and the first fired.

I gathered a small group of about five young black men to discuss the possibility of forming a credit union in our community, and in July 1944 we received our charter from the Ontario government under the name Fellowship Credit Union, Windsor.

The bond of association was intended to be residents of the area in which black people were concentrated, but the Ontario government required a more specific name and bond of association. Since it was hoped that this credit union would draw many members from the five "coloured" *(sic)* churches in the area, the group agreed, after considerable exchange of correspondence with the government department, to accept the name "Fellowship of Coloured Churches Credit Union". The bond of association would be the members and adherents of the "coloured" churches.

The effects of opposition to the campaign of the Windsor Council on Group Relations against discrimination in southwestern Ontario extended into my activities as treasurer of the credit union. I received educational information about life insurance from the central office of the credit union movement in North America, CUNA Mutual Insurance Society. The information revealed that most working people were spending more on insurance premiums than they should have been. For instance the twenty-five cents a week industrial life policies that my mother had taken out on all eight of us children were payable to age sixty-five, with a maximum benefit of two hundred dollars. Although this type of insurance policy was the most costly available, the small weekly premiums made them attractive to low income families with children.

Furthermore, I discovered that all the larger insurance companies refused to sell certain types of insurance coverage to blacks and those policies that were available to blacks had higher premium rates than for whites. The companies gave as their reason the lower life expectancy rates for blacks. However, the life expectancy figures for blacks was based on the mortality rates for Negroes in the United States — over 90 percent of whom lived in the slums of the big cities and in the poorest areas of the deep South. I reasoned that the mortality rates for blacks in Canada should be based on the rates for the general population as they were for all Canadians with the exception of being non-white.

In addition to the above, most working people, both white and black, were over insured, paying for policies that they couldn't afford or for which the premiums were disproportionately high for the benefits received. For example a Twenty Pay Life policy, which many parents had purchased to provide for the future needs of their children such as for education or training, would require premium payments over the twenty year period far in excess of the amount required each month to save the amount of the insurance benefit!

I began to suggest to our credit union members that they should cash in their industrial life policies, and instead take out term insurance in an amount sufficient to cover any debts, including their mortgage, plus one year's wages or salary. The year's wages was suggested because a man of up to forty-five years of age had a life expectancy to be approximately age seventy. If he should die before age fifty-five his widow would likely remarry in either a year or so or be established in some kind of employment. The idea that a working man should ensure himself for five or ten times his yearly earnings was considered impractical.

The local manager of one of the largest insurance companies in North America called me into his office one day. He accused me of selling insurance without a license and threatened to report this to my employer if I didn't stop. I explained to him that I did not sell insurance; I had merely explained to our members how the insurance companies were discriminating against them. I added that I would continue to do so until his company and all the others changed their way of treating non-white people. I never heard from him again. It gave me a great deal of satisfaction to see many of our members benefit from their savings and insurance policies with the credit union that they could never have received from the mainline companies.

One of the ongoing difficulties the credit union encountered was increasing its membership. I had been urging the pastor of the BME church, Rev. Stewart, who had consented to act on our supervisory committee, to encourage his parishioners to support the credit union. One day he approached me and said, "You know, Lyle, I've been trying to get my people to join the credit union, but they just don't seem to respond. Just the other day one man told me that he believed that the reason you started the credit union was to get a hold of money to pay off your mortgage."

We both considered the man's remark a big joke in view of the small amount of capital the credit union had at the time and passed it off as such. However, in 1947 the credit union was in a financial position where I could borrow the few hundred dollars I needed to pay off my share of our mortgage on the duplex that my brother Andy and I had purchased five or six years previously. In order for me to obtain the loan it was necessary for me, as an officer, to obtain the unanimous approval of all the other officers of the credit union.

After the loan had been approved and granted, I had occasion to talk to Rev. Stewart again. "Rev. Stewart," I remarked, "do you recall our little discussion when we were trying to get the credit union started? I mean the one in which you told me that one of the members of your church had expressed his opinion that I was organizing the credit union in order to get money to pay off my mortgage?"

"Yes," he replied, "I do recall that conversation."

"Well," I continued, "you can tell that man that I am just about to pay off my mortgage with a credit union loan. In fact you can tell the whole congregation that if they will just become shareholders they too will be able to obtain loans to pay off mortgages and other debts."

After seven years the board of directors was able to persuade the government to accept the name Coloured Community Windsor Credit Union, but the bond of association had to remain the same: i.e. members and adherents of the five black churches.

Seven more years passed with little growth in either membership or assets compared with other similar credit unions in the city. By this time, with the publicity and promotional campaign conducted by the credit union's board of directors, many blacks accepted the credit union idea but decided to join the credit unions at the places of their employment. It was only in the Coloured Community Windsor Credit Union that they didn't have confidence. It seemed that there was a common belief that the black men who organized the credit union were not capable or reliable enough to hand other people's money. A residual slave mentality by which blacks had been taught to mistrust one another was responsible for this belief. It had been a way for the master to control his slaves. Added to this there was the aforementioned rumour circulating that I as the principal organizer started the credit union to obtain money to pay off my mortgage.

After twenty-one years of mediocre success and after several of the officers had been involved in the city's civil rights campaign, the government was persuaded that requiring the words coloured or Negro in either the name or the bond of association was a violation of Ontario's Human Rights Act. This was also in violation of the Credit Union National Association's prescribed bylaws. Accordingly, the board was allowed to change the name to Eastside Windsor Credit Union Ltd.:

From "The President's Report" for 1964

.... There has been a number of reasons advanced for abandoning our present name, ranging from an inferiority complex with regard to it, to a feeling that we are discriminating against persons of white origin — it is a historical fact that organizations of Negro orientation are seldom joined by persons of white racial origin in any significant numbers...

Mahlon C. Dennis, President

The threat of a discrimination complaint had worked, but it was too late. The die had been cast. The annual report for 1976 showed a mere 156 members, shares of $94,000 and total assets of $105,080. After so many years of struggling to survive, the members voted in 1981 to amalgamate with a larger credit union. Here are some excerpts from the notice sent to the members:

May 15, 1981

DEAR MEMBER:

East Side (Windsor) Credit Union and Mororco Truck Division (Windsor) Credit Union are now about to complete a purchasing agreement in the very near future.

... The final date for members doing business with East Side (Windsor) Credit Union has been set for June 15, 1981...

Glenn C. Dennis,

Secretary of the Board

I had been treasurer/ manager from 1944 to 1970 when I left Windsor to become a human rights administrator with the federal government in Ottawa. Thus, I was an active participant for twenty-six years in the credit union's struggle to overcome the hurdles of both the historically ingrained attitudes of the black community and the institutional racism prevalent in Canadian society.

THE OTHER UNION – THE UAW

The second largest automobile factory in Windsor, Chrysler Corporation, had never hired a black employee in almost thirty years of operation. The Council on Group Relations, in cooperation with leaders of the United Auto Workers' Union (UAW), had approached the company several times trying to get them to hire blacks. The management would not even discuss the matter with them. Company policy had been established and it was not going to be changed in spite of the fact that the Fair Employment Practices Act had been on the books for almost a year. The Canadian Congress of Labour Convention was scheduled to meet in Winnipeg in the summer of 1952. At a meeting between the executive of the Council on Group Relations and regional representatives for the UAW, Bill McDonald, director For Fair Practices for the UAW was chosen to present a resolution before the convention demanding that the company change its discriminatory hiring policies and practices.

The newspapers and the radio gave the resolution national publicity. The next morning the president of the local union received an urgent telephone call from the company president. The company wanted fifteen black men to report to the employment office immediately. The community was searched for fifteen able-bodied men who wanted work. On such short notice it was not easy to find fifteen such men, but somehow almost that number responded and eleven were hired. Some of those original black employees became longtime workers for that company. Still other blacks, both male and female, have been employed in their office and/or in professional categories, and at least one I know of was made a supervisor.

During my time at Ford's many significant things happened in my life. When the UAW became the official bargaining agent for the hourly rated employees, I became quite involved in that union's activities as a union organizer/recruiter. There were several strikes during the forties and fifties, the longest lasting 121 days.

The most spectacular strike and the one that received the widest public attention was the strike for union security near the end of World War II. It is significant that the bitterest dispute between the union and the Ford Motor Company was not over wages, but over the right of the union to collect dues from all the employees who benefitted from union activity.

During each strike I acted on a committee that looked after unusual financial issues of the workers' families such as threats of eviction and requirements of food and clothing for larger families for whom the strike allowance was insufficient to meet their needs. The committee worked in the union hall located on the corner of Wyandotte Street and Ouellette Avenue from 8:00 a.m. until 5:00 p.m. every day.

As the strike dragged on from September to November, the tension mounted. Someone overturned the company president's automobile as he was attempting to drive through the main gate one morning. The picketers claimed that he had tried to run into the picket line. He claimed that they were blocking his legal access to his office. The problem the picketers saw was that the entrance to the president's office was not through that particular gate.

This incident sparked a strong demand that the mayor, Art Reaume, call upon the RCMP to maintain law and order. Having been elected with strong support from thousands of factory workers in Windsor, Reaume was openly sympathetic to the Ford workers. Finally he gave in to the pressure and called for help from both the Ontario Provincial Police and the Royal Canadian Mounted Police.

The RCMP detachment of about fifty men was billeted in the Burroughs Adding Machine building at the corner of Elliott and McDougall Streets. Around 8:00 a.m. each morning the detachment, in full dress uniform, i.e. red tunics etc., would march out of the building, down McDougall Street and west on Erie Street to the HMCS Hunter building on Ouellette Avenue where they would have breakfast. I made a point of watching this parade every morning and reported this to the picket captains who assembled in the union hall every morning.

A few days after the arrival of the RCMP officers the chief picket captain called me aside. "Do you know what happened to the strikers in Winnipeg at the end of World War I?" he asked. I replied that I had heard how the Mounties had broken the strike by attacking the picket lines on horseback and how the horses came at the picketers with front hooves flailing.

"Well, Lyle," the captain stated, "we don't want anything like that happening here. So if you notice anything unusual about the dress or actions of the Mounties any time when they go for breakfast, let me know, will you?" I assured him that I would.

A couple of days later, after there had been another scuffle on the picket lines between strikers and management personnel, I noticed that the Mounties emerged from their billet dressed in dark brown jackets, with riot sticks hanging from their belts and wearing riding boots and spurs. I reported this to the picket captain.

At about the same time a phone call came in from the town of Tecumseh, ten miles from the main gate, stating that the Mounties' were saddling their horses there. Immediately messengers were dispatched to the picket lines at the six gates. They told every man who had a car to go home, get it and drive to the two main gates. The idea was to form a barricade around the picketers so that the horses could not attack them as they had done in Winnipeg a quarter of a century earlier.

While the strikers were driving their cars to the main gates, someone got the bright idea of directing all the traffic travelling on Riverside Drive, Wyandotte Street, Walker Road, Strabane Avenue and Drouillard Road toward the two main gates. The picket captain intended to have the strikers park their cars in a jigsaw pattern so that there would be no access to the gates for horses. What happened was that approximately four hundred vehicles, including buses, trucks, citizens' cars, service vehicles, taxis and transports formed an impenetrable blockade within the space of an hour and a half.

I don't know whether the Mounties ever tried to approach the gates, but I do recall that it took four days to unravel the tangled mass of vehicles after it was agreed to submit the case to an arbitrator. I also know that Mr. Justice Rand was called in immediately to attempt a settlement of the strike. He came up with the now famous Rand Formula whereby every hourly rated employee in the company had to pay union dues whether or not he chose to join the union. The strike ended just before Christmas and I recall that every child in every Ford workers family received toys, clothing and goodies from the citizens of Windsor who were glad to see the city getting back to normal.

Despite the popular notion that strikes cost the worker irreparable losses, I personally emerged from every strike more financially stable than before the strike began. Now in 2012, more than sixty years after the first strike at Ford of Canada, I am still reaping the benefits gained through the collective bargaining process.

Benefits Gained Through Collective Bargaining

Paid Vacation	1940
Union Security	1943
Seniority Rights*	1943
Paid Holidays	1948
Cost of Living Allowance	1950
Annual Improvement Factor	1950
Pensions	1950
Medical-Hospital-Surgical Coverage	1954

Supplemental Unemployment Benefits 85percent of take home pay	1955
Wage Parity with U.S. workers	1967
Dental Coverage	1968
Optical Coverage (Lens and Frames)	1973
Hearing aids	1976
Paid Personal Holidays (Birthdays/Anniversaries)	1976
Paid Education Leave**	1977
Paid Maternity and Adoption Leave	1982
Childcare on the premises	1983
Equal Pay for Equal Work	1983
Prepaid Legal Services	1984
Fitness Facilities	1984
Pension Indexing	1987

*This guaranteed employment for me when I might otherwise have been laid off as a result of discrimination as my father had before the union.

**The Tuition Refund Plan that I benefitted from in 1965 was not this plan.

A MODEL FOR TRANSPORTATION

Our family did not have a vacation prior to 1948. Even after the union negotiated paid holidays in 1942, we still couldn't leave town because we didn't own a car. Then in 1948 Marietta and I and our two daughters, Marilyn and Carol, accompanied my brother George, his wife Margaret and their children, Ralph and Jimmy on a week's holiday in Idlewild, Michigan, at a small resort where Margaret's aunt owned a cottage.

Three years later we had our second holiday. We travelled north with my brother Andy, his wife Kathleen and their two sons, Emerson and Teddy. The toddlers, our Gerry and Andy's Teddy sat on their mothers' laps in the back along with Marilyn and Emerson. Carol sat between Andy and me in the front. After we had travelled north for about four hours on the Blue Water highway along the shore of Lake Huron, I assumed the driving of Andy's car, a 1939 Graham Paige I think it was. A couple of miles south of Kincardine the right rear tire suddenly blew out and the car began rocking out of control. It turned around three times as Andy and I squished young Carol as together we tried to get the car back under control. Finally it came to a stop in the middle of a narrow bridge across a fifteen foot wide ditch. I believe the Lord had guided the car to this spot when I could no longer control it.

Andy and I mounted the spare tire; then Andy decided that he'd better drive since the blowout had shaken me up a bit. He started down the highway as we all breathed a sigh of relief. We hadn't gone a quarter of a mile when a young man walking towards us started waving his arms. I remarked that the folks around there must be friendly people, but I happened to glance back through the rear window and the young man was still waving his arms. "Maybe we'd better stop," I suggested; "I think that guy is trying to tell us something. He's pointing at our car." Andy came to a stop in the middle of our traffic lane and I got out to look around. My heart took a leap as I walked around to the back of the car and saw that the left rear wheel was sitting precariously right on the end of the axle shaft.

I removed the hubcap and found that the lug nuts that were supposed to hold the wheel were lying in the hubcap. We decided that Andy would hitchhike into town to get a tow truck while I stayed and directed the traffic around our vehicle. We spent the next three hours in a garage while the mechanic replaced the wheel, hub and all the lug nuts with new ones. All of the old ones had worn beyond usefulness from travelling while loosened. While we were waiting I asked Andy if he had had his car checked for safety before we left home. He replied that he hadn't because he hadn't thought it necessary. At least our wives and the kids had a break playing in a nearby park.

Our destination was Waubaushene, on Georgian Bay. At about 6:00 p.m. we came to a fork in the highway. One arrow pointing to the left read, "8 miles to Waubaushene." The arrow pointing right read, "11 miles to Waubaushene." As Andy took the left fork he remarked, "Why go eleven miles when we can be there in eight miles?" We found out why in a few minutes when the left fork led over hills, around S shaped curves and became a rough gravel road after a couple of miles. We came to the top of a hill where the roadway sloped steeply downward ahead of us. As we started down the hill the car began to gain momentum. "Put on your brakes!" I exclaimed.

"I am!" Andy yelled back. But the car, with its load of four adults and five child occupants, continued to accelerate. The brakes weren't holding! At the base of the hill the road took a hairpin curve to the left, and there in front of us was a single lane wooden bridge over a gully. Somehow Andy managed to make the turn and cross the bridge at a high rate of speed, and then he brought the car to a stop on a level piece of road. In a few minutes we arrived at the small resort at Waubaushene on a minor bay at the south end of Georgian Bay.

We were a little apprehensive as we drove up to the office even though Marietta had written to the woman who owned the cottages and had asked her if she would rent one to coloured people. The only reply she received was that our cottage would be ready for us. In 1951 in southern Ontario, at least, there were very few, if any, resorts where a black family could rent a cottage, so we weren't sure that it would not be the same farther north. However the woman welcomed us warmly and we spent an enjoyable ten days of fishing and swimming before heading back home except for one concern Marietta had.

In those days before the civil rights movement, the affirmation of a positive black identity was non-existent in our community. Blacks carried an inferiority complex as a result of the history of oppression, discrimination and non-acceptance by the white mainstream. One way they tried to overcome this was to try to find ways to emulate the white standards of beauty and our hair was one aspect of our appearance that was a victim of these efforts. To achieve a semblance of straight hair, black people (mostly the females) used a process involving a hot comb (an iron comb heated in the flame of a gas stove) and well oiled (greased) hair. Of course this was not a technique willingly exposed to white persons. When a grease spot inadvertently got on the wall of the cottage, Marietta was much distressed when she could not completely remove it. This seemingly small incident is symbolic of the greater ramifications of a negative history on a people.

As noted, we were able to take those two holidays due to the generosity of my brothers, but otherwise we did without a car the first thirteen years of our marriage. That being the case, going shopping for groceries was a real challenge. At first, when Marilyn was an infant, we would load the pram with groceries that we couldn't carry in our arms the eight blocks from the A&P store where we shopped to get the best bargains. After we bought the children a wagon I would take the wagon to hold the groceries on the trip home. There were also times when I would get off the bus at the A&P on the way home from work, do the shopping and then get back on another bus with two or three bags of groceries and ride home thankful that the bus drivers were so patient with me.

Then one day in the summer of 1950, while walking down McDougall Street, I saw a 1931 Model A Ford roadster with a rumble seat with a For Sale sign on it. The young man wanted fifty-five dollars for it, and I was able to convince Marietta that I could convert the car to a transportation form more suited to our needs. At that time Dad Wilson, Marietta's father, was making concrete lawn ornaments like birdbaths, flower urns, and benches to sell. He even designed and created a unique sundial and a miniature lighthouse. I was able to follow through on my idea to replace the rumble seat with a pickup box that I was able to get at the auto wrecker's lot.

We used that old Model A to deliver groceries, Dad Wilson's lawn ornaments and whatever else we needed to transport. We also used it to take the family on picnics to Colchester Beach on Lake Erie, one of the few beaches where blacks were allowed to swim. We often loaded the kids, their bicycles and groceries in the truck and went to visit Marietta's folks in Amherstburg on several occasions. For those trips Marietta, the girls and I would crowd into the cab with little Gerry stretched out along the back of the seat. Sometimes, much to their delight, we allowed the girls to ride in the pickup box when we had no load to carry. Fortunately the police never stopped us.

One Saturday afternoon I was taking a load of sand and cement to Amherstburg for Dad Wilson. All at once, while driving along the back road, I saw a tire rolling down the highway beside me, and in the same instant the right rear side of the pickup truck dropped to the pavement with a dull thud. I couldn't get the jack under the axle, so I looked for something along the ditch that I might use as a jack. I found a tree branch and a large chunk of wood with which I fashioned a lever to raise the axle. I retrieved the tire and rim, installed them, and we continued on to Amherstburg.

Another time Marietta's brother, Herman, had bought a piano from his mother-in-law's neighbour in Windsor. He asked me if I would take it to his house in Amherstburg and I agreed. With the help of two other men we loaded the piano onto the pickup. It hung over the end of the box about a foot, but we figured that if we tied it down good and two men rode with it on the back, we could manage. About ten miles out of Windsor, the highway took a ninety degree turn to the left. I slowed down to what I thought was a safe speed and started to make the turn. As I slowed the piano began to rock back and forth causing the pickup to rock with it. The men on the back couldn't stop the rocking because the whole pickup truck was rocking with the piano. Before I could come to a stop the piano rolled over the side of the box and landed on the gravel shoulder. Somehow we managed to get it back on the pickup and proceeded on to Amherstburg. I can't remember whether the piano survived the spill enough to carry a tune.

Still another time, we were travelling home from somewhere when the Model A became overheated and steam spurted from under the hood. I stopped to let it cool off while Marietta walked along the side of the road. About twenty yards in front of us she found a little pool of clear water and a one quart tin can with which I was able to fill the radiator after I tightened the petcock that had come loose. With that adjustment we were on our way again.

Whenever the battery was weak or on very cold days, I used to be able to get it started by jacking up one of the rear wheels, putting the gearshift in low gear and giving a quick pull with the hand crank. One cold winter morning after we had bought a Studebaker, I went to get the Studebaker started to drive Marietta to work, but it wouldn't start. The oil in the transmission had gotten quite stiff overnight. The starter on the Model A wouldn't turn that vehicle over either. I jacked up a rear wheel on the Model A, gave the crank one quick jerk and got Marietta to work on time.

Finally, when we were building our house in 1955-56, that old pickup served us well in carrying all sorts of materials to the building site. After the house was finished I parked the Model A in our driveway, and for a few weeks it stayed there with some sort of ignition trouble. In other words, it wouldn't start. Over the previous six years I had managed to keep it running, having been coached in the art of tuning a Ford by two of my neighbours who were master mechanics. One day I discovered that our son Gerry and his friends had put sand in the gas tank. I decided that the old buggy had served its time, and when a junk man happened to come by he offered me eighteen dollars for the pickup. I reckoned that the thirty-seven dollar difference from the purchase price wasn't a bad investment for almost six years of transportation.

BLACK IS BEAUTIFUL

Minstrel shows were somehow much funnier to white audiences if the white participants blackened their faces and wore top hats, white gloves and white spats. They were a popular form of entertainment and proved to be a good way to raise money for churches and other worthy causes. As far as white Ontario was concerned, there was no problem with those shows.

Even as late as the 1960s many Canadians were defending them as harmless entertainment. They couldn't understand why black folks got so upset over them. No harm was intended and the jokes were not malicious. People told Scottish, Irish, French, Italian, Jewish etc. jokes and no one seemed offended. Why were blacks so sensitive? My answer to such questions is to say that none of the other ethnic groups, apart from our aboriginal people, has suffered from racism as long as blacks have simply because they are what they are. Those other ethnic groups could afford to say, "I don't care what you call me as long as it's not late for supper." Blacks were not being called for supper, late or otherwise. The name calling for them was directly associated with the discrimination, oppression and suppression that they were experiencing every day of their lives.

Besides, tell me please, what did the blackened face add to the humour if it were not that white people were laughing at the condition of being black itself? Blackness to them meant laziness, dirtiness, slothfulness, insobriety, ugliness, ignorance and a number of other derogatory stereotypes. They were laughing at the plight of black people; it was laughter of derision and contempt. In addition, why was it that Buckwheat, the black member of the Our Gang group later named The Little Rascals, always got so much more frightened at things than his playmates? Was it that it was common knowledge that blacks were more easily frightened?

The minstrel show was the first form of humour based on the apparent representation of persons of black African ancestry. As noted above, this representation was blatantly derogatory and demeaning in its portrayal of blacks. The minstrel show was followed by vaudeville, the movies and radio with the Amos and Andy, Pick and Pat, Honeyboy and Sassafras stereotypes in which whites blackened their faces and attempted to mimic blacks. The next development in black humour was the appearance of the Stepin Fetchit and Eddie Rochester Anderson type characters. These were African Americans who continued the stereotypes, but who added the dimension of often outsmarting or out maneuvering their white bosses or antagonists. At least this was a way for blacks to get into the lucrative world of show business.

Since the emergence of the civil rights movement, black humour evolved from white people making fun of blacks to becoming humour in which blacks made whites laugh at them. Further evolution led to the stage where blacks laughed at themselves. Finally it reached the stage to where blacks could laugh at whites, often portraying white society as the oppressor and the perpetrators of the last vestiges of racism in North American society.

The complexities associated with this evolution of black humour provide an effective paradigm for the issues of identity and self-esteem relevant to the Afro-Canadian psyche. Practically all whites and a large number of blacks have been unaware that for a black in Canada to be confronted with the race issue adversely is of such overriding significance that all else fades into insignificance at that moment. As long as a black person's experience is limited to interaction with other blacks, which in Canada is only in infancy, he or she may be practically oblivious of a problem. However, the first unpleasant racially based encounter impresses him or her with the whole weight of his or her blackness. No amount of the black is beautiful rhetoric can totally erase the stigma of such experiences.

In the days before World War II, "passing", in black vernacular, was a process that Canadian black people generally accepted. It was the term applied to the process of the light-skinned person renouncing his or her blackness, usually for socio-economic reasons, and identifying as a white individual. In my experience other blacks never took any action to betray the one who was passing. Passing, the ultimate rejection of one's blackness, was an effective vehicle toward upward mobility, but it was also a response to society's failure to recognize the worth of black people.

Interracial marriage is another situation that Canadian blacks have historically accepted. The white partner is usually welcomed into the family and social circles of the black partner. In fact, in the folklore of the black community, the children of mixed marriage were expected to be more intelligent, more beautiful, and more talented than so-called pure children of either race. This is yet another sign of the racial insanity in North America.

Whites felt that their racially mixed child would experience more frustration than the all- black child would. Blacks felt that the children of mixed marriages would have fewer problems than all-black children primarily because it was anticipated that these children would be light-skinned in colour, with straight or curly hair and thus more easily accepted by white people. Underlying these differences in opinion between blacks and whites there is an interesting phenomenon. The white parent was comparing the probable experiences of the mixed race child with the average white child. Blacks were comparing the child's experiences with those of the average black child, hence the opposite perceptions.

Just as humour was historically distorted to appear consistent with society's perceptions of blackness, history also was distorted so that Canadians would not even think of blacks as having been historically significant. How many of us who studied the American Civil War were told that John Brown had a company of black soldiers from Canada with him in his ill-fated attack on Harper's Ferry? How many knew that the first Canadian to receive the Victoria Cross was William Hall, a black soldier from Nova Scotia? How many learned that Harriet Tubman, the famous Black Moses who helped more than three thousand slaves escape to freedom, operated the Underground Railroad from her home in the St. Catherines, Ontario, area? How many were taught that in the middle of the nineteenth century blacks in Canada had erected more than thirty church buildings, many of which are still standing today? How many realize that blacks were the organizers and builders of the First Baptist Churches in at least ten Canadian cities? How many heard of that whole community of blacks from Jamaica, known as Maroons, who refused to be shunted off a tract of practically barren land in Nova Scotia after they had fought hard for their freedom? White Canada got rid of some of these ungrateful rebels by shipping several thousand of them to Sierra Leone.

In light of the above observations it is not surprising that many blacks in Canada have suffered from identity confusion. They have been a people suppressed, isolated, alienated and victimized, but who refused to go away or give up, and whose very presence in Canada has been but a pinprick on the conscience of this country for over a century and a half. Black is beautiful.

A NEW HOME

In early 1955 Marietta and I began to become dissatisfied with living upstairs in the duplex on Howard Avenue with my brother Andrew and his wife Kathleen living in the lower flat since their marriage in 1943. Our dissatisfaction stemmed from several things. I was weary of living upstairs, having done so since our marriage in 1937. In addition, our relationship with Andy and Kathleen, while it was generally congenial and pleasant, would become tenuous and unpleasant every time something needed to be done to our part of the building. For example, when our hot water tank sprang a leak during the war and new tanks were scarce, I patched the leaks several times myself. When new tanks became available we thought that Andy and Kathleen should share the cost with us but they disagreed. However, when their son Emerson dropped something in their toilet and cracked the bowl, I not only volunteered to pay half the cost of a new toilet, but I also agreed to install it for Andy since he had no experience with plumbing.

I found a lot owned by the city in the west end of town on Matchette Road. The price set by the city for the lot was eleven hundred dollars but we had only a few hundred dollars in our savings account at the Credit Union that I had helped to establish in 1944. I happened to go by my parents' house a day or two later and I mentioned to Mom about the lot and the price. After we had discussed the location and other related things, Mom excused herself, went into her bedroom and shut the door. In about two minutes she emerged with an envelope in her hand. "You recall that you and George helped Dad and me financially a couple of years ago when Dad had the stroke? Well," she continued, "I kept track of the money you gave us, and now that we are back on our feet with Dad's pension and the rent from Phil and Elsie, I am able to pay you back. Don't open the envelope now. Just take it home with you."

My mind flashed back to other times when Mother had gone into that bedroom and shut the door, and then had come out with just enough money to meet a crisis in our family affairs. Now, I thought, she's done it again. I expected that the envelope might contain three or four hundred dollars. I had not kept account of the amount we had given them and did not want, nor did I expect any of it back. Imagine my amazement when we opened the envelope and counted out exactly eleven hundred dollars!

Marietta and I had been looking through housing magazines for weeks. We figured that we couldn't afford a very costly house, and we didn't like the prefabricated models that were advertised. We had also obtained Dad Wilson's promise that he would build a house for us, with a little help from us of course. Mr. Wilson had been in the building trade for several years. He was a master fire-brick mason, having worked at the Bruner Mond, Allied Chemical plant for over twenty years building and maintaining ovens used in drying soda ash.

We found the design for a precut, not prefabricated, ranch style bungalow that we liked, and since the lot we were buying had ninety feet of frontage, we chose that design — with Dad Wilson's approval, of course. We planned to begin work on the construction on the first of September, so one Sunday afternoon in mid-August I drove out to stake out the foundation with Marietta, her dad and our children (three in number by now as we had adopted Marietta's nephew, Gerald (Gerry), born in 1949).

We had been there but a few minutes when the neighbour to the north of the lot came out of his house obviously quite agitated. "Get off my property!" he shouted as he approached us. Dad Wilson calmly informed him that his daughter and son-in-law had purchased the lot and were planning to build a house on it.

"We'll see about that!" the neighbour threatened as he retreated toward his house and we continued to stake out the foundation.

Early in the next week we received the plans for our house. The seller assured us that the materials would arrive in time for us to begin construction right after Labour Day. With the blueprints in hand we returned to the site and began to recheck the stakes. The neighbour came out again, but this time his demeanor was completely different from the first time.

I had the end of a 150 ft. measuring tape in my hand when he walked up. He spoke to Dad Wilson. "Let me help you with this. These young pups (nodding in my direction) don't know what they're doing." He apologized for his rudeness on the previous occasion explaining in his pronounced French Canadian accent that for twenty years he had been using our large lot for his garden. City hall had not informed him that his garden permit was no longer valid.

"You'll find this land the best anywhere," he claimed. "It's good black sandy loam and I've been fertilizing it with manure every year."

He led us around to the area where his vegetables were still growing beautifully, stooped down and thrust his hand up to his elbow in the rich soil. We expressed our understanding that he would hate to lose such a wonderful garden plot and told him to continue using the garden for the rest of the season. From that time until he passed away in the mid-1960s we were the best of neighbours. He often expressed a dislike for priests who, he said, were just after his money, but at his funeral mass the priest had nothing but good things to say about the kindness and generosity of this parishioner. It was my impression that Mr. Charette's coarse belligerence was just his way of expressing his manliness.

There were many memorable events during the construction of our house. First we had to have a mortgage. As late as 1955 it was extremely difficult for a black family to obtain a mortgage. This was the situation for me as well even though I had worked continuously at Ford's for fifteen years and had paid off our previous thirty-year mortgage in six years. I approached every bank and trust company in town, including the trust company from whom we had purchased the duplex on Howard Avenue and which had been the bank for the credit union that I managed for about ten years. The last bank I visited was the Royal Bank. The loan administrator here listened to my request, and when he began his response with "I'm sorry . . ." I anticipated the same response that I had been getting everywhere else.

He continued, "I'm sorry that I don't have the authority to approve your mortgage, since your father-in-law is not a registered contractor. However, I expect Mr. Miller, the district manager, to be in town next week; I'll speak to him about your case. In the meantime have Mr. Wilson make a list of some of the buildings he has constructed. Here's my phone number just in case you need to contact me."

At one o'clock on Friday of the next week I was working at my job in the foundry lab when a telephone number kept flashing in my mind. I checked in my wallet and found that it was the number that I had been given at the Royal Bank. I completed the test I was performing and on impulse I dialed the number in my mind. The loan officer answered and when I identified myself he remarked, "Mr. Talbot, I was just about to dial Ford's and ask for you when the phone rang. Can you come down right away? Mr. Miller is here and would like to see you right away as he has to catch the train for Toronto this afternoon."

My supervisor happened to be in the lab at that moment, so I asked the loan officer to hold while I got permission to take time off. "You know this is Friday, and we're short a man. I don't think . . ."

I spoke up, "But this is very important to me, Jim," and I quickly told him the predicament I was in.

"How long do you think you'll be gone?" he asked.

"Well, by the time I get my car, drive down to the bank and back, it won't take more than an hour." That was cutting my time with Mr. Miller to a few minutes, but I was afraid to ask for more time.

"Okay. One hour. And don't forget to punch out." Punching out, of course, meant that I wouldn't be paid for the time I was gone.

Mr. Miller at the bank was very helpful. He had checked the list of buildings that Dad Wilson had worked on. It included a bank branch, a store/office building, alteration to a large building and several houses and cottages. "This is an impressive list. I'm sure the Central Mortgage and Housing Corporation will approve of your father-in-law as the builder. Now about collateral." My heart sank as he told me that we would need 10 percent of the mortgage as collateral, and I had but a few hundred dollars.

We couldn't use our share of the value of the duplex because we shared joint ownership with Andy, and he didn't want to mortgage it. While I was searching my mind for a solution, Mr. Miller asked, "What about your father-in-law's wages? They're worth something?"

"But he won't accept any pay," I explained; "he's building the house for his daughter."

"His labour is still worth something. If we calculate a thousand hours at a brick layer's wages, it comes to more than you need; let's make that your collateral." That's how we got the mortgage money.

During the next six months I learned much about the building trades. I dug trenches, mixed mortar, carried blocks and bricks and did many other tasks that I had never done before or since. We also had help from many people including four brothers-in-law.

When the foundation had been dug and they were about to pour the concrete footings, a Biblical question came to mind. I remembered the story that Jesus told about the wise man who built his house on a rock and how it withstood the rain and the floods while the house of the foolish man who had built his house on sand fell. I expressed my concern to Dad Wilson that the foundation of our house was being poured on sand.

"Will it not shift with the heavy rains we get in this part of the country?" I asked.

"Now that's an interesting question," Dad replied. "The sand that Jesus was talking about was the shifting dry sand found in Palestine. It would be unwise to build a foundation on that kind of sand." Picking up a handful of the sand from the base of the foundation, he pressed it into a ball. "See how firm and hard this ball of sand is? This is very sharp sand, you see, and there is just enough moisture in the soil to pack the sand so that it will be as hard as a rock with the weight of the house on it. Don't worry; your house won't shift. Trust me."

Sixteen years later when we moved out of that house, the only evidence of settling was one small hairline crack in a corner of the kitchen wall just about at the centre of the building. The lesson Jesus taught is a true one; only the comparison that is more accurate for our part of the country would be between sand and clay, according to Dad Wilson. Clay will shift with excessive flooding and will crack with excessive dryness. I had learned once again from a practical example that one cannot always generalize from a particular parable or Bible lesson.

One Friday the city inspector came to examine the work up to that point. After he had tested the foundation with his instruments, he called Dad Wilson over to where he was and said, "Norm, there's something I have to tell you. According to my instrument this foundation is perfectly level, but it's one eighth of an inch out of square." When Dad showed him the old wooden spirit level that he used, the two men had a good laugh over this. They recalled the argument of a few days before over whether weeping tiles should be brought in through the wall into the centre drain of the basement. Dad Wilson's argument was to let the water drain directly into the storm sewer. The inspector had won that argument, up to a point. Dad Wilson did bring the tile into the basement, but he adjusted the slope of the drainage in such a way that the water would flow naturally toward the storm sewer and not into the basement sump. Even with the heaviest of rains, the only water we ever got in our basement was from the storm sewer backing up in flash floods. As soon as the storm was over, the water ran out quickly from our basement floor.

On the Saturday that we had planned to place the plate around the top of the foundation wall, my brother-in-law Al came to help us. Al was a journeyman carpenter, so when he offered to set the plate for us, we were pleased to accept. Dad Wilson and I worked at another task while Al was laying the plate. At one point, when Al had almost completely bolted the plate to the pre-set bolts in the foundation, Mr. Wilson took me aside and said, "I realize that Al is a good carpenter and knows how to read blueprints, but he has put the plate a full inch too far toward the rear of the foundation."

"Do you want me to tell him?" I asked.

"Oh, no! It will just upset him," Dad said. "He has in mind a frame building, but this is going to be a brick one. We'll just let him finish and on Monday morning we'll correct it."

I pictured us disassembling the plate and assembling it over again in the proper place. On Monday morning Norm had me remove all the large nuts that held the plate. With the help of the neighbour who had come over to see how his new friend and the young pup were doing, we re-drilled the holes where the bolts should go, lifted the entire plate in one piece and set it in its proper place. Al never found out about his mistake.

On another Saturday afternoon in the fall of 1955, a couple of our friends came to help us spike together the precut outside wall sections in place. The last section to be spiked was the twenty-foot long front wall with the picture window and two side windows already placed in it. It was late in the day, so when we got the wall in place we nailed a support plank at one end from the floor joist to the end of the wall. Then we proceeded to spike the wall to the floor. We had not noticed that a brisk breeze had begun to blow while we were busy at the other end of the wall. One of us happened to glance down the wall and saw the support plank swinging back and forth with the wall section swaying precariously in the breeze. We rushed to re-nail the support, expressing our thanks to the Lord. If that long wall had rocked a little more, the weight of it would have torn it from the floor smashing it, along with the windows, on the rubble outside the foundation.

A week after this, Marietta and I were in Detroit at a party at her cousin's house. There were five or six couples present, and the subject of our house building came up. I mentioned that we were ready to put the interior walls in place. The next day, Sunday, Marietta and I came home from church and found several cars parked in front of the duplex. It seems that after we left the party, our friends, some of whom we had just met, had decided to come over to Windsor and give us a hand. We hadn't planned to work that Sunday, or any other Sunday for that matter, but when all these people arrived with their hammers and saws, and with food enough for dinner for all, we couldn't refuse their offer to help.

One of the fellows worked for a contractor as a nailer. We found out what a nailer does when he scurried along the tops of the partitions nailing them together as fast as we could put them in place. Norm had difficulty reading the blue prints fast enough to make sure that each partition was in its exactly right location. We built the walls, for "the people had a mind to work." This quotation from Nehemiah 4:6 (*King James Bible*) describes what happened that Sunday afternoon before we all went back to our house and partook of the elegant display of food that our wives had prepared.

With that kind of help and with the Lord blessing us with favourable weather that fall, we were able to close the house in from rain and snow before winter set in.

Dad Wilson had hired a mason's helper to assist him in erecting the fireplace from the footing up to the chimney so that we were able to build a fire in it to warm the building. He had also brought a small wood burning cook stove from his shop in Amherstburg to heat coffee, soup, etc. Once, on a day when our then six year old son, Gerry, came out to the house with us, Dad Wilson made a soup using chicken feet, potatoes, and vegetables. Gerry wouldn't touch the stew, but we had a group of plasterers there of Czechoslovakian origin. They had brought a lunch that included European style meats, pickles, salads and other foods common to their culture. We all sat down to eat on boxes, planks or whatever we could find, but when the lid was lifted off the pot of chicken foot stew, the aroma proved too tempting to our plasterers. They offered to share their lunch for some of our stew, and we all feasted together.

Finally, at the end of March 1956, six months to the day after we staked out the foundation, we moved into our new home on Matchette Road, where we were to live for the next sixteen years. After the final inspection by a representative from Central Mortgage and Housing Corporation, Norman Wilson received a citation from the Corporation designating him as an A1 building contractor. Norm took pride in showing his letter of commendation to his old friends and cronies in the town of Amherstburg. We also enjoyed telling all and sundry who came to see our new house about the citation. Incidentally, our house was the last building that Norm Wilson ever built, even though he remained able

Figure 8
Home on Matchette Rd

bodied for ten years or more. Rather than trying to make a fortune as a contractor, he was content to stay at home and just do small jobs for his friends and neighbours.

I must not leave this episode in my life without saying that during the six months that we were building the house I worked full time at Ford's and managed the Credit Union's business on Friday evenings. I was able to switch shifts with other men in the lab so that I could work in the daytime at the building site and midnights at Ford's. Happily this heavy schedule did not cause any incidents such as the close call I experienced on the night shift in 1941 while working on the rear axle assembly line.

My duty at that time was to test the torque on the housing's nuts, hook the three hundred plus pound axle with a hoist and hang the axle on the conveyor to go through the paint shop. At about 2:00 a.m., the time I would usually be the sleepiest, I didn't have the axle hooked properly. I hung it on the conveyor, so I thought, and as I began to turn around to do the next axle, the one I had just hung toppled to the floor less than six inches from my foot gouging an inch deep hole in the concrete floor. That narrow escape completely woke me up thanking God for his guardian angel!

Many days, when we were at a critical point in the house construction, I worked from ten in the morning after I came home from the 12:00 a.m. until 8:00 a.m. shift, had some breakfast and then went to work on the house until dark. I went to my job many times after only one or two hours sleep and a few times with no sleep at all. Fortunately my job at Ford's during those days was such that from 1:30 a.m. until 5:00 a.m. I had no work to do. We had a dark room with no door for developing spectrographic plates, but it had an S shaped hallway that excluded any light when developing was in progress. Someone had put a sheet metal slab in the hallway to let the person in the dark room know that someone was coming into the dark room. The heavy, steel-toed work shoes that we all wore made quite a noise when we stepped on this sheet metal. There were two of us on the shift and we both spent our free time in the dark room, usually catching up on the rest we hadn't gotten the day before. The thump of a sample container falling down the chute from the furnaces at about 5:00 a.m. would always alert us to our responsibilities.

HOUSING AND INTERRELATED ISSUES

In parts of the country like Nova Scotia and Southwestern Ontario, black families are among the oldest residents, but as a racial group they neither enjoyed the resources available to others nor the freedom of choice to live wherever they desired.

Migrating groups tend to group together geographically in cities. This can be a potential source of support and positive motivation provided the group members establish facilities and services designed to work toward the solution of common problems. Lacking these resources geographical concentration becomes a potential source of maladaptive self-defeating behavior. In Canada, as in other countries, racially segregated housing has been an important factor in perpetuating structural racism since it did not lead to solidarity among blacks and yet persisted through several generations.

Many blacks said that they preferred to live in the downtown areas of a city close to the bulk of their people. However, Helling found that 95 percent of his sample in Windsor in 1965 gave racial discrimination as their reason and 14 percent would not move to the suburbs for the same reason. Those blacks who did move to previously all-white neighborhoods were not free from the subtle and often overt forms of racial bias which middle class society practiced. Behind the facade of politeness and respectability that is the hallmark of middle class social interaction, there can still be racial name calling of children, naive claims of color blindness and other indicators of prejudice that blacks have learned to recognize immediately. The first black families to move to the suburbs usually found that they had the task of educating their neighbours as to what blacks were really like, but perhaps more importantly what white society was really like in its treatment of blacks.

Blacks who were concentrated mostly in lower tax paying and rental housing areas of the cities did not have equal educational opportunities when one sees education in its total environmental contexts. Moreover, the education of children, whether black or white, involves more than access to well equipped schools. McDiarmid and Pratt, in their book *Teaching Prejudice,* affirmed that education as it functions in most cultures permits the dominant group to shape children's attitudes by patterns that it has set. They confirmed the argument that blackness, if it had any meaning at all in Canada, carried with it negative connotations which ignored and denigrated blacks, an attitude that is perpetuated through generations. In Canada, social studies textbooks were written from the point of view of white middle class values. These values were the basis for the judgment of all people within the society.

An examination of the list of books about blacks in the Nova Scotia textbook analysis revealed that if one were to read all the books and articles and view all the films listed, one would have a fairly comprehensive picture of American blacks but almost no knowledge of Canadian blacks. Formal education in Canada was not programmed to eliminate the effects of established social arrangements and behavioural patterns or to change attitudes that have been transmitted through generations of misinformation.

The housing situation of blacks had a direct relationship to limitations in employment and career opportunities. These limitations varied from city to city and from one occupational group to another. In industrial establishments employing more than two or three hundred people in Halifax, Nova Scotia, St. John, New Brunswick, Owen Sound and Windsor, Ontario, there were no blacks in middle management or executive positions as late as 1970. In professions in which academic skills and knowledge cannot be easily disregarded in an open society, blacks achieved a measure of success and recognition. This is not an indication of an equal opportunity structure, but rather a reflection of the public's recognition of professional credentials.

A report of the Windsor Advisory Committee on Employment in 1969 claimed that racial discrimination was a major problem for blacks in Windsor. In fact all available studies showed that the number of black skilled tradesmen was disproportionately low relative to the black population. Blacks were undeniably at the lowest end of the employment scale.

Even in such a menial occupation as stevedoring, the International Longshoremen's Association in Halifax excluded blacks from membership prior to 1962 including those who were able to get the occasional work assignment through the union hiring hall. Even if the union members voted to lift the colour bar, or if the government ordered them to do so, the local could not have admitted blacks to full membership as late as 1977 because so many white dockworker members needed work. Henry found that Halifax blacks earned less than the mean income, were unemployed for more weeks than the average for the city and were concentrated in menial jobs.

Blacks faced a dilemma. White society ignored them, placed limitations on their access to upward mobility and then denied that race had anything to do with the treatment they received. Out of frustration many blacks understandably developed various responses to the situation of being powerless members of a small minority group. Some became apathetic, dropped out of school, accepted menial jobs and attempted to make the most of a bad situation and survive; others developed skills of manipulation and became small scale social brokers. Others pursued what they were told was the most viable means to success as defined by white society, the academic/professional career path. A few attempted to counteract the racism of society by becoming social activists while a few others who were not visibly black tried passing, separating themselves from the black community in order to be accepted as white Canadians.

In the mid-1970s human rights agencies developed a new strategy known as affirmative action. This concept was an attempt by a few white decision makers to do something about the injustices of historical racism by attempting to even the score in the marketplace. However, the concept was slow in catching on. A handful of government agencies, corporations and trade unions accepted the principle and took steps to implement these programs on behalf of blacks to the same extent as they did for women. This is evidence that the black presence in Canada had neither yet been adequately recognized, nor the socio-economic needs of blacks taken seriously.

NOTHING VENTURED NOTHING GAINED

In 1953 the Ford Motor Company advertised a position in the foundry laboratory. High school chemistry, physics and mathematics were the principal criteria for the position. The job paid more than my stock picker's job, and since my brother George had worked in the lab for several years before moving into the plant manager's office as a clerk, I discussed the job with him. Convinced that I had the qualifications, even more so than my brother who had only finished grade 12, I decided to apply for the job.

By this time I had thirteen years seniority, and hence was the senior applicant. When I appeared for the interview one of the first things that the laboratory foreman said to me was that he didn't think I could do the job of chemically analyzing metals since I had had no previous experience in that type of work. I immediately asked to have a union representative present for the interview. I sensed that I might once more be facing possible discrimination on the grounds of my race. While I had been waiting for the interview one of the other technicians whom I had known through the union confided in me that a young man who had been laid off due to a cutback had held the job for which I was applying. The layoff had extended beyond the callback meaning that it had to be advertised plant wide.

When the union representative appeared I reported what the technician had told me. He addressed the foreman saying, "Listen, Jim, I know that you would like to have your own boy back on the job, but we've got a contract to be observed. The applicant with the highest seniority, who possesses the qualifications for a position the company has posted plant wide, must be given the job subject to the usual ninety days probation. The job belongs to Talbot." Accordingly, I got the job, and not long afterward the young man who had been laid off was also recalled to work.

After working for a few months as a lab technician and finding it challenging and fascinating, I came to the conclusion that, apart from the skilled trades such as tool and die maker, electrician, steam fitter, etc., our job was the highest paying job in the company's collective bargaining unit. I had the opportunity to convey this thought to Jim who was superintendent of quality control after having worked twelve years in the lab.

One day during my time in the lab, Jim came rushing into the lab (Jim always rushed at everything he did). He handed me a sample of already pulverized cast iron, a procedure which was part of my job, and told me to rush the carbon analysis on the sample because the pouring line out in the foundry was being held up. He stood behind me looking over my shoulder as I weighed out the allotted portion. I was as careful as possible since this was obviously an important sample. Next I placed the sample in the testing furnace and waited for all the carbon to burn off. Bubbles in the measuring vessel next to the furnace would indicate this result. Finally I brought the bottle down from its holder and placed it beside the calibrated tube that measured the volume of carbon dioxide emitted from the sample. I was about to convert this volume into the percentage of carbon in the sample when Jim, peering over my shoulder, nervously questioned me.

"What is it? What is it?" He demanded.

At that precise moment the reading I had just taken before releasing the carbon dioxide into the air left me. "I'm sorry, Jim!" I apologized. "I'm afraid I just lost it."

Jim was furious as he ran out of the lab. When he returned about three minutes later, I handed him the results of the test that I had run again. He said, "Thanks," but the way he snatched the test slip from my hand said something else.

The next day Jim summoned me to his office. "Lyle," he said, "I haven't been entirely satisfied with your work for some time. That incident yesterday is an example. First of all you work too slow, and secondly you spend too much time in your books."

"Before you say any more, Jim," I asked, "have you checked the worksheets to compare my daily output with those of the other guys?"

"I don't have to," he claimed, "but I've got them right here on my desk."

"May I see them?" I requested.

Jim handed me the worksheets and I made a quick calculation noting that my average daily output was virtually the same as for the other men doing the same work on the three shifts. I knew that this would be the case since we share the work equally on every shift.

Jim commented, "You may be doing as many tests as the others, but I don't like your style of working. You don't show any enthusiasm for the job. Obviously you're not happy here. Maybe a transfer would be good for you. If you want a transfer just identify the job you'd like and I'll see that you get it."

I realized from past experience that Jim could not make good his offer, and so I took a different approach.

"You say that I don't show enthusiasm for my work and you're probably right. I have never liked factory work and I never will, but you know that factory work was all our people could get when I started in 1940. Just look at the other Jim (the black chemist); he's no doubt the most knowledgeable foundry chemist and metal technician in the entire Ford empire and has been sought after for advice and counsel by Cleveland, Detroit and elsewhere. Nevertheless, because he's black, what is he doing — the same job that he was given when another black employee pointed out to Superintendent Blackwood that the man he had working on the hot, dirty shakeout was a graduate chemist. That was twenty-five years ago.

You're offering to help me get a transfer, and I really believe you would do everything you can to get me out of your area of supervision. But let me tell you,

Jim, I know my way around this company as well as anyone, and from where I stand I've got the best job there is outside of an office or supervisory position. Thanks, but no thanks! I'll just stay here and do my job until I retire, God willing." Jim and I never discussed my work from that date until I retired in 1970.

The books that Jim referred to earlier were my materials for my university studies. In 1965 the company circulated a letter outlining a tuition refund plan. Through the plan the company could reimburse an employee for a large percentage of the tuition fees for any post-secondary courses taken to enhance the employee's career. I didn't think that I could qualify for the plan since my interest in higher education had little direct relevance to my job in the lab. I wanted to study sociology. Both of our daughters, Marilyn in 1961 and it Carol in 1962, had graduated from university, and when I observed how they were able to handle their courses with time for other social and recreational activities, I thought that maybe I could do it too. I wasn't going to apply for the program, but Marietta insisted that I might as well try; the worst they could do was say no.

I applied, and I believe it was an act of Providence that the person who handled my application was a former lab employee named Matti Holli. He was also the conductor of the Windsor Symphony orchestra and had given Marietta a few piano lessons. As well, he had been on the advisory board of the Windsor Council on Group Relations for which I had been the treasurer manager.

When I approached my supervisor, Jim, to sign the approval for my bursary application, he was reluctant to do so questioning whether the company would approve it. "What can we put down for the way that the courses in sociology will benefit you as a lab technician?" he asked. I thought for a moment.

"How about saying that they will enhance my career in dealing with people or something like that?" Jim agreed that that reason might be worth a try.

When Matti received my application he called me on the phone. After acknowledging our acquaintance he said, "Your reason for taking courses in sociology is the strangest I have handled. I don't know if it will be accepted, but I'm going to submit it to the committee with a recommendation for approval."

My application was approved. At fifty years of age and after a break of thirty-two years in my academic career, I enrolled in the general arts program at the University of Windsor in the summer of 1965. Four years later I graduated with a double major in theology and sociology with a B+ average. I was encouraged by my professors to continue my studies in theology, and in the fall of that year the university accepted my admission to the Department of Graduate Studies.

Figure 9
Lyle's Graduation Photo

FAMILY AND FAITH

After Dad's retirement he and Mom moved to Dresden where he was then the full time pastor of Queen Street Baptist, his home church. The congregation was building a new manse for him and Dad helped with the construction in any way he could. One Friday afternoon he decided to go to the house about 2:00 p.m. to do some work after all the men had gone home for the weekend. Sometime around 5:00 p.m. he came staggering home like a drunken man to their temporary residence. He was bleeding from a swollen cut on his forehead, and Mom discovered a big lump on the back of his head.

Dad couldn't tell her what had happened, but we were able to make an educated guess. My dad was a person who ran at almost everything he did. When he worked at Ford's he would run from our house to the corner where the streetcar travelled. If the streetcar was coming he would board it and ride to work. If there was no streetcar in sight he would start out jogging. Many times he had run so far by the time the streetcar came that he would just continue running all the way to work, a distance of about two and a half miles from his home. When he was over fifty years old he entered the open hundred yard dash for men at the company picnic and won!

On that Friday afternoon in Dresden, our family thinks that he ran down the plank that had been placed from the main floor to the basement before the steps were built. He must have bumped his forehead on the bottom of the stairwell wall, fallen backwards and hit the back of his head on the concrete floor. He never fully recovered from that mishap. Over the following years he suffered three strokes, but he found it difficult to accept the idea that his preaching days were coming to an end.

He resigned as pastor in Dresden and he and Mom moved back into the house on Lillian Street in Windsor. He began to attend First Baptist church again, but he couldn't understand why the pastor never asked him to preach or even lead in prayer. Around 1956 he became ill with uremic poisoning, and for several months he was in and out of the hospital.

One day as I was going into the hospital on my way to work for the four to twelve shift, I met a former co-worker of mine, Jack, from Ford's coming out with two women. He introduced the women as his wife and his sister-in-law. When I told them that I was on my way to see my dad and that he had uremic poisoning, Jack's sister-in-law said, "You might as well prepare for the worst." uremic poisoning is incurable. My husband died from it."

"In that case," I responded, "we'll have to take it up with a higher power."

Inside the hospital I met Dr. Brien, Dad's doctor, coming from Dad's room. "I'm glad I met you, Lyle," he said; "your father is fading rapidly. We can't give him any more blood transfusions and his system doesn't retain intravenous feeding. I think you should let your family know. They will want to come and pray with him tonight, I'm sure, because he may not survive." I thanked the doctor and went in to see Dad. He was still conscious, but barely. I prayed with him and went on to work. That night the family members came, stayed as long as they could, had prayer and went home.

The next morning I went back to the hospital to ask about my dad, not knowing what to expect. The nurse at the station seemed unusually pleasant as I inquired, "How's Rev. Talbot?"

"Why don't you just see for yourself?" she said, pointing in the direction of Dad's room.

When I entered the room, Dad was sitting up in bed, eating his breakfast. The doctor was standing beside him. "I don't quite understand it, Lyle," he said, "but your father seems to have passed the crisis. We'll be taking more tests, but it appears that the symptoms of uremic poisoning are no longer pronounced. The Lord must have answered your prayers." You see, Dr. Wilbert Brien, my high school friend, was a fine Christian and a deacon in Temple Baptist church.

Dad did recover from that illness. He lived for fifteen more months, and when he did die, it was from arterial sclerosis due to aging. I knew my father was fading fast the evening in December 1959 when I visited him at his home. I said to him, "Dad, I would like to repeat the Twenty-third Psalm with you and then pray with you. Can you say 'The Lord is my Shepherd' with me?" He nodded in assent, but when I began to say, "The Lord is my shepherd, I shall not want . . .," he couldn't repeat the words after me.

Two days later, on December 29, 1959, Dad slipped away into the bosom of his Savior. People packed First Baptist church to overflowing for the funeral. Throughout the forty years of his ministry he had led many scores of those in attendance to a saving knowledge of Jesus Christ. Moreover, they had come from all the churches where he had ministered to pay their last respects.

Dad had requested "It is Well with My Soul" be one of the hymns sung during the service. To this day, whenever we sing, "When peace like a river attendeth my way,/ When sorrows like sea billows is roll,/Whatever my lot, thou hast taught me to say/ It is well! It is well! With my soul!" (Text by Horatio G. Spafford), memories of my father, a mighty soldier in the army of the Lord, flood through my mind.

My mother divided Dad's sermon notes among us three sons, about one hundred sermons each. I typed copies of those I received and made a book of them. Then I gave them to my nephew, Henry White to deposit in the Museum of Black History in Amherstburg for posterity.

Whenever I read one of Dad's sermons I am impressed anew with the priceless heritage of faith that my Great Grandfather Samuel Henry Davis, my Grandmother Sarah Ann (Davis) Talbot, and my father, Henry Lorenzo Talbot passed on to me.

On Marietta's side of the family, Herman Wilson, her youngest brother, was a WWII veteran. When he came home after serving overseas he thrilled our daughters with a gift of some coins of overseas currency. They kept those mementos for many years in Marietta's button jar (along with buttons saved from old clothes for future repair projects).

When Herman and his wife Wanda lost two small children in a fire that destroyed their home in the early 1950s, we took in two of the older children, Ralph and Gordon, to help out during that tragic time. Somehow we managed to fit them, along with our two girls and baby Gerry, in our two bedroom duplex. In the interim the people of Amherstburg joined together and built the family a new house on the site of the one that had burned down. It was a demonstration of how a community can come to the aid of their neighbours in time of trouble.

A few years later, after we had moved into our new home on Matchette Road, Wanda died in childbirth leaving Herman to look after seven children on his own. The decision was made for one of his sons, Mark to come and live with us. Violet, Marietta and Herman's youngest sister, took another boy, Blake, to live with her in Detroit. Herman's fifteen year old daughter, Gail, helped her dad with the other small children for a while, and then she too came to live with us. By then Mark had been with us for about seven months and during that time we were able to teach him about the Lord, taking him to Sunday school and church every Sunday. Both Mark and our son Gerry came to acknowledge Jesus Christ as Savior while Mark was with us. When Gail came, however, problems arose because she was a very emotionally disturbed girl. She was probably suffering from what we now know to be post-traumatic stress, and we were not competent to deal with her problems. The situation came to a head after Mother's Day.

Mark and Gerry both gave Marietta lovely Mother's Day cards with the usual note of gratitude contained therein. Gail became very upset, reminded Mark that

Marietta was not his mother and insisted that he should go back home with her. Mark gave in to her and went back home two months later.

We didn't have much more to do with Mark until about 1985, over twenty years later. We were living in London, Ontario, when we received a phone call from Mark who said he wanted to come and visit us. He arrived with his wife and their son and we had a very good visit for a couple of hours. During the conversation Mark said something like this, "Uncle Lyle and Aunt Marietta, there's something I want you to know. I want to thank you for introducing me to Jesus Christ. If you recall, I accepted him as my Savior while I was going to church with you all and Gerry. Well, over the years I have grown to love him more and more. I am now teaching a Bible class and I have you to thank." We expressed our praise and thanks to the Lord for His grace and as Mark was leaving I gave him a few copies of bible study material that I had prepared. Mark endeared himself to us in a unique way because of the bond of Christian love that we share. Over the years he has continued to keep in touch.

Ethel Wilson, Marietta's mother, was another important person in our lives. She was a woman of simple but profound faith. Once, when she was visiting us for a few days, I noticed that she was reading a rather difficult passage in her Bible. I asked her if she understood the passage. Her reply was that she just read until she came to something that she did understand, and then she would think about it. I'm sure that her method of Bible study was not unique. She felt that there was enough that she did understand to guide her in her Christian life.

One afternoon in the summer of 1965 Marietta was in our backyard moving some soil from around the above ground pool that we were having installed. She mentioned to me that there was a very strange aroma of flowers all around her, yet there were no flowers in bloom in that area. Early the next morning we received a message from Amherstburg that Marietta's mother had passed away suddenly at her blind daughter Marguerite's house where she had gone to stay while Marguerite's husband was away on business. She had gotten up in the night to go to the bathroom when Marguerite heard a thud, but since her mother had not called out Marguerite hadn't thought any more of it. When she got up in the morning she stumbled over her mother's body where she had fallen at the bathroom door. It was determined that she had suffered a heart attack and died.

After her death Dad Wilson's health began to deteriorate adversely affecting his lifestyle. He had contracted emphysema from the combination of working as a firebrick mason at the Allied Chemical Plant, and from a lifetime of smoking cigarettes. His job at the chemical plant involved constructing and repairing ovens used to dry a product called soda ash. He once told me that when they needed an oven repaired in a hurry, he and his helper would often have to work in temperatures of 115° to 120°F. As well the oven would be filled with the hot fumes from the chemicals that had been in it.

As his emphysema gradually grew worse, Dad Wilson began to drink alcoholic substances to take his mind off the pain and discomfort. Whether or not the alcohol ever eased the pain is questionable, however it became a matter of great concern to Marietta and me as well as to other family members. He had also developed cataracts in both eyes, but after they were surgically removed he was able to read large print with the aid of the glasses he wore. Marietta and I found a large print New Testament and encouraged him to read it.

Every Sunday, after our morning church service, Marietta would pack up our Sunday dinner and we would take it to Amherstburg to share with Dad Wilson and the extended family that lived with him at that time. Included in this extended family were all of the following: Marietta's Aunt Emma (then in her seventies and crippled from a fall suffered in her childhood when no medical help was available to them), our son Gerry who had left our home to live there with his birth mother (Marietta's sister, Isabel) and Gerry's half-brother, Wayne. Marietta's sister, Violet, was also often there as she came regularly to visit her dad. We would spend the afternoon with all these family members, but we tried, that is Marietta especially tried, to get a few minutes with Dad Wilson to talk about the Lord. She would refresh his memory of his past experience as a faithful member of the church and reassure him that God wanted to reclaim him as his own child.

One Sunday during our visit Dad Wilson told Marietta that he was giving up alcohol. He realized that it was doing him more harm than good. We went home that day rejoicing in the fact that Dad Wilson had made that decision on his own. But Marietta was not yet satisfied. She wanted to hear him testify of his faith. One day as she was spending time in prayer and meditation, she prayed, "Lord, I thank you that my dad has vowed to quit drinking. I pray that you will enable him to keep his vow, but I would love to hear him give a testimony of the faith that he has regained in you and in your son Jesus Christ."

While she was still worshiping, the phone rang. It was her dad. He had something he wanted to say to her. He said, "I just want you to know that my body is still suffering from my sickness but my soul is walking on air. A heavy weight has been lifted from my heart." Marietta could hardly wait for me to come home from work to share the good news.

In the next few months Dad Wilson was in and out of the hospital several times. When breathing became extremely difficult and painful from the emphysema, he would be taken to the hospital in Windsor for oxygen treatments. The nurses noticed the change in his attitude even though they said he had always been a good patient who tried not to be troublesome and worked to cheer up the other patients in the ward. One day when we visited him there was a young man in the next bed who had become quite friendly with Dad Wilson. This young man told us that Norm had shared his faith in Jesus Christ, but that he didn't know much about such things having been raised in a non-Christian home. On our next visit we brought the young man a copy of the *Good News for Modern Man New Testament*. When Norm was ready to go home a relative of one of the patients in the ward insisted on driving him to Amherstburg.

During this time the old folks in our lives were not to be our only concern. On a Friday afternoon in 1968 as I was brushing my teeth in preparation for going to work, I felt a sharp pain in the lower left-hand side of my skull behind my ear. The pain lasted for about ten or fifteen seconds and then left, and so I thought nothing of it and proceeded to eat my dinner, picked up my bag lunch and left for work.

I drove to the corner of our block and stopped for the stop sign. At that point I couldn't remember where I was supposed to be going. Then I noticed my lunch on the seat beside me and thought, "I must be going to work."

Somehow I managed to drive through the Friday afternoon rush hour traffic and made it to work. At that time my duty was to perform certain physical tests on molding and core sand samples of sands being used in the foundry. It required that I weigh precise amounts of the samples to be put through certain tests for tensile strength, hardness etc., but on that Friday afternoon I couldn't remember any of the weights for samples that I have been using for several months. After several attempts to complete that task, I called my coworker, Walter, over and told him that something was wrong with me and that I'd better go see the company doctor.

The doctor examined me and told me to go see my family doctor whom he had already called. It was probably about 5:30 p.m. when I left the plant and drove to our doctor's office. From there I went to the Kmart pharmacy near our home to get the doctor's prescription filled. I don't remember how I got from the plant to the doctor's office. I don't remember being in our doctor's office. I don't remember driving from there along Tecumseh Road for about four miles to the Kmart. I remembered only that I had the prescription to be filled and I remembered roaming around Kmart waiting for it. I finally arrived home sometime around 9:30 p.m. to find Marietta beside herself with anxiety. Walter had called to tell her that I was on my way home at about 5:30 and here it was 9:30. Normally it wouldn't take more than twenty or twenty-five minutes for me to drive home from work.

Sunday morning I felt well enough to go to Sunday school and church. Marietta and I had a record of more than ten years of perfect attendance at Sunday school and I didn't want to spoil our record. During the Sunday school hour prior to the worship service, I met Dr. George Willms, a close friend of ours, in the lower auditorium. As we exchanged greetings George noticed something wrong about my demeanor, and in a few minutes he approached me again.

"Listen, Lyle," he began, "I hope you're not offended, but I just called Dr. Carter, your doctor, and he tells me that you've suffered a cranial spasm, bordering on a stroke. He said that he told you to go to bed and stay there. You had better do that right now. I'll drive you home and Marietta can bring your car home."

The next five or six days were total blanks. It was two weeks before I was able to return to work. I had to learn the weights required for the sand tests all over again.

That year, 1968, was significant for another very important reason. The Windsor Star had been publishing a daily feature article entitled "Today's Child" with a photograph and resume of a child being placed up for adoption. Although I was in my fifty-third year and Marietta in her fiftieth year, the Children's Aid Society had accepted us as potential adoptive parents. Being black and willing to take older visible minority children probably worked in our favor.

Marietta had been drawn to a photo of a little five-year-old aboriginal girl named Bernice, but somehow we found ourselves going through the adoption procedure for a different child. Sandy, as we call her, had just had her third birthday when she came to us and she did not relate well with me right away. She did relate immediately with our teenage son Gerry probably because in the foster home where she had lived since infancy there was a teenage boy. The foster mother had spoiled her with goodies, but the foster father had had very little to do with her.

Sandy immediately fell in love with our reddish brown collie type dog, Lady, and they got along from the start since Lady loved children. Lady wouldn't let adult strangers into our yard, especially the meter reader for the gas company, but children could come and go at will. All Lady wanted was for them to pet her and play with her.

On Sandy's first Sunday with us we took her to church with us. Marietta sang in the choir, so I sat with Sandy in the family pew, second from the front on the left side of the sanctuary right in front of the pulpit. Sandy was somewhat restless, not only because it was a strange place, but also because this was the first time that she had been with me without Marietta. Halfway through the sermon Sandy stood up in the pew beside me and announced, "I gotta go pee pee!" I tried to quiet her down, but she just spoke louder and more urgently. "I gotta go pee pee!"

Imagine my embarrassment as I took her up in my arms. In a split second I had to choose between going down the aisle to the rear stairway, a route that would mean facing the whole congregation, or taking the front exit to the left of the pulpit at the front of the sanctuary. I chose the path of least embarrassment, out the pulpit exit.

Two years later, in February 1970, at a dinner given by Windsor's Black Heritage Society, my friend, George McCurdy, approached me. He had been involved with us in the sit-ins in 1949 and had been the provincial secretary of the Carpenters' Union for several years. George had gone to Ottawa about a year before our meeting to take on the responsibility for human rights administration for Labour Canada, administering the Canada Fair Employment Practices Act. He had found the work more demanding on his time and energy than anyone had anticipated, and accordingly he had convinced the director of that Fair Employment Practices Branch to hire another administrator to work with him. After much prayer and discussion with Marietta, who had absolutely no desire to leave Windsor and the house that her dad had built, I was able to negotiate a starting salary with Labour Canada that I could not refuse. We began to prepare for the move to Ottawa.

It is my belief that the sovereign hand of God was again working in our lives. June 30, 1970, I would accumulate sufficient years of service at Ford's to qualify for a pension, but I wasn't old enough to retire, fifty-eight being the earliest eligible retirement age for a full pension. I had turned fifty-five on June 27. Once more the union came to my aid. My committee member told me that the ex-president of our local had recently negotiated a special early retirement at about age fifty-six based on a hernia from which he had suffered for some time. He asked me if I had any physical disability that we could submit on an application for a pension.

We talked about my weak left hand, my trick right knee, my lazy left eye, and the chronic sinus problem brought on by an accidental inhalation of phosgene gas during laboratory tests I had performed a few months before. None of these disabilities appeared to be sufficiently serious enough since none of them hindered the performance of my duties. Then the committee member asked, "Lyle, what's your real reason for wanting to leave the company?"

Half jokingly, I responded, "I want to leave because this place is driving me up the wall."

"That's it!" the committee member exclaimed. "That's what we'll put down; 'irreparable psychological damage caused by continuous stress and anguish on the job.'"

This time a friend whom I had made during my years as a credit union organizer and as civil rights activist handled my application. When he received it he called me on the phone. "Are you serious about the reason you've given for wanting to retire?" he asked.

"Very serious," I replied. "If I continue to work here much longer I'll probably have another attack like the one I had two years ago." He knew about the time in 1968 when I suffered a seizure or mild stroke and was off work for two weeks.

"This is the first request of this kind that we've received, but I'll submit it to the committee with a recommendation for its acceptance. Let's see what happens."

The committee, consisting of himself as company representative, the committee member from the union, and a neutral person from the public sector accepted my application and they granted me the special early retirement pension effective June 30, 1970.

Meanwhile Dad Wilson had not only quit drinking, but also he had regained the ability to keep his financial accounts. On one of our visits he sat us down and went over the budget that he had prepared to manage the meagre income that he received. He said he was surprised at how much farther his pension cheque went. In June of 1970, however, his health took a turn for the worse and by about the middle of the month he had to be hospitalized again.

By this time we had committed ourselves to moving to Ottawa. I had reported for work on June 15, but returned to Windsor a few days later to finalize the sale of the house and arrange for moving our furniture. We had told a friend of ours in the real estate business that we had to sell our house. She had replied that a former resident of Windsor who had attended our church was moving back and his mother was sure that he was interested in purchasing our house. He had visited our home several times as a member of the youth group. Hence, when the date for our departure was settled the house sold within a week.

The remaining serious problem was who was going to take care of Dad Wilson's needs after we left. There didn't seem to be an adequate answer to this question. None of Marietta's sisters and brothers was in a position to do all the things that we had done. Her oldest sister, Alva, had been critically ill with cancer for about three years. Marguerite, her next sister was blind, having lost her sight a couple of years previously due to detached retinae. Isabel had recently married and was living in Detroit and her youngest sister, Violet, also lived in Detroit and could only visit on Sundays. Her brother Arnold was separated from his wife and widowed Herman had his seven children to care for. All we felt that we could do was to pray that somehow God would take care of the problem. On the eve of July 1, 1970, exactly one month before the closing date for the sale of our house, we were called to the hospital. Marietta's dad had taken a turn for the worse.

As the family gathered around his bedside I began to pray saying, "Dear Lord, we thank you that you have heard our prayers on behalf of our father and our friend. We thank you for the way he has changed his life in recent months and for his words of testimony of his faith in your Son. Now, Lord, in this hour of his great suffering, I pray that he will know the power of your Holy Spirit comforting him and easing his pain. We pray for his healing."

And then I heard myself saying these words, not of my own volition, ". . . His final healing."

Early the next morning, we received the message that Dad Wilson had passed away peacefully in his sleep during the night. He had indeed been blessed with his final healing. This came just a few weeks after Marietta's Aunt Emma had gone out in the backyard to feed Wayne's dogs and had been found lying dead just outside the dog kennel. God had taken care of both of his dear children in the best of ways. He had taken them to be with Himself.

The move to Ottawa was not without its dramatic moments. The Sunday after Dad Wilson's funeral Marietta and I were scheduled to take a flight to Ottawa for a week of house hunting. The Talbot family had chosen that day to have a combination family reunion and sendoff for us. We spent an enjoyable afternoon greeting, eating and chatting with relatives, some of whom we had not seen for several years. Just before we had to leave the park to prepare to catch our flight, the news came over the radio that a DC9 aircraft had crashed at or near the Toronto International Airport killing a large number of passengers and members of the crew. Our reservation was for a DC9 flight from Windsor to Toronto, then on to Ottawa.

Marietta had been on an airplane before, but after this news she was quite apprehensive about our upcoming flight. Her apprehension turned to anxiety when the family members gathered around to bid us farewell choosing to sing:

God be with you 'til we meet again;
By his council guide, uphold you;
With his sheep securely fold you.
God be with you 'til we meet again.
'Til we meet at Jesus' feet;
'Til we meet, 'til we meet,
God be with you 'til we meet again.
(Lyrics by Jeremiah E. Rankin)

I had to reassure Marietta that the words, "'Til we meet at Jesus' feet" could just as well be taken to mean when we meet in prayer and worship at Jesus' feet. Now I realize that indeed there were several relatives at the reunion in 1970 that we wouldn't meet again until we met at the foot of the throne of King Jesus in heaven.

A week later Dr. and Mrs. George Willms invited our friends from the church, the credit union, our family and our neighbours to a garden party at their large home also to bid us farewell.

In May of that same year, the adoption of Cheryl Bernice, our seven year old full blood Ojibwa daughter was finalized. We barely had time to get acquainted with her when we decided to let her and Sandy go to Parry Sound with Carol and her family. We planned to pick them up on our way to Ottawa in our car.

On July 30, 1970, we set out for Parry Sound, 350 miles from Windsor, with our dog Ginger, (Lady had died two years before this after having gone blind), our two cats — seventeen year old Fifi and two year old Hobo. I had made a makeshift cage for Hobo because he was a very nervous animal, and we believed that he wouldn't stay calm on such a long trip even with the help of tranquilizers.

We stayed overnight in Parry Sound and headed for Ottawa across Algonquin Park on July 31. When we arrived in Ottawa at about 3:00 p.m. we found our way to our lawyer's office thinking that we would get the key to our new house on Quincy Avenue. The lawyer informed us that the key had not yet been turned over to him because the balance of the down payment had not arrived from Windsor. "Legally," he said, "you don't have possession of the house until tomorrow, August 1."

That day was sunny, hot and sultry. We had parked our car on the street while our two children, two cats and our dog remained in the car. We implored the lawyer to do something to get us into the house immediately. No hotel or motel would allow three animals and two small children to stay overnight even if we thought we could control them.

Realizing the plight we were in, the lawyer agreed to call the real estate agent handling the sale of the house to see if she would let us into the house. He was able to persuade her to give us the key, but by then it was 3:45 p.m. and she said her office closed at 4:00 p.m. I had no idea how to get from the lawyer's office to the real estate office, so he started to give me directions, north on this street, east on another street, south on a third street, east on . . .

I broke in, "In case I get lost, just tell me where the office is."

"Well, it's five blocks down on the street in front of my office and a block and a half to the left, but . . ." I didn't wait for the rest of his description because to me time was of the essence. I had parked our car on a side street around the corner from the entrance to his office, so I made a right turn at the corner, passed the front entrance to his office and started to count the blocks. Just as I passed the second block I noticed that all the traffic on that street was going in the direction opposite to us. I glanced at my watch. It was less than five minutes before four o'clock. I made my way against the traffic the remaining couple of blocks, turned left and arrived at the real estate office just as a woman was coming out.

"Are you Ms. . .?" I asked.

"Yes," she replied. "And you must be Mr. Talbot. I was just about to leave. I have an urgent appointment, so I couldn't wait any longer." As she handed me the keys to the house she cautioned me that we really shouldn't be in the house before the sale was finalized.

We offered a prayer of thanksgiving and made our way to Quincy Avenue. Four o'clock is the time that a majority of government offices closes. That meant that we had to drive in rush hour traffic from the centre of downtown Ottawa for about five miles to the area known as Beacon Hill North, where our house was located.

We got there just before five o'clock, and it was a good thing that there were two bathrooms since everyone was in a rush after four hours without a rest stop. We put the animals down in the basement and left to find a restaurant. When we returned to the house we decided that we might as well try to get some sleep lying on the floor.

Just after dark someone rang the doorbell. I opened the door to face a man in uniform. I identified myself as the new owner of the house, but the officer said that according to his information the house wasn't to be occupied until the next day. What further complicated matters was the fact that our furniture had not yet arrived from Windsor, and there we were sleeping on the floor in an empty house. My explanation was too fantastic to have been fabricated and so the officer left after suggesting that we leave the lights off to avoid any further disturbance.

Our furniture and the cheque both arrived the next day from Windsor, and we began a new phase of our life's experience — a new career for me, a new family member and a new house in a new neighbourhood.

In the fall of 1971 my mother became ill with a virus that caused one side of her body to swell greatly. She had been living with my oldest sister, Luella, for some time, but when her condition worsened she moved in with my brother George and his wife Margaret. It was in November when Marietta's sister, Alva, died after a four year battle with cancer. We were in Windsor for the funeral and the day after the service I decided to visit Mom before we left for Ottawa. We had a loving visit and as I was about to leave her room she beckoned for me to bend down to her. "I'm very tired, Lyle; I'm ready to go home. Here, let me give you a kiss, and one for Marietta, one for Marilyn, one for Carol, one for Gerry, one for Cheryl and one for Sandy. Tell them all that I love them." After that, I left and drove back to Ottawa.

Two days later my brother George called to tell me that Mom had been taken to hospital. When my office telephone rang the next morning, I somehow knew that those goodbye kisses were really goodbyes. Mom had lived to be eighty-five years old loving her family and loving her Lord.

A dear woman once said to me, "Lyle, my dear, I have felt for some time that you are the one who is going to follow in your father's footsteps and become a great preacher. After your talk this morning I'm convinced that you are called to be a preacher."

"I believe that I've been called, too," I replied, "but not to be a preacher. I've been called to be a Christian layperson, a layperson who can teach God's word, who can lead God's people, who can live a life that brings honour to our Lord. Such laymen are needed today."

My desire to be a good layperson led me to study the Bible, following the instructions of my dad and of my mentor, Rev. C. Wells. It led me to attend conferences and seminars to improve my knowledge and my skill in being a witness for my Lord. It led me to return to formal education at age fifty so that I could follow the biblical injunction to "Study to shew thyself approved unto God, a workman that needeth not to be ashamed, rightly dividing the word of truth (2 Tim. 2:15, *King James Bible*). It led me to compile many Bible studies on subjects that are vital to living a Christian life in today's world. In addition, it led me to write many poems based not only on passages from the Bible, but also on the experiences that I have shared with family and friends.

As I near the end of my journey to faith I cannot say with the apostle Paul, "I have fought a good fight, I have finished my course, I have kept the faith" (2 Timothy 4:7, *King James Bible*). I can, however say, as in Philippians 3: 13, 14 (*King James Bible*), "Brethren, I count not myself to have apprehended: but this one thing I do, forgetting those things which are behind, and reaching forth unto those things which are before, I press toward the mark for the prize of the high calling of God in Christ Jesus."

CHAPTER 25

VOICES IN THE WILDERNESS NO MORE

Voices in the wilderness raised in protest against racial discrimination in one city, Windsor, Ontario, had actually become shouts from the housetops heard across the land in a single decade. It was tedious work on the part of a small but dedicated band of activists. A survey taken 1957 demonstrated this, i.e. ten years after that first "Community Audit" mentioned in a previous chapter.

In addition to the factory that began hiring blacks in 1952, factories with union agreements no longer refused to hire blacks. Seniority and ability to perform a task became the primary criteria for upgrading and promotions within the bargaining units. Company-wide posting of openings made it possible for all employees to bid for jobs that they felt they were able and willing to perform. Some qualified black office workers were also able to find work. A few stores were hiring black clerks and some of them were offering opportunities for promotion.

There were blacks working in some provincial and federal government offices in Windsor, but none worked as customs or immigration officers on the Canadian side of the Detroit River. The city promoted its black assistant solicitor to city solicitor. As well, Canada's first fully authenticated police constable, Alton Parker, who had been hired while Art Reaume was mayor in the mid-1940s, had been promoted to detective and another black was a special constable working with the youth of the city. Two more police constables, one firefighter and several office workers were on the city's payroll.

These were signs of progress yet there was one humiliating aspect related to the city's one black firefighter. The reason given for not hiring black men as firefighters in the past was that the on duty and off duty firefighters shared the beds in the fire halls, and it was considered unfair to require a white man to use the same bed as a black man. When a black man was eventually hired in the 1950s as a firefighter, after working for several months he discovered, and then verified, that none of the white firefighters shared his bed on the days that he was off duty. They did share all the other beds.

In 1960 a group of young black professionals led in the organization of the Guardian Club whose purpose was to protect the rights of blacks. They had become caught up in the enthusiasm of the American civil rights movement that had such notable leaders as Martin Luther King, the Freedom Riders, Malcolm X and Stokely Carmichael. Later they joined with others, principally in Toronto and Montreal, to form the National Black Coalition of Canada. This organization hoped to be an umbrella organization representing the interests of blacks from coast to coast. The Coalition faced difficulties right from its formation in 1968, and after ten years of struggling to survive, it failed to become a viable national forum.

There was another development taking place at the same time in the Maritimes where the spirit of the civil rights movement had spilled over into the cities and towns of Nova Scotia and New Brunswick. Africville, a black community on the edge of Halifax, became an eyesore in the Maritimes and literally a black mark on the conscience of Canada. The authorities believed that they had to eradicate it because of the bad publicity it was generating. By 1965 Africville had been destined for redevelopment. The story of Africville in the 1960s gained as much notoriety as the Dresden story of the 1950s and the Sir George Williams Affair of the 1960s.

A national race problem was becoming more visibly evident as blacks arriving in Canada by the thousands from the Caribbean sought jobs, housing, education, recreation and other services. Once again the city of Windsor provided leadership in this movement. At the founding conference of the National Black Coalition held in Toronto, the attendees elected Dr. Howard McCurdy, a biology professor and president of the Guardian Club in Windsor, as the first national chairperson. These were tense times in Canada's racial history. In 1968 some black students at Sir George Williams (now Concordia) University in Montreal accused a professor of racism in grading them. Students everywhere were in the midst of a student revolution and the situation at Sir George Williams touched off the infamous computer riot.

In St. John, New Brunswick, Joe Drummond was conducting what amounted to a one man campaign for human rights. It was this Joe who wrote in a brief to the mayor of St. John in 1970, "Blacks are climbing a molasses mountain dressed in snowshoes while whites ride the ski lift to the top." On one occasion Joe went to one of the larger department stores to try to obtain employment for young blacks as clerks and salespersons. When he met with resistance from the manager, Joe told him that he had eleven children and all of them were expert shoplifters. He added that if the store didn't hire a black person at once he would turn all eleven of them loose in the store. The threat worked because, even if Joe's children were not shoplifters, I'm sure that management did not want eleven black children roaming around their store all at one time.

Prior to 1970 the black population was composed of a majority of Canadian born persons with several generations of Canadian ancestry and a minority from the Caribbean area. It can be said that the leadership in human rights among blacks emanated almost entirely from Canadian born blacks in southwestern Ontario, Toronto and the Maritimes and blacks of West Indian origin in Toronto and Montréal who had come to Canada either to work as porters on the railroads or as domestic servants.

By 1970 the presence of almost 200,000 Afro-Caribbean people had drastically changed the interracial situation. In cities like Toronto, Montreal and Ottawa, immigrant blacks rapidly outnumbered the Canadian born blacks. The black population of Toronto, for example, mushroomed from less than 10,000 prior to 1960 to more than 50,000 by 1970 and to 150,000 by 1980.

During the decade of the 60s, either immigrant blacks seemingly did not face overt discrimination except in housing, or they were reluctant to complain to statutory authorities. Several factors could have contributed to this. Since most of them had entered Canada with skills or professions that were in demand on the labour market, they may not have had a great deal of difficulty in finding a job. Some may have been obliged to accept employment for which they were overqualified, but being new in the country they would be inclined to accept this as normal. They came from a society in which they were a part of the majority racial group to one in which they were suddenly members of a numerically small minority (even smaller groups when one takes into consideration the various parts of the Caribbean from which they emigrated). They were unlikely to be psychologically prepared for such a drastic change in status.

In many respects they were strangers to Canadian born blacks and even to blacks from other Caribbean sources. Hence, there was minimal interaction and communication between the various groups. Indeed, they had little in common! Many members of each group have interpreted this strangeness as unfriendliness, jealousy and in some cases, outright open hostility. Canadian born blacks have often seen West Indians as Johnny-come-lateties who neither knew about, nor appreciated the struggles and deprivation Canadian blacks have had to endure throughout their history in Canada for over more than a century. West Indian blacks, on their part, have sometimes perceived Canadian born blacks as backward, docile and passive. This social distance between the various black groups was the principal factor in the inability of the National Black Coalition or any other black organization to become an effective umbrella for blacks at the national, regional or local level. It takes some time for immigrant blacks to recognize, comprehend and deal with the kinds of subtle and evasive discriminatory patterns and practices that have manifested themselves in Canada. Among the semiskilled, skilled and professional groups it takes even longer because it is only when they have attempted to achieve higher levels of socio-economic status that they may have encountered these forms of racism.

Among professionals their status gives them so many of their professional peers' privileges that they are not aware of those aspects of privilege which result in differential treatment because of race. Wilson Head, a West Indian sociologist who had been in Canada more than ten years, observed that the West Indians in Toronto in 1975 were at the same stage in black/white race relations that the blacks in Windsor were in the 1950s. He suggested that Torontonians would have to develop the same sort of strategies and tactics that the Windsor Council on Group Relations had used. He cited as an example the situation that existed in reference to the Ontario Human Rights Commission. While most West Indians recognized that the Ontario Human Rights Commission had been relatively ineffective in guaranteeing equal socio-economic opportunity for blacks, as West Indians they did not come together to present a single strong voice to either the provincial or the federal government. It was not surprising that by 1982 neither the federal Human Rights Commission nor the Anti-discrimination Directorate of the Public Service Commission of Canada had a single black officer in their Toronto offices where the largest portion of their discrimination complaints based on race originated.

The belief that there is no racial problem for the hard working, successful, sophisticated person, and then those with such a belief behaving accordingly, widens the psychological distance between blacks and whites even if it appears to be otherwise on the surface. The crowning insult that one can pay to an intelligent Canadian white person is to suggest that he/she might be motivated in some action or inaction by racial considerations. For Canadians it is a matter of self respect to be considered free of racism.

UNFAIR EMPLOYMENT PRACTICES

My job as a human rights administrator involved a lot of travelling across Canada. In the first year I made over fifty trips by airplane from Ottawa to cities from Halifax to Vancouver. During the twelve years with the federal government, I visited every province except Newfoundland as well as the Yukon Territory. One reason that I never visited Newfoundland and the Northwest Territory was that the only times I might have received an assignment in either of these places was in the middle of winter and I was able to decline in favour of another officer who really enjoyed winter travelling.

Air travel had its traumatic times as well. On a scheduled trip to Windsor from Ottawa, heavy fog conditions delayed the plane's departure for about two hours. Then about a half hour into the fifty minute flight to Toronto, the captain announced that fog still covered the Toronto airport but that he was still hopeful that we would be able to land. As we approached the Toronto airport the fog was still dense, so the captain announced that we would have to circle the airport for a while. A few minutes later he announced that another plane had landed and we would probably be following it shortly. Presently I could tell that the plane was in its descent, and in a minute or two as we were about to enter the fog bank I could see the smoke stack of a factory just outside the landing field. I estimated that the fog bank must be less than 150 feet deep. Suddenly the plane's engines roared and we rose above the fog. Instead of the scheduled landing in Toronto flew on to Windsor!

Fifteen months after I started at Labour Canada, George McCurdy, the friend who had been instrumental in getting the job for me and had invited me to come and work with him, accepted an offer to become the director of the Nova Scotia Human Rights Commission and moved to Halifax. This left his position at Labour Canada vacant and I presumed that I would be the logical person to succeed him. But it was not to be. The top brass in the department decided to leave the position vacant. When I inquired as to why they were not advertising the vacancy, they told me that no staffing action was being taken for the time being. That "time being" lasted four years.

In fact there were two positions for which I was the logical candidate, but neither one was filled. The director tried to fill in for my division head by attempting duties for which he had no previous experience or training. Three other officers and I shared the duties of the other position without direct supervision. In my opinion the work of our division suffered severely just because our department heads chose not to appoint another black man to replace the one who had left.

During that whole four years I was given no meaningful productive assignments. I was asked to write reports that were never read by anyone in management. I prepared position papers on such subjects as "The Strategy of Inclusion in Employment and Upgrading." I wrote several articles on discrimination in employment and affirmative action, none of which received any response. In the fourth year of this situation I filed a grievance with management claiming that I was being denied my right to advancement and upgrading. I also filed a complaint with the Public Service Commission stating that the position for which I should have been the best qualified candidate was not being filled. I claimed that my racial origin was the ground of my complaint. As a result of my grievance I was given an upgrading of one level since two other officers in the directorate had received such upgrading.

The complaint of discrimination was a different matter. The irony of the situation was that I was claiming that the very branch of the government that had the responsibility to investigate complaints of discrimination was itself being accused of a discriminatory practice. It took eight months before I received the finding of the investigation. The finding was that since no action had been taken to staff the position in question there could not have been any discrimination. The finding reflected a kind of circular reasoning: no staffing action, hence no discrimination. No one had been appointed: therefore my career in the public service had not been adversely affected.

That was the very essence of my complaint. The failure to staff the position was discriminatory since I was available and the person best qualified to fill it. Not long after that finding was handed down the Canadian Human Rights Act was enacted and steps were undertaken to organize the Canadian Human Rights Commission. Because of my experience in human rights as an activist, an investigator and an administrator, I was placed on assignment to assist in setting up the Commission. However, during the entire year that I worked there my assignment was never made official. I continued to be on the payroll of Labour Canada in spite of my repeated requests to for and official transfer.

When it came time to staff the position of chief of investigations, I applied for the position but soon learned that an African born man had received the appointment. I was told that they preferred someone more visibly black than I am.

While working at the Human Rights Commission, one day I had occasion to meet with a former colleague of mine at Labour Canada who was at the time the director of the Anti-Discrimination Directorate at the Public Service Commission. At the end of our meeting as he was about to leave my office he asked me, "Hey Lyle! How would you like to come and work with me?"

I thought he was joking, so I jokingly replied, "Des, if I was out of a job and you offered me the only job in the government that I could do, I wouldn't take it. Two years of putting up with you is enough."

We had a good laugh over some of our experiences together in Labour Canada and he left. The next day a large envelope showed up in my IN basket. Upon opening it I found a notice of a proposed staffing action for a senior investigator at the Public Service Commission, an application form and a note which said simply, "I wasn't kidding."

I applied and was appointed to the position. In a few months I was promoted to the supervisory position called a review officer. In this position, the one and only promotion I ever received in the forty-five years of my working life, I was responsible for assigning cases for investigation to four officers at headquarters and two officers in our regional offices in Toronto and Vancouver. It was also my responsibility to review the findings of their investigations and determine with them the appropriate actions to either uphold or deny the complaints filed.

The first year in the position was perhaps the most enjoyable year of my working career. The four officers at headquarters relied upon my judgment and followed my instructions in conducting their investigations. Two of them found it difficult to finalize an investigation and make comprehensive, yet concise reports, but I was able to deal with such problems. One of the officers at headquarters, a black native of Trinidad, had an incorrigible habit of writing voluminous reports containing much irrelevant verbiage. When I repeatedly returned his reports for him to abbreviate, he became frustrated and on one occasion asked me what he could do to please me. I suggested that a department like National Defense would really appreciate his particular writing skill. "You know," he commented, "I've been thinking of applying for a job there."

"Why don't you?" I asked in as serious a tone as I could. He did apply, and a couple of months later he announced that he was leaving to accept a position at National Defense.

After that young man left the branch the director confided in me that he had been trying to get rid of him for a couple of years. He wanted to know how I managed to do it. "I didn't really do anything but demand the kind of reports we expected of him, and when he found it too much of a hassle, I merely suggested to him where his expertise would be more appreciated. I'm sure he'll be happier in his new position." The director agreed, and a few months later when I met that former officer on the street, he thanked me for my suggestion. He felt quite comfortable at his new department.

The last year of my employment was not so pleasant. I had been scheduled to retire at the end of June 1980, but the branch was still in the process of organizing the regional offices in Toronto and Vancouver and I was asked to stay on a year to oversee this project. When we were in the process of staffing one position of senior investigator, one junior investigator and three support staff positions at each regional office, my problems began. The branch director, a staffing officer from the personnel branch, a senior investigator from headquarters and I made up the selection board for all the positions.

We had been in Vancouver all week interviewing candidates, so the director decided that I should stay in Vancouver over the weekend while he and the other two board members returned to Toronto to interview some candidates for the support positions. They were supposed to return to Vancouver Sunday night to resume the interviews on Monday morning. We finished the interviews in Vancouver and returned to Ottawa. My understanding was that we were going to proceed on to Toronto the next day to interview candidates for the senior investigator position there, but the director informed me that the other members of the board had completed the interviews on the previous Friday while I was in Vancouver.

I wasn't at all happy with the decision to interview candidates for the senior investigator position without me, but the staffing officer assured me that it was all in order. I really became concerned when I saw the board's report. They had not selected the person who, from his application and resumé appeared to be the best qualified. The candidate that they had selected had been a personnel officer in a large post office. In that position he had been the respondent in a successful complaint of discrimination in which the investigator's report described him as arrogant and overtly racially biased.

It wasn't until I was in the position of being that successful candidate's immediate supervisor that I found out for myself what he was like. From the outset he ignored every instruction, every suggestion, every memorandum that I gave him, doing only what the director himself told him to do. In one instance he told me point blank that he didn't have to take any instructions from me. He said that Des was his boss and he would be responsible only to him. Furthermore, if there was anything about his work or his reporting methods that I didn't like I could take it up with Des. I soon learned that he, Des and the director general, Tom, were all drinking buddies. When the situation became intolerable for me, I brought the matter to Des' attention who responded with, "Don't let it bother you, Lyle; Norm's a good man. Just leave him alone. He'll be all right."

"But Des," I protested, "I'm only trying to get him to abide by the directives that you yourself have issued. He ignores every memo that I write to him."

"I repeat," Des concluded, "don't let it bother you."

However, it did continue to bother me, so I decided that since Des would do nothing I would discuss it with Tom, the director general. Instead of supporting me, Tom suggested that I should stay at home until my retirement date occurred in June 1982, and the Commission would have my pay cheques delivered to my home.

Thus, the only white male who was supposed to work under my supervision during my working career refused to be supervised by me. Such is the merit system in Canada, and such is the operation of structural racism with the kinds of circumstances that shaped my career and the careers of a multitude of blacks in Canada. Their life stories, like mine, can best be described as The Anatomies of Failure.

TOWARD A BETTER UNDERSTANDING

The expressed ideology of fair treatment for all has obscured the subtlety and covertness of the Canadian racial situation. This characteristic provides a significant differentiation of the racial situation in this country from other countries. Canada's official policy proclaimed to be non-discriminatory with respect to race, colour and ethnic origin. Ironically, having made the proclamation, Canadian power holders proceeded to determine their actions based on patterns and social arrangements which were intrinsically racist. Our immigration policies and practices were founded on a spurious myth about blacks — i.e. the idea that they could not survive the winters despite the fact that many thousands of them had been living here for multiple generations. This resulted in the virtual exclusion of blacks from other countries until the mid-1960s. At that time the need for technical and professional skills in the labour market and a decline in immigration from western Europe brought about the largest wave of non-white immigrants in Canada's history. This increased our black population from about 60,000 to more than 200,000 in the short span of ten years. Even with this influx the percentage of blacks has remained below two percent of the total population both nationally and in areas of the greatest urban concentration.

Historical patterns and practices in housing, employment, education and services have made blacks the victims of discrimination since the arrival of the first escaped slaves, and these patterns persisted for decades. Furthermore, the physical isolation emanating from historical segregation affected all areas of blacks' socio-economic lives. The concentration of blacks in low skill, low pay menial occupations with limited career opportunities have been due to racial factors rather than from purely social class factors.

In education, religious affiliation, accommodations and such services as those offered by hotels, restaurants, amusement centres etc., it has been shown that blacks have been relatively disadvantaged. The merit principle espoused in overt policies has been demonstrated to be a virtual myth because the vicious circle of perpetuation affects all aspects of Canada's socio-economic structure. Whites who accepted the status quo or been reluctant to take the initiative to change in interracial situations have defined and limited the extent of mobility for blacks.

The failure to implement Canada's official policy of fair treatment for all has meant that white power holders and decision makers, who have had little or no education or socialization in interracial interaction, have been constrained by this same policy to deny not only their own racism but also the racism of society as well. Most Canadians have failed to see that they have been predisposed to discriminate on racial grounds by the very nature of this society and by the kinds of behaviour and social arrangements that have become institutionalized. Overt discrimination is rejected because it is contrary to society's avowed denial of its racism. This denial of racism further enhances its perpetuation. If society does not face up to the fact that one does not have to be a racist in order to function as a racist, then society will maintain the status quo in this regard.

Although blacks who can be identified as such are highly visible, they can suddenly become psychologically invisible. This can occur when a promotion or an upgrading is being considered, in school when the teacher fails to recognize the hand of the bright black student in response to a question or when the textbook implies that all of Canada's heroes and celebrities are white and blacks are either forgotten or pictured in demeaning terms.

The subtly concealed ways in which racism is expressed usually frustrates blacks who experience discrimination. From early childhood they learn that in order to achieve even a minimal degree of success they must expect to work harder, wait longer and develop special skills in interracial social action not only to advance in life but also just to survive physically, socially, economically and psychologically. The socialization of the black child includes early recognition of his difference from the majority of Canadians and figuring out how he can cope with that difference. Unlike white children, who learn little or nothing about blacks, black children learn a great deal about whites with whom they must interact all their lives.

The situation which has been described in this book is a complex one, but one about which every Canadian thinks he is knowledgeable. Almost everyone will admit that there may be isolated cases of discrimination in Canada, although none will admit that he/she is guilty. Furthermore, few Canadians realize that this underlying societal characteristic, racism, has adversely affected the lifestyle of many blacks in various ways across the length and breadth of this country.

In a complex urban society like Canada's, the interactions and related roles of the individual can be represented by the rooms in a mansion, each one representing an area of activity and involvement. The rooms in this mansion interweave in varying degrees and according to ever-changing dynamic patterns that move about, interlocking and disengaging as the person goes from one activity to another. The journey reported through the experiences described in the foregoing chapters provides an opportunity to open a number of doors in Canada's mansion, put one foot on the threshold and take a look inside for the meaning of being black and Canadian

It is not always easy to conceptualize the complexity of roles and situations in which any individual in society may be found. When the individual is a member of a subgroup further complexities are added. The black person has to learn unique role-playing skills to use according to the circles in which he finds himself at any given time. Often the same situation will call for two or more dissonant roles at the same time. This is true for a member of any disparate group in varying degrees.

Most blacks who were born and reared in this country have developed a kind of cat like psychological reflex system, either consciously or subconsciously. A cat can be sleeping peacefully on the floor, apparently oblivious to its surroundings, but let the slightest disturbance occur — the rustle of a newspaper, the closing of the door, the motion of a person — and instantly the cat is alert; its back arches, ears perk up, neck fur stands on end. If the disturbance calls for action, it acts quickly and spontaneously. If the disturbance turns out to be just a momentary, passing, nonthreatening one, the cat immediately resumes its nap as though nothing has occurred. The cat behaves this way by instinct. In interracial relations, however, if the black person demonstrates a comparable psychological reflex action, whites perceive him as being over sensitive or too self-conscious with regard to his race. Whether cats have a memory or not is debatable, but human beings do, and the memory of traumatic or tenuous past experiences can induce a spontaneous reaction even when there is no apparent concrete reason for it.

Many black Canadians have white friends who have told them about some racist or prejudicial attitudes and opinions that have been expressed, often quite freely, when no blacks were present. Hence the black person cannot be sure just when, where, how or why racism will rear its ugly head. When it does, the black person must be alert to handle the situation spontaneously. It is a matter of psychological survival. Maybe he will act; maybe he will do nothing. Whichever decision he makes he must make it instantly even if the decision is to deal with the matter at a later more opportune time.

I have held many discussions with blacks who came to Canada as professionals from other countries. Hardly any of those who had been in Canada for ten years had given much thought to the problem of being black in Canada. They invariably presumed that their professional accreditation was all that they needed to make it in this country. If there was any search for an identity, that search was almost exclusively for identity only as a black, not as a Canadian. Having a meagre knowledge of the historical experiences of Canadian blacks, since so little has been written about us and since interaction between foreign born and Canadian born blacks has been very superficial and formal, these new Canadians have sought their roots in Africa, the United States or their countries of origin.

It is my hoped that all blacks in Canada will come to know themselves and their black brothers and sisters better and will be able to find common grounds for identity, a commonality of experience and a common cause which may serve as a unifying force and focus for organized action toward common goals and aspirations. We must acknowledge that white society does not differentiate between Canadian born blacks and immigrant blacks. As a rule, they can neither tell, nor do they care one whit whether we originated in Nova Scotia or Barbados; Windsor, Ontario, or Windsor, Nova Scotia; Kingston, Ontario, or Kingston, Jamaica. Whether our ancestors came to Canada via the Underground Railroad or whether we arrived via Air Jamaica is only a matter of passing curiosity to the vast majority of white Canadians. Just as white Canadians tend to lump all blacks together and fit them into whatever stereotypes they hold, so too many blacks born in Canada do the same with all foreign-born blacks.

The model of a multicultural mosaic as distinct from a melting pot model presents an interesting question for blacks. Are the black tiles in the mosaic representative of individuals? Of families? Of communities? Of islands? Each person's answer to this question within his own mind is a reflection of his attitudes and behaviour patterns on matters of race and colour.

Do all the black tiles really look alike, Canada?

Since language, food, mannerisms, lifestyles and ways of interacting are all intrinsic to a people's culture and heritage, what does this say about black identity and black culture in Canada? Can we really repossess our common African heritage?

What I think will happen is that a synthesis of cultural traits and elements will evolve over time, not only adulterated by the many sub cultural backgrounds from which blacks in Canada have come, but also by the influences of the majority white society in which we live and by ethnic and racial miscegenation.

The concept of black and Canadian or Canadian and black means to share a common experience of being both black and Canadian. The focal point of that common experience, whether or not we are fifth generation Canadians or newly arrived Canadians, is the discrimination and the failure of white society to recognize that we blacks are as Canadian as they are. It is this common experience, not in our differences or in our remote African heritage that we who are blacks and living in Canada will eventually find our true identity.

What does it mean to be black and Canadian? It means that we are both being and becoming. In a sense we have just arrived and are just beginning to get acquainted with one another. We should continue to get to know one another better. We should continue in our search for identity as blacks in Canada for black is beautiful!

***

There was a tribe of Hebrews enslaved in Egypt for several hundred years. Somehow they gained their freedom and eventually, after a couple of generations of aimless wandering in the desert of Arabia, they began to settle in Canaan and eventually became the nation of Israel. After they were well established, their poets, sages, prophets and historians gathered bits and pieces of the oral tradition of the many tribes and wove them into a single history known as the Pentateuch. The Pentateuch binds together the folklore, legends and myths of their oral tradition into a single internalized document.

In the time honoured black spiritual tradition I offer this parallel to that Hebrew experience through the following paraphrase of Deuteronomy 26:5-9:

A wandering African was my father, who sojourned in bondage in many lands for three hundred years. He became a nation, great, mighty and populous. The white man treated us harshly, afflicted us and laid on us hard bondage . . . The Lord heard our voice and saw our affliction, our toil and our oppression, and the Lord brought us up out of bondage with a mighty hand and an outstretched arm. With great terror, signs and wonders and he brought us to this place . . . .

To the next generation I pass the torch to continue our saga . . . .

You Are a People

When our people stood helpless on Afric's sun drenched shores
And watched their strong, healthy, virile sons and daughters
They had hope and surety that life would continue
And that tribe and race would not be lost in the jungle of forgetfulness —
Suddenly those children were snatched from them
 Ruthlessly chained and transported like cattle
Disappearing into the sunset never to return . . .

When our forebears bent their backs 'neath the yoke of bondage
Stripped of possessions family   friends
Song   music art dance banned . . .
Under the lash   no land   no kin   no home
Daughters   sisters   mothers   wives   ruthlessly   raped   ravished
Reduced to chattels   possessed   used   traded   bought   sold

Four thousand moons changed faces but the face of bondage refused to change
While man wrangled animal human soul to save mind to think
Noble savage   beast of burden   half-human   human   human   but
Four thousand moons bound beaten branded but only in body
Free spirits will not be slaves
Free spirits will not hold slaves
The soul of freedom makes us free but not quite free
For men love darkness rather than light . . .
Some would blind us by invisible chains
forever . . .
So we remain half slave   half free
Shores once outstretched with open arms from sea to sea
Inviting beckoning . . . Come to me
Set foot within my gates and be at liberty

My father stepped on board the Underground Railroad
Your father joined the Maroons or Toussaint l'Ouverture —
freedom bound
Thus we came from Africa all, 'tis true
But as the sons of Jacob wandered five hundred moons
In the Wilderness of Zin in search of Canaan
We have come via diaspora from Carib lands British and Dixie soil
What land e'er gathered blacks within its bounds from so many places
To a true mecca for us to reunite and claim our heritage
Freedom   justice   equity   when once the yoke is lifted
And black men say in truth and action,
"YOU are my brother!"

We can join hands with a free voice loud and clear and shout "BLACK!!!"

Bibliography

Reproduced from "Black and Canadian: Inside Looking In"
(unpublished manuscript by Lyle Talbot)

Act for the Promotion and Protection of the Fundamental Rights of the People of British Columbia, commonly cited as the Human Rights Act, 1969.

An Act Respecting Human Rights and Freedoms, Quebec, 1975.

An Act Respecting Human Rights, Prince Edward Island, 1969.

An Act to Establish the Newfoundland Human Rights Code and toProvide for its Implementation, 1969.

An Act to Establish the Saskatchewan Human Rights Commission, 1972.

The Adoption of Negro Children, Social Planning Council of Metropolitan Toronto, 1966.

Affirmative Action: Guidelines for Employers. Labour Canada and Manpower and Immigration, Ottawa, 1976.

"Africville Relocation Report". Halifax, Institute of Public Affairs, Dalhousie Univ., 1971.

Antonovsky, Aaron. "The Problem: The Social Meaning of Discrimination" in Mass Society in Crisis, ed. B. Rosenberg et al. New York: Macmillan, 1964.

Boydell, Grindstaff and Whitehead. Critical Issues in Canadian Society: The Evolution of an Immigration Policy.

Binstock, R. H., and Ely, K. Politics of the Powerless. Cambridge: Winthrop, 1971.

"Brief to the Royal Commission on Provincial Municipal Relations." by the Black United Front of Nova Scotia, unpublished, Halifax, 1971.

"Brief of the New Brunswick Association for the Advancement of Coloured People to the Senate Committee on Poverty." St. John, N.B., August, 1970.

Brill, Harry. Why Organizers Fail: The Story of a Rent Strike, Univ. Of California, Berkeley, 1971.

Broom, L. and Selznick, P. Sociology: Third Edition. New York: Harper and Row, 1963.

"Canada Labour Code, Part I, Fair Employment Practices." Ottawa, 1953.

"Canada's Negroes, An Untold Story." U.S. News and World Report. May 11, 1970.

Canadian Human Rights Act. Ottawa, 1977. Clairmont, D. H. and Magill, D. Africville, The Life and Death of a Canadian Black Community. Toronto: McClellan and Stewart, 1974.

Clairmont, D. H. and Magill, D. Nova Scotia Blacks, an Historical and Structural Overview. Halifax Institute of Public Affairs, Dalhousie University, 1970.

Clarke, Austin C. "A Black Man Talks About Prejudice in White Canada." Social Problems, a Canadian Profile, ed. Richard Locking. Toronto: McGraw-Hill, 1964.

Comer, James P. Beyond Black and White. New York: Quadrangle Books, 1972.

Crowell, George H. Society Against Itself. Philadelphia: Westminster Press, 1968.

Davis, Morris, and Krauter, Joseph F. The Other Canadians: Profiles of Six Minorities. Agincourt: Methuen, 1971.

D'Oyley, Vincent et al. Black Presence in MultiEthnic Canada. Vancouver and Toronto: U.B.C. and O.I.S. E., 1976.

Encyclopedia Canadiana. Vol. VII, Ottawa: Grolier, pp. 261 ff.

Fanon, Franz. Black Faces, White Masks. tr. Chas. L. Markman. New York: Grove Press, 1967.

Harrison, Phyllis and Wyden, Barbara. The Black Child: A Parent's Guide. New York: Wyden 1973.

Head, Wilson. The Black Presence in the Canadian Mosaic. Toronto: Ontario Human Rights Commission, 1975.

Helling, Rudolph. The Position of Negroes, Chinese and Italians in the Social Structure of Windsor, Ontario, in a report submitted to the Ontario Human Rights Commission, Univ. of Windsor, 1965.

Henry, F. J. "Perception of Discrimination among Negroes and Japanese Canadians in Hamilton," a report submitted to the Ontario Human Rights Commission, 1965.

Henry, Francis. Forgotten Canadians: the Blacks of Nova Scotia. Don Mills: Longman, 1973.

Hentoff, Nat et al. Black Anti-Semitism and Jewish Racism. New York: Baron, 1970.
Hill, Daniel G. Human Rights in Canada: A Focus on Racism. Ottawa: Canadian Labour Congress, 1977.

---. Negroes in Toronto, A Sociological Study of a Minority Group. Ph. D. Diss., Univ. of Toronto, 1960.

Hodge, John L.; Struckman, Donald K.; Trost, Lynn D. Cultural Bases of Racism and Oppression. Berkeley: Two Riders, 1975.

Hoffman, Hans, The Theology of Reinhold Niebuhr. New York: Chas. Scribner's Sons, 1961.

Howie, Don. "The Origins of Racism." Negro Digest, Vol. XIX, No. 4, February, 1971.

"How Does Our Town Add Up?" Windsor Interracial Council Community Audit, 1947.

"How Does Our Town Add Up Ten Years Later?" unpublished study, Windsor Council on Group Relations, 1957.

Hughes, David, and Kallen, Evelyn. The Anatomy of Racism, Canadian Dimensions. Montreal: Harvest, 1974.

The Human Rights Act. Manitoba, 1970.

The Individual's Rights Protection Act. Alberta, 1972.

"International Covenant on the Elimination of all Forms of Racial Discrimination." Part I, Article I. United Nations.

"International Labour Conference, Convention III, Convention Concerning Discrimination in Respect of Employment and Occupation." Geneva, June, 1968.

Jenkins, Dwight. "Blacks Still Feel Scars of Racism." Montreal Star, November 4, 1972.

Johnson, Elmer. Social Problems of Urban Man. Georgetown, Ont.: Dorsey Press, 1973.

A Key to Canada, Parts I, II, III, IV. Published by the National Black Coalition of Canada, Inc. Montreal, 1976.

Krech, David, Crutchfield, Richard S.; and Ballachey, Egerton L. Individual In Society. Toronto: McGraw-Hill, 1962.

Let's Take Affirmative Action. Fair Employment Practices Branch, Labour Canada, 1970.

Living In Canada. Department of Manpower and Immigration, Queen's Printer: Ottawa, 1971.

London, Ontario, City of. The Pioneer Period and the London Of Today. London Public Library Board, 1900.

MacIver, R. M. The Web of Government. Toronto: The Free Press, 1965.

McDiarmid, G., and Pratt, D. Teaching Prejudice: A Content Analysis of Social Studies Textbooks Authorized for use in Ontario. Ontario Institute for Studies in Education: Toronto, 1971.

Mason, Robert W. "The Dilemma of Black Mobility in Management," Business Horizons, August, 1972.

Neibuhr, Reinhold. An Interpretation of Christian Ethics, New York: Harper and Brothers, 1935.

---. Leaves From the Notebook of a Tamed Cynic. New York: World, 1929.

New Brunswick Human Rights Act. Undated, but repeals the Human Rights Act of 1967.
Nova Scotia Blacks, An Historical and Structural Overview. Halifax, Nova Scotia: Institute of
 Public Affairs, Dalhousie Univ.,1970, 1971.

Nova Scotia Human Rights Act. 1969, amended 1972.

Ontario Human Rights Code. enacted 1962, amended 1970, 1972

Pathfinders of Liberty and Truth. A History of the Amherstburg Regular Missionary Baptist
 Association, 1940.

Porter, John. The Vertical Mosaic. An Analysis of Social Class and Power in Canada. Univ. of
 Toronto, 1965.

"A Preliminary Report of a Review of the Literature on Migrating Indians." Department of
 Citizenship and Immigration, Ottawa, 1971.

Report of the Owen Sound Human Rights Committee. 1970.

Report on Negroes in the Maritimes. Dalhousie Univ. Institute of Public Affairs, 1962.

Report of the Windsor Advisory Committee on Employment. 1969.

Rosenberg, Stuart E. "The Jewish Community in Canada", Vol. II, In the Midst of Freedom.
 Toronto, McLelland and Stewart: 1971.

The Senate of Canada: Proceedings of the Special Committee on Human Rights and
 Fundamental Freedom, No. 7, May 9, 1950, King's Printer, Ottawa, pp.253-258.

Semler, Michael. "The Blacks in Canada; The Forgotten Minority." Unpublished paper, Washington
 Univ., St. Louis, 1971.

Shand, Gwendolyn V. "Adult Education Among Negroes of Nova Scotia." Journal of Education,
 Institute of Public Affairs, Dalhousie Univ., Halifax, 1961.

Social Policies for Canada, Part I. A Statement of the Canadian Welfare Council, Ottawa, 1969.

Stonequist, E. V. "The Marginal Man: A Study in Personality and Culture Conflict." in
 Contributions to Urban Sociology, eds, E. W. Burgess and D.J. Bogue. Univ. of
 Chicago Press, 1964.

"Study of the Level of Education and Unemployment Among Adult Blacks in the Inner City of
 Windsor." Unpublished, 1971.

Talbot, Lyle E. "An Analysis of Human Rights Legislation."Ottawa, Labour Canada, 1975.

Tarnopolsky, Walter S. "The Iron Hand in the Velvet Glove." The Canadian Bar Review, Vol. XLVI, 1968.

Terry, Robert Y. For Whites Only. Grand Rapids: Erdmans, 1970.

---."Racism Isn't Just . . ." Detroit Industrial Mission, Vol. 13, No. 2, 1971.

Textbook Analysis: Nova Scotia, Halifax, Nova Scotia Human Rights Commission, 1974.

Trudeau, Pierre E. A Canadian Charter of Human Rights. Ottawa: Information Canada, 1968.
Tulloch, Headley. Black Canadians: A Long Line of Fighters. Toronto: New Canada Press, 1975.
Warsen, Albert. "Rising Tension and Conflicts in the City Streets." Human Relations. Toronto: May, 1969.

Whitton, Charlotte. Immigration Problems for Canada. Kingston: Jackson Press.

Williams, Donald S. "The Dynamics of Community Work In Human Rights: A Sociological Analysis." Human Relations, Vol. 13, August, 1973, Toronto.

Winks, Robin. Blacks in Canada. Montreal: McGill-Queens, 1971.

Winter, Gibson. Being Free. New York: MacMillan, 1970.